THE POLITICS OF BENEVOLENCE

Revival Religion
and American Voting Behavior

MODERN SOCIOLOGY:
A Series of Monographs, Treatises, and Texts

Edited by
GERALD M. PLATT

THE POLITICS OF BENEVOLENCE

Revival Religion and American Voting Behavior

JOHN L. HAMMOND

Hunter College

ABLEX PUBLISHING CORPORATION
Norwood, New Jersey

Printed in the United States of America

Library of Congress Cataloging in Publication Data

Hammond, John L
    The politics of benevolence.

    (Modern sociology)
    Bibliography: p.
    Includes index.
    1. Revivals—United States—History. 2. Christianity and politics—History. I. Title. II. Series.
BV3773.H35   322.4′4′0973   78-16050
ISBN 0-89391-013-9

Grateful acknowledgement is made to the following for permission to
reprint previously published material:

    American Academy of Religion: material which appeared in differ-
ent form in "Revivals, Consensus, and American Political Culture" by
John L. Hammond, *Journal of the American Academy of Religion* 46 (September, 1978).

    American Sociological Association: material which appeared in dif-
ferent form in "Revival Religion and Antislavery Politics" by John L.
Hammond, *American Sociological Review* 39 (April, 1974).

    Harcourt Brace Jovanovich, Inc.: excerpts from *The Life of the Mind
in America* by Perry Miller, © 1965 by Elizabeth Miller. Reprinted by
permission of Harcourt Brace Jovanovich, Inc.

    Yale University Press: excerpt from *A Religious History of The Ameri-
can People* by Sydney E. Ahlstrom, copyright © 1972 by Yale University
Press.

Ablex Publishing Corporation
355 Chestnut Street
Norwood, New Jersey 07648

To My Parents

Contents

Preface

Sometimes people hold ideals so strongly that they feel obligated to realize those ideals in their own action and in the world around them. But when their ideals call not for inner perfection but for improving the condition of the world, they discover that they must come to terms with the world, and they may find that the effort to change the world changes themselves or their ideals at least as much.

This book is about one such group of idealists. They experienced conversion in a religious revival movement, and conversion taught them to look at the world in a new way: they became certain that they could identify sin, and they believed that they had the ability as well as the obligation to eliminate it. The obligation they called the obligation of "benevolence," because they believed that eliminating sin would benefit other people, even some who had not experienced conversion as they had. In the early nineteenth century the greatest sin which the duty of benevolence turned them against was slavery. They founded a movement through which they hoped to abolish slavery by persuading public opinion and by organizing political parties to win public office.

I became interested in the movement for abolition and its idealistic inspiration at a time when I was devoting some energy to the civil rights movement and even more to the effort to end the war in Vietnam. It appeared to me that the ideals that inspired those movements were similar to the ones that inspired the early abolitionists, and I found that their movement and ours even undertook similar activities. My thinking about revivalism and its political consequences was influenced by the aspirations (and the illusions) I shared in those years.

There is another way in which my participation in the movements of the 1960s influenced my view of the earlier movement. What interests me most about movements is their ordinary participants: what brings them in, and how they develop and sustain their ideals. This book is not about movement leaders; it attempts to measure and account for the participation of average members. Such questions are hard to answer for the nineteenth century, but I have devoted most of my attention to voting statistics, for they represent the behavior of ordinary people better than any other kind of records.

Many commentators have argued either that most American voters in the nineteenth century cared little about the manifest issues of politics or that the positions they adopted were a reaction to social tensions in their own communities; that antislavery politics, in particular, had little to do with feelings about slavery but derived instead from local political and cultural rivalries. This book shows that, on the contrary, the political sentiments of antislavery voters were based on strong religious convictions. Opposition to slavery was a conscious part of their value system.

Those whom the revivals inspired to enter politics faced a reality for which their ideals had not prepared them (just as we in the twentieth century did): they would not be able to put their ideals into practice automatically. The revivals had taught them that if they struggled hard and with sincerity they would win. They learned, however, that their society was resistant; that the benefits that slaveowners received from slavery also gave them the political power to resist pressures for its abolition, and that they, the abolitionists, would have to find allies who were as powerful as the slaveowners and who had self-interested reasons for opposing slavery. They found, in other words, that the search for political power forced them to compromise the very ideals which had led them to seek political power in the first place. The sincerity of their benevolence was not enough to assure them success.

If my sympathy with the first generation of people whose politics was inspired by the revival movement becomes evident in these pages, so too will my lack of sympathy with revivalism's major political manifestation after the Civil War, the prohibition movement. The word "benevolence" becomes ironic when those who practice it fail to ask whether their presumed beneficiaries want their help.

Collective political action arising from conviction faces the dangers of ineffectiveness, of compromise, and of self-righteousness. The political movements which grew out of revivalism encountered all these dangers, and did not always overcome them. But despite the mixed record which these and other movements have achieved, collective action inspired by conviction remains necessary to force government to respond to the will of the people.

As the author of a work on disinterested benevolence, it is especially gratifying to acknowledge how often I have been its beneficiary. While working on this book I have received all kinds of help—intellectual, personal, administrative, and financial—for which I am very grateful.

When I was working on it as a dissertation, Duncan MacRae, Jr., gave me the extraordinarily generous, thorough, and perceptive advice and criticism which he has given so many students. I thank him. James Fennessey and Donald Scott also contributed valuable advice from their diverse perspectives.

Bill Hodge originally suggested the project which grew into this book (I wonder if he will remember that). Gordon Adams, Michael Edelstein, Eric Foner, Dall Forsythe, Bob Handy, Jonathan Kelley, Pat Molloy, Pat Peppe, Bob Richard, and Don Treiman all commented on parts of the manuscript or discussed it with me. My discussions with Jerry Finch were particularly valuable.

Gaylord Albaugh gave me his unpublished bibliography of early religious periodicals and advice on how to consult them, providing essential assistance in locating reports of revivals. Ellen Brennan collected and coded much of the revivals data. Most of the political and demographic data were provided by the Inter-University Consortium for Political and Social Research, whose data archive has vitally assisted many scholars of voting behavior.

My research has been supported financially by the University of Chicago and the Columbia University Council for Research in the Social Sciences, whose grants permitted me to acquire different portions of the ICPSR data. An especially generous grant from the National Institute of Mental Health permitted me a year's leave from teaching to complete the research. The Center for Policy Research bore many of what would otherwise have been my administrative burdens. I salute the Center's efficient and cheerful administrators, Stephanie Clohesy, Judy Johns, and Dena West, and my typists Margery Budoff, Toni Goldsmith, and Evelyn Ledyard.

On important occasions, Herb Klein and Hoby Spalding stimulated my flagging enthusiasm. Dan Jones helped me to concentrate on the right things at the right times.

Hilah Thomas had the good fortune not to know me during most of the years I was working on this book, but I have enjoyed having her company in celebrating its completion.

JOHN L. HAMMOND

1
Revivalism as a Political Ethos

A phenomenal wave of religious revivalism swept several northern states in the late 1820s. Though the area had seen periodic outbursts of revivals dating back to Jonathan Edwards's first Great Awakening, these were the most intense. They were inspired by the evangelist Charles Grandison Finney, who brought new doctrines and new methods to revivalism. His preaching and that of his followers led many unchurched people to a conviction of their own sin and their salvation. These converts accepted not only religious faith but a commitment to changing their world and a confidence in their ability to do so. The revivals taught them new beliefs, not only about what was wrong with the world but also about how to go about correcting it. These new ideas affected them and their communities for many generations.

The doctrine preached in the revivals created a tradition which became part of those communities' belief system. That tradition has endured and been particularly important to their politics. When, in subsequent generations, people in those communities have been called on to make new political choices, the revivalist tradition has influenced them on several occasions.

The first manifestation of an unusual political tradition in revival communities was their support for abolitionism. Abolitionist preachers toured the area, drawing on revival rhetoric and revival emotions to call upon their (obviously nonslaveowning) audiences to renounce the sin of slavery. In 1840, abolitionists who had been influenced by the revivals organized the Liberty party, which called explicitly for the abolition of slavery and which won far more votes in revival communities than elsewhere. Those communities continued to give their votes to the nonabolitionist opponents of slavery in the Free Soil and Republican parties in later years. The vote for the Republican party was not distinctively revivalist, however, for it grew only as the party diluted the abolitionist platform.

Some revival communities continued to express a unique political tradition after the Civil War. When the temperance movement became political in the late nineteenth century, revival communities supported it through the ballot, and later voted to institute and maintain prohibition in the twentieth. When Populism came east with the presidential campaign of William Jennings Bryan in 1896, he was supported not by depression-impoverished agrarians but by voters attracted to his moralistic appeal. When New York State attempted to liberalize its gambling laws in the mid-twentieth century, revival communities voted against the proposals. More recently, when the Republican party nominated a man who opposed the extension and enforcement of civil rights in 1964, these same communities were even more inclined than other northern communities to abandon the Republican column in which they customarily marked their presidential ballots.[1]

Slavery, prohibition, Populism, gambling, civil rights—a heterogeneous collection of issues—are not usually regarded as parts of a single political tradition. But they are, for all are derived in different ways from the teachings of Finney and his followers in the revival movement. The revivals inspired a new set of religious beliefs whose specific content led converts (and their descendants) to adopt these positions and whose general orientation led them to advocate their views politically.

The communities in which the revivals were most common, and in which this political tradition took root, were rural. They were found in the newly opening frontier, covering western New York and the region beyond the Alleghenies, all of which in those days was still known as "the West." These areas were largely unopened to settlement until the end of the eighteenth century, but were soon populated by the New England invasion in the early years of the nineteenth. The settlers brought with them a Yankee culture, which had grown out of Calvinist puritanism and included a tradition of revivals. Western New England had seen several waves of revivalism in the previous century, and a portion of western New York became known as the "Burned-Over District" because of the frequent and intense outbursts of religious fervor there (Cross, 1950). The revivals inspired by Charles Finney drew on a tradition that was already known in those communities.

---

[1]The relation between the anti-Goldwater vote and pre-Civil War voting patterns was first noted by Burnham (1968, pp. 20–23).

But Finney's revivals and the religion they spread were different. The Calvinist tradition had undergone a gradual modification until it was now almost unrecognizable. The central element of Calvinist belief had been predestination, the doctrine that since one's salvation was decided upon by an inscrutable God, nothing that one did in life could affect that decision, and that furthermore one could not even be certain of being among the elect. This austere belief led to austerity in life. Calvinists, seeking assurance that they were among the elect, had to grasp for earthly signs of salvation. The way in which they assured themselves was to engage in a life the hallmark of which was discipline—whether by striving in an earthly calling or by attempting to establish a severe moral order.[2]

Discipline became the central principle around which Calvinists attempted to organize their moral life. However, by the early nineteenth century, and especially under the impetus of Finney and his predecessors in revivalism, discipline grew less important because the belief in predestination that underlay it was abandoned in favor of a belief in free will. The new central principle on which the moral life was based was the principle of benevolence.

The revivals themselves influenced the change of doctrine. If conversion could occur at a revival and in response to a preacher's emotional exhortation, predestination made little sense. The convert, of his own free will, renounced his sinful past and accepted conversion. That experience had to mean that he was saved, so it could not be true that his salvation or damnation was decided in advance. Free will and assurance of salvation were both experienced directly and emotionally in the revival, and the disciplined ordering of life was no longer necessary for assurance.

But confidence in salvation did not lead to complacency. Belief in both the sinner's ability to save himself by his own free choice and the revivalists' ability to bring others to salvation through their preaching encouraged the belief that the acts of individuals could change the world, and whoever had the ability and knew how God wanted him to use it surely was obligated to act to bring about God's will on earth. That obligation was fulfilled by acts of benevolence.

In principle, benevolence neither won salvation for the Christian nor even assured him that he was saved; both the salvation and the assurance came from repentance and conversion, and benevolence was only supposed to follow from them. But for earlier Calvinists the disciplined life, in principle, had no such effects either. In each case,

---

[2]The social consequences of Calvinist belief have had different interpretations, but the element of discipline is central in most of them. See, for example, the very diverse views of Hill (1967), Weber (1958b), and Walzer (1969).

however, obedience to the moral principle came to be taken as a sign to others that one was truly saved, and individual believers probably came to regard it as such for themselves. In any case, the obligation to benevolence created by the revivals was a strong one.

The duty of benevolence incorporated some specific duties. The first of these was to present to others the opportunity to be saved, by supporting revivals and missionary efforts. The idea of benevolence, however, came to imply duties not directly related to the religious life. The most important obligation in the northern United States in the mid-nineteenth century was to work to free the slaves, for slavery was an abominable institution which deprived blacks of their God-given free will. The importance of freedom in the new religious doctrine made lack of freedom in the earthly state unacceptable to revivalists as it was not to other Christians.

Another benevolent duty was abstinence from alcohol, for drunkenness, too, deprived one of freedom. The missionary impulse inherent in the principle of benevolence made Christians concerned not only about their own abstinence but about the abstinence of others, and they organized temperance societies and promoted temperance revivals to convince others to give up drinking as well.

The benevolent impulse led in several other directions. Concern for abolition of slavery led to concern about northern racism and the condition of free blacks, and abolitionists established schools and attempted to achieve civil equality for them. Revivalists also supported Sabbath observance and opposed gambling. Many of them became antimasons.

The duty of benevolence required them to work for these goals in a variety of ways. Initially they believed that their ends could and should be achieved by individual persuasion; they had come to adopt those goals of their own free will by conversion, and so should everyone else. But a combination of circumstances led them to regard the political system as an appropriate place to channel their efforts, so they created and voted for political parties which espoused the same principles.

One source of the politicization of revivalism was the character of the American political system. It was new, it was open, and every citizen had the right to advocate his views. But the nature of revival religion particularly predisposed converts to act on their religious convictions in the political arena. Revival preachers were pragmatic and experimental, consciously developing effective techniques of conversion. Converts applied the same experimentalism to their secular goals and found in the possibility of political influence an obviously available method which was worth trying. And just as revivalism made them pragmatic about means, it made them absolutist about ends. The sins they saw around them were grievous. Even if politics meant coercion (as only some of them recognized), they were willing to use political means to eradicate sin.

The beliefs inculcated in the revivals therefore led to the growth of abolitionist politics very soon after the revivals had occurred. People in revival communities undertook the drive to end slavery, and pursued it even when it led to disunion and to Civil War. Evangelical Christians were not the only abolitionists, but they were the ones who made abolitionism a political movement and organized a new party explicitly dedicated to it. The revivals made slavery so intolerable to them that they supported the movement with intense dedication.

Revival beliefs were also incorporated into the culture of revival areas, and affected politics in later generations. Those later generations did not learn those beliefs from specific revivalist exhortation but acquired them as part of their general cultural heritage. Revivalist politics accordingly has not usually had the character of a movement during the later period. Instead, its expression has generally been limited to unusual voting patterns based on the political predispositions which revivalist beliefs created. But the votes of revival communities for abolition, prohibition, and even (in the mid-twentieth century) civil rights are part of a coherent tradition derived from the religious beliefs they adopted at the beginning of the nineteenth century.

The tradition these revivals formed is different from most political traditions, not only in the apparently heterogeneous set of positions to which it leads but in the form in which it affects political behavior. First, it is not a party tradition. Party loyalty is probably the most common sort of political tradition in the American system. Communities, especially stable ones, tend to adhere to a long-lasting norm of partisan choice, and attachment to a party can be much more constant than political interests seem to justify. Over periods of forty years or longer (and sometimes as long as a century), differences between counties of a state in the outcome of elections have been remarkably constant, not only in the rank-ordering of counties but also in the absolute levels of vote for each party. The regular support of a county for one major party rather than the other attests to the existence of political identifications independent of other identifications. Rural areas tend to be especially stable in their voting patterns (Flinn, 1962; Key & Munger, 1959; MacRae, 1955).

MacRae (1955) has attributed rural voting stability to the existence of community integration and a stable prestige structure, allowing "political party identification [to] become assimilated to and be perpetuated by [the] value system" (p. 334). Such a political tradition, he suggests, does not determine the attitude of the community on issues of the moment; rather, it maintains identification with a party name and allegiance to the party's symbols (MacRae, 1955, p. 339).

The communities in which the revivalist tradition has lasted are indeed integrated and stable, and they have a traditional party allegiance: most are strongly Republican. But it is not their partisanship that makes them—at least some of them—distinctive. The voting patterns of revivalist communities have most often been distinctive in their support for minor parties, especially "one-issue" parties promoting abolition or prohibition. They have occasionally been distinctive by being even more Republican than their traditions would lead one to expect, at times when other Republican constituencies have shifted to the Democratic party. On some occasions (1896 and 1964) their distinctiveness has been in an unexpectedly high Democratic vote.

The political tradition of revivalist communities is also unusual in that it is not a constant influence on voting behavior. Revivalist communities vote distinctively only in some elections. Revivalism defined its benevolence in specific ways, and so it relates only to a limited set of issues. Because these issues become matters of political controversy only infrequently and sporadically, the occasions for the revivalist tradition to influence political choice are rare. But this very infrequency attests to the tenacity of the tradition. Even though the revivalist heritage is not called on regularly it still influences votes when relevant issues arise.

Such a political tradition, with such unusual characteristics, I call a *political ethos*. I define a political ethos as a system of political attitudes and beliefs held by a group which defines itself in other than political terms; received through socialization processes; accepted early in life and relatively without question rather than rooted in contemporary structural or political discrepancies and accepted by choice in maturity; relatively independent of variations in personality and position in the social structure; and furnishing a set of standards and values motivating politically relevant decisions. The present study will show that the revivalist tradition is a political ethos and that it was formed and became part of the culture of the communities where it exists as a result of the religious experiences of those communities in the early nineteenth century and the new beliefs those experiences taught.

A political ethos is a particular kind of political belief system. To explain the concept, it will be useful to contrast it to two other kinds of political belief systems, political culture and ideology. "Political culture" and "ideology" both refer to belief systems about politics and about the holder's participation in politics. But the two concepts differ significantly on a number of dimensions.

Almond and Verba (1963) define a political culture as "the political system as internalized in the cognitions, feelings, and evaluations of its population" (p. 13). More specifically, the political culture is the distribution of orientations toward political objects in a population. Almond and Verba's typology of parochial, subject, and participant political cultures is based on orientations to the political system as a whole and to oneself as a participant. In the parochial political culture, the average member has no orientation to the political system; in the subject political culture, the member conceives of himself as a beneficiary in relationship to the political system; and in the participant political culture, he sees himself as a participant as well (Almond & Verba, 1963, p. 16).

For Almond and Verba, the nature of the political culture depends not on the political system but on the general culture. Almond and Verba imply that political culture is determined by general psychological and attitudinal patterns of participants, and that the political culture in turn determines participants' patterns of relations to political institutions. For Pye, too, the political culture encompasses general political orientations which are shaped by the modal personality (Pye, 1962, p. 158). Specific political behavior stemming from cognitive processes is of little concern to these writers.

The general orientations they describe, however, leave room for a wide variety of views on such matters as the functions of the state, the boundaries of legitimacy, and appropriate forms of participation, as well as other matters that might be part of the contents of a political culture. Elsewhere they pay more attention to the specific contents of political cultures (Almond & Powell, 1966, p. 52; Pye, 1962, pp. 122–24), but still the concept remains diffuse, involving general orientations rather than specific beliefs.

An ideology differs from a political culture in being more clearly articulated. For Geertz (1964), the primary characteristic of an ideology is that it is a system of symbols and meaning by means of which people interpret their political environment. Ideology is consciously employed in an active process of perception and evaluation. Ideologies and other symbol systems are "extrinsic sources of information in terms of which human life can be patterned." Their function is to "make an autonomous politics possible by providing the authoritative concepts that render it meaningful" (pp. 62–63).

Systematic ideological formulations render ambiguous social situations meaningful and make possible purposive action within such situations. They arise in times of social uncertainty when events call accepted political traditions into question. Geertz (1964) notes that the French revolution led to a crisis of legitimacy because it destroyed the apparently hallowed and permanent principle of monarchy. He concludes that "it is when neither a society's most general cultural orientations nor its most down-to-earth, 'pragmatic' ones suffice any longer to provide an adequate image of political process that ideologies begin to become crucial as sources of sociopolitical meanings and attitudes" (p. 64; see also Lane, 1962, pp. 413–16).

The concepts of ideology and political culture differ on several dimensions: an ideology is usually thought to be held by individuals or by formally and politically defined groups while a political culture is a property of whole societies or subgroups, usually ascriptively defined, within a society; an ideology is voluntarily adopted while a political culture is accepted as part of the environment; an ideology provides opinions on substantive issues and criteria for decisions in concrete situations while a political culture frames the decision-making process and sets parameters which are normally not called into question; an ideology is usually specifically formulated while a political culture is more pervasive and often unarticulated; an ideology functions primarily in extraordinary times, while a political culture provides a pattern for behavior in all politically relevant situations. Ideology is focusing, while political culture is enveloping.

The differences between the two concepts are summarized in Table 1.1. However, these two sets of polarities do not appear to contain the only possible combinations. Culturally transmitted thought patterns include concrete cognitions which condition attitudes toward

TABLE 1.1
Contrasts between Political Culture and Ideology

	Political culture	Ideology
Degree of articulation	Low[a]	High[a]
Bearer	Society or ascriptively defined subgroup[b]	Politically defined formal group
Source for individual	Cultural transmission[b]	Conscious decision
Locus	Personality dispositions	Symbol system[b]
Scope	Procedural norms	Substantive issues[b]
Application	Unconscious assumptions behind decisions	Standards for concrete decisions[b]

[a] A political ethos occupies an intermediate or fluctuating position on this dimension.

[b] Characteristic shared by political ethos.

specific political events as well as to political institutions. Concrete decisions are required in normal as well as in extraordinary times, and surely the criteria for such decisions may be unarticulated as often as they are precisely formulated. Aspects of each member of this pair of concepts appear relevant to an interpretation of the role of revivalism in American political behavior.

They will therefore be combined into the concept of a political ethos, defined as a political orientation culturally transmitted and accepted as part of the recipient's environment rather than deliberately indoctrinated and accepted or rejected on the basis of a specific decision, but in which cognitions and evaluations of specific objects occupy a central place and determine behavior toward those objects.[3]

Though a political ethos is institutionalized and culturally transmitted, it originally arises as an ideology, a set of beliefs which a group consciously acquires and holds as a matter of personal commitment. But even after it has been institutionalized, a knowledge of its history is necessary to understand it: the elements which are brought together in a political ethos have coherence only because they arose out of a specific set of historical circumstances. The term culture is often used to imply that behavior patterns are static, because culture is fixed. The term ethos, on the other hand, has a dynamic implication. Weber used the term, according to Bendix and Berger (1959), because he

> wanted to emphasize that each man's participation in his society involved a personal commitment to the behavior patterns, the ideas, and the interests of a particular status group. . . . Weber construed the culture of a nation as an outgrowth of group power and group conflict in their historical development. Accordingly, the analysis of historical legacies is an essential part of the interpretation of culture. (pp. 106–07)

A political ethos is rooted in specific historical events and group conflicts. To understand it, then, one must examine the historical situations in which a political ethos arises and declines.

An ethos is in the first instance a system of thought. The ideas

[3]The term "political ethos" has been given another meaning, by Banfield and Wilson (1963, p. 234), who discuss the public-regarding and private-regarding ethos as factors in city government. They do not define the term explicitly except as "conceptions of politics." Their examples place it, perhaps, midway between the concepts of political culture and political ethos as used here: it refers both to general orientations toward political institutions and to attitudes on specific issues (but principally, it seems, as stemming from those general orientations).

The imprecise definition of the concepts has given it limited usefulness in empirical research, and it has been criticized by Hennessy (1970) and by Wolfinger and Field (1966). The usage has not been so well established that its use here in a precisely specified but different sense should cause confusion.

which compose it must be internally consistent if social groups are to find them acceptable as a package (Converse, 1964, pp. 209–13; Lane, 1962, pp. 426–28). They need not be logically or deductively consistent, but something must make them appear to hang together. The consistency of the ideas may inhere in their manifest content, but it may also arise from the fact that the ideas arose under the same historical circumstances. Such a system may contain conceptual bonds between elements which appear disparate to those who do not share the premises of the ethos.

An ethos must also be consistent with the cultural premises of the people exposed to it. The tradition of revivals grew out of and flourished in the Puritan culture of New England. Though there were revivals in other parts of the country as well, the revivals in New England were different, producing a unique theology with specific political implications.

Though necessarily consistent with preexisting cultural premises, a newly adopted ethos must not match them exactly. New views arise out of critical experiences (Goldrich, Pratt, & Schuller, 1967, pp. 14–15; Mannheim, 1969, pp. 363–64; Zeitlin, 1966), and to the extent that they amend those premises their adoption requires a special stimulus. Though revivals were part of a cultural tradition, they had a transforming effect at the same time. Calvinist Protestants were led to expect the experience of conversion through the revival, but were also led to interpret it as a life-changing event. When new political beliefs were explicitly associated with the doctrines preached in the revivals, their converts were ready to accept those beliefs as part of a single transformation.

The revivals did not cause a social upheaval of the kind Geertz describes as the usual occasion for the development of ideological thinking. But events critical in the life of an individual need not be cataclysmic to a society. The United States was a new society relatively lacking in political traditions when the revivals occurred, and the areas in which they were most common were even more recently settled. The wide diffusion of revivals in an area and at a time when no traditions were fixed allowed the adoption of new beliefs as a consequence of common individual experiences rather than a society-wide shock.

Although no national cataclysm was required for those beliefs to be adopted, one soon occurred, partly as a consequence of those beliefs. Revivalism contributed to the growth of the antislavery movement, which in turn led to secession and Civil War. Since revivalism, in part responsible for those events, offered an interpretation of them, its beliefs readily became part of the standards by which converts evaluated political choices. It is likely that the ethos became culturally embedded because it was urgently required to interpret political reality during the 1840s and 1850s. It later survived as a political tradition even when it was detached from its religious roots.

The embedding of a political ethos into a group's cultural patterns means that its consistency need no longer be called into question. Culturally received ideas are perceived to have consistency because of the manner in which they are learned. Once institutionalized, such ideas are passed on from generation to generation rather than adopted as a matter of individual commitment. In the process these ideas are transformed. The revivalist ethos, which had revolutionary consequences in the antebellum period, later became a tradition whose maintenance implied, and depended on, stability in the communities in which it prevailed.

The relative absence of political traditions in the early years of the nation's political life, and in particular the absence of traditions on the frontier, may have left a vacuum which the revivalist ethos was able to fill. But a political ethos can take root only when an area has achieved some stability, for if rapid change and immigration continue, the events giving rise to the ethos will not have been shared by the newer arrivals. It was in areas becoming relatively stable after emerging from frontier status that revivals were most common (Cross, 1950, p. 12; Sweet, 1933).

If critical events are necessary for an ethos to emerge, it will best be preserved in the absence of such events. Cultural traditions once established, including a political ethos where one exists, are most stable when populations do not experience major changes. Two kinds of changes might destroy an ethos. First, new critical events might require a new adjustment of thought patterns. Even if the group is preserved, its previously held thought patterns will no longer be sufficient. However, no such disruption has threatened American institutions since the crisis of the Civil War period during which the revivalist ethos became institutionalized.

Alternatively, gradual changes may lead to the destruction of traditional cultural patterns. If a culture is shared by a group which is geographically concentrated and whose conditions of life do not change, successive generations will be able to maintain that culture. If, on the other hand, new groups move into the area and social and economic conditions alter, the increased heterogeneity may extinguish the culture.

The revivalist political ethos will be studied through its influence on the politics of New York and Ohio. Though revivals affected the politics of many other states during the same period, several characteristics make these two the most appropriate sites for the study. The Finneyite revival movement was centered in New York, and probably stronger in Ohio than in any other state but New York. Second, the history of political abolitionism was written primarily in these two states and in Massachusetts. William Seward and Salmon P. Chase, Lincoln's chief rivals for the 1860 Republican nomination and subsequently members of his cabinet, were from New York and Ohio, respectively. Furthermore, the two states were among the first to give solid support to the Republican party when it emerged.

In the mid-nineteenth century both states were divided into fairly distinct geographic sections, one of which was settled principally by New Englanders. Further, both were reasonably fully settled by the time the Finneyite revivals began, and had been states long enough to have a tradition of voting predating the onset of revivalism.

These two states later experienced different developments with opposite consequences for the preservation of the revivalist ethos. By the middle of the nineteenth century New York's pattern of urban development was already established, and the areas where revivalism had flourished remained rural. In Ohio, on the other hand, the area where revivals were concentrated (the Western Reserve) would later become the most urbanized and industrialized section of the state. The stability of the revival district in New York permitted the ethos to remain a strong cultural element there, while in Ohio it ultimately vanished.

The evidence for the existence and influence of a political ethos is to be found in political behavior. The people presumed to share the ethos should act politically to support its principles. The influence of the revivalist ethos can be traced in the political behavior of two groups of people: activists and ordinary citizens. Political activists motivated by the revivalist ethos organized new political parties explicitly dedicated to the secular principles derived from revivalist preaching. But political activists are by definition few in number. Even if their behavior was due to religious beliefs they acquired through revivals, therefore, revivalism still may not have formed a cultural pattern.

To show that revivalism became a political ethos one must show that it influenced the general population of revival areas. Its influence, then, must be found not only in the political behavior of identifiable individuals; it must also be shown that the general public held and acted on political beliefs derived from revivalism. The most common form of political behavior for the general public is of course the vote, and its records can be examined to see if revivalist communities voted differently from other communities. Most of the evidence for the revivalist ethos, then, will be found in voting records.

Voting data provide the most comprehensive records of past opinion on political questions. The vote is an overt expression of political choice, and insofar as it determines the outcome of an election it is potentially binding; therefore it is likely to be a more definitive expression of political belief than a casually expressed opinion. Moreover, vote totals do not suffer from the selective survival and representativeness of most historical documents (Benson, 1969, pp. 57–61). The high level of voter turnout throughout the nineteenth century also means that the vote represents an unusually complete canvass of the opinions at least of eligible voters (Burnham, 1970a, pp. 198–201).

To demonstrate from voting patterns that revival belief developed into a political ethos which influenced political opinions and behavior, several points must be established: it must be shown that revivals had an impact on the way people voted, and that the impact was due to the beliefs they espoused and taught; it must further be shown that certain political acts (notably, the vote for particular candidates in particular elections) are in some way an enactment of the principles of revivalism; and finally it must be demonstrated that those acts are determined by culturally shared beliefs rather than by motivations restricted to individuals.

The first of these matters is dealt with in Chapters 2 and 4. In Chapter 2, I consider various possible explanations for relationships between religion and political behavior, among them that political behavior is determined by religious belief. In Chapter 4, I show that it is that explanation rather than others which best accounts for the political behavior of revival communities.

To show that political acts are enactments of revivalist principles (or any other principles) one must be able to show that votes were determined by voters' positions on particular issues. The relation between policy position and party choice is difficult to assess: the relatively loose articulation between them has often been demonstrated for the mid-twentieth century, so one should not readily assume that the vote for a particular candidate represents an endorsement of his party's platform (Bower, 1948; Campbell, Converse, Miller, & Stokes, 1960, pp. 202, 212–15).

But some inferences can be made. If a political ethos influences the voting decisions of people in certain areas, the way in which they vote will demonstrate a consistency in supporting political positions derived from its prescriptions. The areas of revivalism will support candidates and measures representing the ethos's principles, most importantly, abolition and prohibition, but also other policy goals and particular candidates who represent the ethos more than their opponents.

The distinct policy preferences of voters motivated by a political ethos can influence their votes both in referenda and in partisan campaigns for office. Referenda offer the clearest indication of policy positions, because a referendum vote is a direct expression of position on an issue and because the decision is relatively free of the influence of party loyalty. The influence of an ethos on partisan vote is more complex, primarily because it occurs in interaction with traditional party loyalty, sometimes reinforcing it and sometimes counteracting it.[4] It has often been argued that through most of American history, voters' party loyalty has been so tenacious as to preclude any influence of issue positions on the vote. While that is an exaggeration, party loyalty must be held in account when assessing the influence of an ethos, or of any policy position, on the vote in a partisan campaign.

A political ethos can be the basis of party affiliation. For two generations after the Civil War, Republican party loyalty in Ohio was largely based on revivalism reinforced by the partisan divisions that developed out of it during the period that led up to the War. If the ethos were identical to party tradition, the term "political ethos" would be superfluous, for one could assume that voters acted merely on the basis of party loyalty rather than of any set of values the ethos incorporated.

That appears to have been the case in Ohio. Traditional Republicanism and issue positions derived from the ethos were most often consistent with each other, but even when the principles of the ethos might have led voters away from the Republican party, they more often stayed with it. But in New York, the effect of the ethos after the Civil War was different. On the basis of positions derived from it, revivalist voters often deviated from their normal party vote.

A vote which violates party affiliation can more readily be interpreted as an expression of position on an issue than a traditional party vote. The inference is still indirect and less clear than in the case of a referendum, for a deviating vote is still a vote for a man or party, and not a direct statement of policy preference. But if it can be related to a position derived from the ethos, it demonstrates an even stronger influence of the ethos than a referendum vote does, because some clear motivation is required to depart from party tradition.

The inference that a vote for a minor party represents a position on an issue is usually fairly straightforward, for the minor parties discussed in this study are clearly one-issue parties. Deviations from

[4]The relationship between ethos and party implied by this discussion will be found in a two-dominant party, plurality-election system. In a multiparty system, it is likely that adherents to an ethos will be represented by their own party.

party loyalty in favor of the other major party are harder to interpret, but in elections in which large numbers of voters systematically deviated from party loyalty there is usually some issue which has been hotly debated in the campaign and which appears to be responsible for the deviation. If the ethos implies a position on that issue, it is reasonable to infer that it was responsible for the deviation.

The normal partisan preference of revivalist areas in New York has been Republican, just as it was in Ohio. But they possess a different kind of "Republican atmosphere" than nonrevivalist areas (Burnham, 1968, p. 29), and have far more frequently voted against the Republican party in unusually large numbers. In particular, when the national or state organization of a major party changes its issue orientation, revivalist areas respond to this change not blindly or automatically but in terms of the interpretations which the ethos provides. Not all normally Republican areas in New York responded alike to the endorsement of Populism by the Democrats in 1896 or to the rejection of prohibition by New York Republicans in 1930. Voters who shared the revivalist ethos acted according to its tenets (in both cases casting an unusually high anti-Republican vote) while voters in other Republican areas did not.

The third point to be established in demonstrating that revivalism acted as a political ethos is that the unusual voting patterns which are identified as its manifestations are due to cultural characteristics rather than individual traits. The effort to prove that proposition from aggregate voting data presents the opposite of the problem usually met in the analysis of aggregate data. Most often, the analyst wishes to use relationships observed at the level of areal units to estimate relationships at the individual level (Duncan & Davis, 1953; Goodman, 1959; Robinson, 1950). Such estimates will be invalid to the extent that areal unit is, or is associated with, a cause of the dependent variable (Hammond, 1973).

If a political ethos is to explain voting behavior, the opposite must be shown, namely, that it exercises a (relatively) uniform influence over people who live in certain areas. This is particularly a problem since the revivalist ethos has more frequently expressed itself in votes for minor parties than in deviations in favor of the other major party. The total vote for any minor party is normally very small; it might therefore be argued that the vote is too insignificant to be taken as evidence of a culturally pervasive political ethos. But minor-party support motivated by the ethos is important out of proportion to its numbers. That support has been instrumental in creating such parties, especially the antislavery parties, and providing the vehicle which ultimately led to a transformation of the American party system.

Moreover, there are factors which depress the vote for minor parties, even though it is an indicator of attitudes more common than the numbers voting for the party suggest.

It appears likely that the vote for a minor party is based on a conscious choice more often than on the kind of unquestioning party loyalty on which the major parties can draw. Especially when a third party is short-lived, the number of automatic voters must be very few; and even for them, issue content is considerably more salient than it is for stable major-party adherents. For most third-party voters, or voters for whom the third party is a live option, it is likely that the decision must be approached anew at each election. They must ask, "Is there a dime's worth of difference between the major party candidates on the issues of greatest importance to me, or might my vote be more effectively given to another candidate even though he has no chance of winning?"

It will be shown in several instances that the base of sentiment favoring a minor party's position extends beyond the few who actually vote for the party, and is rooted in cultural premises shared by larger numbers of voters in the same areas. For example, the vote for a one-issue party can often be compared with the vote on a referendum relating to the same issue. A third-party vote and a referendum vote can be considered as forming a scale, with the choice to vote for a third-party candidate more "difficult"[5] than the choice to support that party's position on the referendum. The choice will be more difficult both because of unwillingness to forsake traditional party affiliation and because of the unlikelihood of the candidate's victory.

This greater difficulty is empirically verified in the data of this study; it is uniformly the case that when voters are offered the opportunity to endorse a third party and a referendum on the issue it stands for, the proportion supporting the party's position in the referendum is much higher than the proportion supporting the candidate. But if referendum vote and third-party vote are highly correlated, and if each is concentrated in the area where the ethos is presumed to prevail, we can infer that there is something distinctive about the area's culture influencing the political decisions of voters, although they are also influenced by party affiliation and the realistic possibilities of victory.[6]

Moreover, though the vote for any minor party is usually quite

[5]The idea of difficulty is derived from the methods of scalogram analysis. See Guttman (1949, p. 70).

[6]Scalability is only suggested, not demonstrated, by a high correlation. For a further discussion of referendum and minor-party votes as aggregate indicators of public opinion, see Hammond (in press).

small, its total can still fluctuate markedly from year to year. If a party doubles (or halves) its total from one election to the next, it can again be inferred that the choice to vote for it was made less "difficult" in the more favorable year by the events of the intervening period. Once again, the pattern suggests a cultural explanation for minor-party support both in the favorable and the unfavorable elections.

A second reason for inferring that revivalism is a cultural pattern lies in the diversity of the elements that compose the ethos. Revivalist communities have been consistent in holding views which occupy very dissimilar positions on a conventional left–right continuum. For example, abolition was a radical position; and prohibition is today thought of as a conservative view (although many of its supporters in the past considered it radical and had radical politics on other issues); Populism has been placed at various locations on the spectrum by different interpreters. But the fact that views so discordant by contemporary standards have been held by the same people in the past suggests that an historical explanation must be sought: they appear to have nothing in common but their relation to revival preaching. So when they have been influential in later generations it appears that a tradition rooted in experiences of the past continues to have important effects.

The strongest evidence that revivalism is a culturally rooted belief system lies in the long period during which the ethos has influenced voting behavior. Voting in New York shows its influence from the 1840s to the 1960s. In Ohio the period is shorter, but still longer than an individual life span. The same voters might be responsible for unusual consistencies in voting patterns separated by forty years, or even longer, but not through more than a century. The length of time precludes an individual-level explanation of the voting of revivalist areas.

This study traces the evolution and the political influence of revivalism during that period. Using the revivalist ethos as an example, the study's principal concern is to establish the force of ideas in motivating political action. But the study also examines the effect which ideologically motivated political action can have on the system as a whole, and finds that it is severely limited. Revivalists found at several periods that the translation of their values into political action raised insoluble problems: the decision to create an abolitionist party and face questions other than abolition confronted the party and led to divisions within the abolitionist ranks. Opposition to slavery could only become a major issue when it gained the support of nonabolitionist forces; the divergence between their purposes and the purposes of the abolitionists led to a dilution of the moral principles on which the latter's political action was based. As a culturally institutionalized ethos after the Civil War, revivalism was unable to initiate political developments; instead, it only reacted when the political aims of other groups led them to adopt positions which happened to coincide with some elements of revivalism. These limits are built into the structure of American politics—to some degree, perhaps, into the structure of politics generally. But it is particularly the American two-party system which forces compromise and coalition on political movements inspired by ideology.

The workings of the revivalist ethos, its effects and its limits, are described in the subsequent chapters. Chapter 2 presents a theoretical discussion of the relation between religious belief and political behavior, analyzing the proposition that religion's influence is due to the beliefs it espouses. The chapter also discusses the types of issues on which religious belief is likely to have an impact.

Chapter 3 describes the history of the revival movement and its development of a doctrine which broke away from its original Calvinist basis to espouse free will and engender the belief that converts could and should use the political system to attempt to transform the world.

Chapter 4 considers the rise of the abolitionist movement and its channeling into electoral politics. It shows that electoral support was strongest in revivalist communities, and that the best explanation for their support of abolitionism is the belief they learned in the revivals.

Chapter 5 describes the transformation of abolitionism into political antislavery after 1848. Abolitionists were unable to achieve their goal until their political movement was taken over by others whose motives were economic and political rather than religious; the influence of revivalists on antislavery politics therefore declined, and their achievements were considerably less than they had hoped.

In Chapter 6, the influence of revivalism on later generations is documented. In the two states of this study, it was transformed in different ways. In New York revivalism became culturally conservative and its principal manifestation was support for prohibition. In Ohio it became completely identified with the Republican party, finally vanishing with the political transformation of the New Deal.

The concluding chapter is a discussion of the place of revivalism in American cultural history. Many commentators have seen in revivalism a source and affirmation of the cultural unity of the nation. That view, however, fails to understand that revivalist politics was derived from a transcendent faith which did not celebrate the condition of the American nation but judged it and found it wanting. Revivalism was also highly divisive in its consequences. The movement for abolition was supported by adherents of revivalism despite its possible destructive consequences because they felt an obligation to make their country more nearly reflect the will of God.

2

Religious Belief and Political Behavior

A political ethos is formed through a series of concrete historical events which force people to reinterpret the world. When these events occur in the sphere of religion, the resulting interpretation may have a religious dimension. In the case of the revivalist ethos, the events brought people to consider political choices in the light of their new religious values.

Many have argued against the claim that religious values have a formative influence on political behavior. If adherents to a particular religion adopt a common political preference or undertake common political activities, their behavior need not be motivated by the beliefs of their religion. For American social scientists, explanations of relationships between religious group membership and political behavior (as well as between religion and behavior in other spheres of life) have more often been of two other kinds: that religion is associated with other traits which affect political behavior (i.e., that the relationship is "spurious"), or that communal involvement in religion provides members with a group identity. The explanation that religious membership and activity provide members with distinctive values and orientations which they apply to political choices—the explanation which I argue applies to the politics adopted in revival communities—has been proposed far less often.

If a relation between religion and secular behavior is explained by the association of religion with other traits, then the initial relation is spurious. For example, the different voting behavior and socioeconomic attitudes of different religious groups may be due to the social class composition of those groups (Allinsmith & Allinsmith, 1948, pp. 379–83; Campbell et al., 1960, pp. 301–06). Not all findings have supported that conclusion (Berelson, Lazarsfeld, & McPhee, 1954, pp. 64–67; Lenski, 1963, pp. 138–42), but clearly the question should be asked: if one proposes that there is a direct influence of religious belief on such decisions as voting choice, then there should be a relationship between measured variables not explainable by socioeconomic status alone.

The explanation of such relations as being due to other, accidentally associated factors also referred to the historical experiences shared by members of the same religious group: that "they were predominantly immigrants, workers, or businessmen, or lived in a certain part of the country" (Lipset, 1964, p. 118). Similarly, the historical circumstances of some religious groups at a crucial stage in the development of political institutions often resulted in the formation of religious parties, so that members of a church or sect supported a party organized around its interests (Lipset & Rokkan, 1967, p. 15).

But such parties do not depend on the beliefs of the religion; rather they are "parties of religious defense," organized to combat a general secularism or to protect the institutional power of the church (Rokkan, 1967, pp. 389, 399). They are likely to assume a religious and moral legitimation, and may take stands (such as opposition to birth control) in accord with the church's teaching. The church, too, may act as a promoter of the party's interests by directly or indirectly encouraging the faithful to vote for it. But the religious beliefs of the members (as opposed to belief in the institutional church) bear only a tangential relation to their political attitudes; in any case, belief is far less a determinant of the strength of these parties than the relative sizes of religious groups in a nation and the relation between state and church (Lipset & Rokkan, 1967, p. 34).

Religious defense parties have never been important in American politics. They might be classified, however, under the second type of explanation of relationships between religion and political behavior, namely, that of religious group membership as a source of identity. Probably the most common explanation offered by American sociology for such relationships is to attribute them to what Lenski calls "communal involvement" in a religious group. Religion provides a basis of association, and common sentiments within groups, which are not necessarily related to any beliefs that particular religions maintain. As a basis of association, a religious group can form a segregated communications network through which it develops and transmits distinctive norms (Lenski, 1963, pp. 335–36).

Considerable evidence shows that there is high unanimity within religious groups on political and other matters, frequently far more than can be explained by the similarity in social status of the members. Further, agreement with the group norm is greater for people more closely identified with the group. In the 1948 election in Elmira, New York, Catholics were more likely to vote Democratic than Protestants, and Catholics who asserted that their religious group was among their "most important" identifications were more likely to vote Democratic than those for whom religious identification was less important. Berelson et al. (1954, pp. 67–69) claim that this was due to in-group association rather than to any direct efforts of the church or Catholic organizations.

Differential voting patterns of religious groups can perhaps be traced ultimately to the average position of those groups' members in the social structure; for example, the lower average status may determine the Democratic affiliation of many Catholics. But association within the group affects the political preferences even of those who do not share the modal status position. And in some instances the effect of in-group sentiment is not determined by the socioeconomic status of the individual or of the group. Catholic candidates of either party draw disproportionate support from Catholic voters (Campbell et al., 1960, pp. 319–21). Herberg (1960, pp. 34–35) has suggested that the tripartite division of religious traditions in the United States is replacing ethnicity as the dominant unit of political behavior.

Thus the understanding of religious group membership as a determinant of political opinions and behavior does not necessarily imply any influence of religious belief on secular attitudes or practices. Lenski (1963, pp. 18–23), in the major American study of the relation between religion and behavior in other spheres, emphasizes the importance of two dimensions of religious involvement, associational (church membership and activity) and communal (association with family and friends of the same religion); they are independent of each other, and each is influential in certain respects. He concludes that "it is both dangerous and misleading to suppose that theology provides the only basis for explaining differences among religious groups" (p. 184).

So it is, but this approach has its dangers as well: in particular, its results are often intellectually unsatisfying, for they reveal the existence of empirical relationships without investigating the causes of those relationships. For the most part, differences between religious groups that cannot be explained by other socioeconomic variables are speculatively assigned to differential socialization and association.

But research adopting this approach does not ask why religion is related to other aspects of behavior: does a Catholic, for example, vote Democratic because he believes that Catholics vote Democratic, or that the Democratic party represents Catholic interests, or does he unreflectively adopt the preference of most of his associates?[1] This research tradition makes no effort to ascertain whether voters perceive any relationship between their religious group membership and their politics.

The final type of explanation is that religions provide their members with distinctive orientations which make particular political attitudes compatible. As I have noted, it is this third explanation, religious belief, which I believe applies to the political consequences of revivalism. Members of a religion may adopt distinctive attitudes either because the religion's doctrine explicitly demands attitudes or behavior of political relevance, or because it creates general dispositions congenial to a secular political ideology (Lipset, 1964, p. 110).

Geertz (1966) defines a religion as

> a system of symbols which acts to establish powerful, pervasive, and long-lasting moods and motivations in men by formulating conceptions of a general order of existence and clothing these conceptions with such an aura of factuality that the moods and motivations seem uniquely realistic. (p. 4)

Religion confronts such characteristic problems of human experience as ignorance, pain, and injustice, and, while admitting that these problems are inescapable, denies that they are characteristic of the world as a whole. The denial that the world is "really" characterized by ignorance, pain, and injustice has two aspects: not only do people interpret the world in accordance with the affirmation of a transcendent reality, they also act to shape the world to conform to it. The "moods and motivations" which religion creates have their greatest impact not in the sphere of religious behavior where they are actually experienced, but in the individual's conceptions of "the established world of bare fact." Those who accept religion as a source of ultimate authority undertake the obligation to attempt to bring the world of their experience into harmony with the world symbolized in religious behavior (Geertz, 1966).

Thus religion establishes an ideal and creates a tension between it and reality which believers must attempt to resolve. Recognizing their obligation, they may act to transform the real (in their own behavior or in the world at large) to bring it more closely into conformity to the ideal.

But religious belief does not affect secular behavior universally or in a uniform way. In the first place, to speak of an effect of "the re-

---

[1]Geertz (1966, p. 41), arguing for the autonomy of religious belief, and Campbell et al. (1960, p. 292), arguing for the autonomy of political belief, make essentially the same point: that whatever the social structural correlates of particular orientations, they must be translated into perceptions before they can serve as motivating factors.

ligious" on "the secular" presumes that the two spheres are clearly differentiated. More important to the discussion of revivalism, it is necessary to specify what kind of behavior is expected. Different beliefs will produce different obligations. Moreover, some types of belief are more likely than others to exercise such influence. Religions vary in the degree to which their beliefs are oriented to the secular world and the degree to which they posit specific behavioral obligations for their members. Johnson (1957) draws a distinction between ethical and liturgical systems of justification: a liturgical system provides for "the transmission of grace through ceremonies performed by qualified priests," while an ethical system demands that its adherents "attempt to realize in their own conduct the principles in terms of which they are united" (p. 90).[2]

If a religion prescribes that salvation is achieved through the performance of ritual acts, there is little likelihood that its beliefs will make specific patterns of secular behavior obligatory. If, on the other hand, salvation is achieved by the performance of acts consonant with a set of religious principles, those principles may well have implications for political behavior, which will accordingly be influenced by religious obligation. One should expect, then, that a relation between religious group membership and secular behavior is more likely to be explained by the group's beliefs if their religion entails an ethical system of justification.

Weber's similar distinction between mystical and ascetic religions underlies his many studies of the relationships between religion, on the one hand, and economic and political behavior, on the other. Particularly in discussing the relation between religion and economic behavior, Weber argues that religion supplies orientations disposing adherents to positive attempts to transform the world. In his major work on this subject, *The Protestant Ethic and the Spirit of Capitalism*, he describes the practical consequences of an ethos of "inner-worldly asceticism,"[3] using Calvinism as his major example (the same Calvinism which, after considerable transformation, produced the revivals of the early nineteenth century). Inner-worldly asceticism views salvation as "the distinctive gift of active ethical behavior performed in the awareness that god directs this behavior [and performed] within the institutions of the world but in opposition to them" (Weber, 1968, vol. 2, pp. 541–42). Calvinism coupled inner-worldly asceticism with the

---

[2]Johnson uses this distinction as the basis for a reformulation of the church–sect dichotomy.

[3]Weber, or his translators, appear to use the words "ethos" and "ethic" almost interchangeably (cf. Weber, 1958b, p. 27).

convictions that God is inscrutable and that people cannot know whether they are saved. The psychological effect of these beliefs was to encourage labor within a fixed calling which might involve acquisitive activity, but without permitting the believer to enjoy the fruits of acquisition. Combined with necessary initial economic conditions, inner-worldly asceticism laid the foundations for the development of modern capitalism (Weber, 1958a, p. 336; 1958b, pp. 97, 155–73).

A systematization of religious belief around ascetic principles attempts to create a meaningful total relationship of the pattern of life to the goal of religious salvation; in this quest it is not governed by any sacred tradition, but only by an inner religious state. It thus acquires the capacity to revolutionize the worldly life of its believers. When people make conscious efforts to govern ("rationalize") their lives by a set of ultimate values, these values have a profound determining effect; and "in a time in which the beyond meant everything, when the social position of the Christian depended upon his admission to the communion [Weber refers, of course, to early Calvinist communities, but these conditions held in early nineteenth-century revival communities as well], religious forces [were] decisive influences" (Weber, 1958b, p. 155. See also Weber, 1958a, p. 287).

Such a belief system can influence specific patterns of behavior. The Puritans' belief system, for example, inspired them to economic productivity but did not allow them to enjoy their riches. These specific effects, however, were part of a larger pattern: "The decisive aspect of [a] religious ethic is . . . its theoretical attitude toward the world" (Weber, 1968, vol. 2, p. 578). Salvation was to be proved not by individual good works, but by a "type of conduct unmistakably different from the way of life of the natural man" (Weber, 1958b, p. 153). This meant not only that one must engage constantly in productive labor, but that one must plan one's whole life rationally in accordance with God's will; family life as well as economic behavior must be directed not toward enjoyment but toward the fulfillment of the will of God. The consequence, which became institutionalized and remained even after the religious ethic had lost its force, was the rational bourgeois economic life (Weber, 1958a, pp. 281; 1958b, p. 153, 174).

A particular characteristic of ascetic religions is that they posit obligations for conduct in the secular sphere; ascetic religions, in contrast to mystical religions, emphasize not the contemplation of God but activity in accordance with his will. In Geertz's terms, "motivations" rather than "moods" are the sought-after consequences of religious participation; the ascetic believes that he is an instrument of God. "The demand [is] implied: that the world order in its totality is, could and should somehow be a meaningful 'cosmos' " (Weber, 1958a, p. 281; see also Weber, 1968, vol. 2, pp. 541, 544–51). This perception applies equally to mystical and ascetic religions, but the contradictory mixture of tenses makes it especially appropriate for the ascetic: one affirms a state of affairs that is eternal, but one's behavior is nonetheless necessary in order to bring that state of affairs into existence.

Weber thus goes beyond the mere statement of association between forms of religious belief and patterns of economic activity. He attempts to account for those associations by interpreting religiously-sanctioned orientations as motivating factors. He pays little attention to religious practices, arguing that it is not religious activity, but the orientations toward the world encouraged by the content of religious belief that determine religion's influence on secular behavior (Weber, 1968, vol. 2, p. 578). But by disregarding religious practices he fails to establish how those orientations acquire their motivating power. Even if an affinity can be established between a set of religious beliefs and corresponding extrareligious activities, the beliefs by themselves are not sufficient to explain why believers act on them. The beliefs will be put into practice only if a strong conviction becomes attached to them, the kind of conviction which arises out of participation in religious ceremonies.

Scholars who examine the place of ceremonial and ritual in religion find in it the social validation of religious belief which gives that belief its compelling character. According to Durkheim (1965), it is through cult that religion affects worshippers' attitudes and motivations:

> The believers, the men who lead the religious life and have a direct sensation of what it really is, . . . feel that the real function of religion is not to make us think, . . . but rather, it is to make us act, to aid us to live. . . . In fact, whoever has really practiced a religion knows very well that it is the cult which gives rise to these impressions of joy, of interior peace, of serenity, of enthusiasm, which are, for the believer, an experimental proof of his beliefs. (pp. 463–64)

According to Geertz (1966), the function of ritual is to generate "the conviction that religious conceptions are veridical and that religious directives are sound." By providing a collective experience validating the truths apprehended, ritual provides men with belief in the authority claimed by religious doctrine. By "placing . . . proximate events in ultimate contexts, ritual sustains the motivations of the religious to transform the world of proximate events" (p. 28).

The revivals were a collective experience of this type. It might seem paradoxical to call the revivals a ritual, for "ritual" has several connotations foreign to revivals. "Ritualism" often means excessive devotion to the form of ceremonies without attention to their meaning. Revivalism explicitly abjured formal ceremonies; the revivals were meant to encourage believers to express their spontaneously felt religious convictions. But the revival was nevertheless a ritual. Though each participant acted spontaneously, revival meetings followed an established pattern.

"Ritual" has another connotation which the revivals did not share. Ritual is often regarded as a mechanism to bind people to society as a whole. Durkheim, in particular, adopts this view because he identifies religion with the total social collectivity. But in a religiously pluralistic society, any one religion may encourage forms of behavior distinct from, and even opposed to, those enjoined by the society's norms, as the revivals did.[4]

Finally, in many religions which emphasize ritual, the performance of the ceremonies is itself the fulfillment of religious duty. Revivalism was not liturgical but ethical: revivals were expected to stimulate convictions which would bear fruit in daily life. But the revivals' ritual pattern of exhortation and conversion was particularly appropriate for conveying the sense of obligation to the norms which were enjoined, for that pattern was permissible only because revivalists believed that individual will was central to conversion. For revival preachers, and for theologians in their wake, the interpretation of the revival was intimately related to the development of a theology which claimed that man might act to free both himself and the world of sin. The power to free the world of sin clearly implied the duty to do so. The doctrine was eventually interpreted to imply that man might use the instruments of government for the same end. Ritual in this case gave content as well as conviction to religious beliefs.

The use of political means to transform the world in fulfillment of religious obligations receives little attention from Weber. Because he defines the state by its monopoly over the use of force, he sees it as an enforcer rather than a creator of norms. Even where Weber suggests that inner-worldly asceticism can interpret political power structures as "instruments for the rationalized ethical transformation of the world and for the control of sin" (Weber, 1968, vol. 2, p. 593), the control which he envisions is exercised through repression rather than conversion. He does not discuss the possibility that religions which propose to change the world by changing individuals' attitudes and values might attempt to use the state as an instrument to that end.

[4]Some American historians have argued that the revivals did in fact help to create a unified national culture. Their arguments are discussed in Chapter 7.

But Weber's treatment of the effect of religious orientations on individual economic behavior can be extended to encompass political behavior as well. People can attempt to resolve the tension between the real and the ideal in various ways. When their political system allows them some measure of influence, they can advocate political ends which they believe will contribute to the achievement of their religious ideals.

The fact that revivals occurred in a country with an electoral democracy made revivalists more likely than Weber's Puritans to organize a political movement dedicated to changing their society. But another difference contributed to the same effect. The Puritans were in constant need of assurance of salvation, which they found by regulating their lives according to the standards of their religion. By the nineteenth century, revivalist Calvinism had largely resolved the problem of assurance; assurance was found in the conversion experience of the revival. Religion created an obligation not of discipline but of benevolence: the obligation to order the world in a manner that would facilitate the conversion of others. In both cases, however, the secular goals came to acquire precedence over the religious goals: the Protestant ethic became transformed from a means of religious assurance to a regulator of economic activity, and the doctrine of benevolence inspired political goals that were not oriented to salvation but to the temporal condition of those to whom it was directed.

Orientations grounded in religion can therefore continue to prevail after they have become detached from their religious roots. The wealth which puritanical ideals helped to accumulate created temptations which were not resisted, and formal correctness in behavior replaced the compulsive flight from uncertainty about salvation. But the Protestant ethic survives, even if it is only historically Protestant (Weber, 1958b, pp. 174–77). Charles Finney's revivals were the last to affect the Burned-Over District, and two decades later revivals had a different constituency and a different political significance, but the revivalist ethos continues to be a part of the region's culture and to affect its voting behavior.

There is an important difference, however: in Weber's interpretation, the Protestant ethic continues to be a pervasive orientation to work as a calling, which in the absence of religious motivation is supported by the rewards and the needs of a large-scale capitalist economy (Weber, 1958b, pp. 179–80). The revivalist ethos, on the other hand, is not a regular determinant of political behavior. The ethos became political in the heat of the controversy over slavery, but though it subsequently became institutionalized, its influence has been only sporadic. Only some elections have evoked the sentiments which make revivalist communities vote distinctively.

There have been three major issues: the position of blacks, temperance, and Populism. These issues, as they were presented in the affected elections, were related (although in different ways) to the content of revivalist preaching. But the three issues share another characteristic: the manifest content of each is unrelated to the everyday affairs of people in the revival areas who apparently based voting decisions on them.

Berelson et al. (1954, pp. 184–85) distinguish between issues of position and issues of style, according to whether the issues directly involve the self-interest of voters. Position issues are based on "self-interest of a relatively direct kind"; they place in opposition "classes, geographical sections, industries, and similar economic organizations"; and they are important for long periods. Style issues, on the other hand, are based on "self-expression of a rather indirect, projective kind," and oppose "religious and ethnic groups . . . and similar cultural groups, as well as opposing personality types," and are topical and of short duration. Berelson et al. suggest that style issues are likely to be created by political parties rather than to emerge as autonomous demands of the population, and to assume importance when economic issues are not important—as it were, to fill a vacuum. Prohibition, for example, was much more important in 1928 than in 1932, when "there were 'more real' issues at stake."[5]

Berelson et al. take for granted that position issues, as matters of direct self-interest, are of interest to voters, but offer no discussion of the reasons why segments of the electorate should polarize on style issues. One answer to that question is offered by Hofstadter, Gusfield, and others in discussions of "status politics" and "symbolic politics," phenomena which bear a clear relation to Berelson et al.'s "style" issues. Hofstadter and Gusfield argue that issues not directly related to economic interest or to the allocation of power have played an important role in American politics. In particular, they argue, such issues become important in status conflicts. They suggest that in periods when the nonmaterial status of groups in society is changing, the groups whose status is declining will reassert their place in the status order by adopting positions that affirm the validity of their own life-style in preference to others. Battles over such issues illustrate one of the characteristic processes of American democracy: that "seemingly ceremonial or ritual acts of government are often of great importance to many social groups" (Gusfield, 1963, p. 6; see also Hofstadter, 1964b).

---

[5]Their study is of the 1948 election, and they offer no evidence for their assertion about the lessened importance of prohibition in 1932. I shall question that view in Chapter 6.

Gusfield and Hofstadter both view the temperance movement as the classic example. They claim that the temperance movement arose among the members of an old middle class whose status was declining as the center of American life moved from the small town to the city, and as the increasing size of government and enterprise seemed to make the Protestant virtues of self-control and industriousness irrelevant.

Gusfield and Hofstadter identify the same process, but call it by different names. Hofstadter, referring to "status politics," emphasizes the fact that changes in the status order can create political issues just as material self-interest can. Gusfield, who refers to "symbolic politics," emphasizes that life-style and value system can become symbols of higher status, and examines the process by which issues can be selected to assert status privileges. Both argue that status anxiety led the old middle class to endorse temperance in order to achieve legislation which would enforce, and thereby legitimize, their stratum's values and enable them to maintain or recover their lost status.

Loss of status is thus one reason why groups might adopt political stands which apparently have no consequences for their material position. These discussions, however, tend to imply that such issues are less important than those which involve tangible self-interest. Berelson et al. characterize style issues as being topical and of short-term importance, while they say that position issues are historical and of long-term importance. But hindsight reveals that the very issues they discuss belie their claim. For example, the Taft-Hartley Act was a highly topical question in 1948, but it soon ceased to be debated, even though the broader issue of labor-management relations which it involved had long been, and continues to be, important. Similarly, any "style" issue of immediate, topical importance also emerges in a context which has been formed over a long period. Their examples of style issues are international relations and civil rights; the events of recent years belie any claim that these are of limited or short-term importance.

Just as Berelson et al. deny the durability of style issues, they also imply that such issues do not reflect strongly felt positions of voters, but are created by political parties when "more real" issues are absent. But for the issues related to the revivalist ethos, the very opposite was the case: they were first raised by movements outside of the party system. The major parties attempted to maintain ambiguous positions until the strength of feeling in the electorate forced them to declare themselves more clearly or, in the case of slavery, be superseded by a new major party which took a less ambiguous stand.

In these and other respects, Berelson et al. tend to see economic (or position) issues as "real" and style (or symbolic) issues as "phony." But the most casual observation of American politics in almost every era reveals that issues are not less hotly contested nor less consequential for being unrelated to immediate self-interest. Nor is the line between issues of position and issues of symbolic importance easy to draw. In *Voting*, style issues are clearly a residual category, covering everything not related to material well-being. But many issues can function as foci both of material and of symbolic struggles (Gusfield, 1963, p. 147), and the allocation of values to status groups can change the balance of power in a political system. For those who brought the slavery controversy into the political arena, it was principally a symbolic issue, but it aroused a conflict whose resolution was of clear and substantial importance to others who engaged in it. The achievement of prohibition likewise represented an assertion of real political power by the groups that supported it.

Those who analyze prohibition as an example of symbolic politics do not deny the real importance of symbolic issues, but their analysis is limited in another way. Any use of the terms "symbolic politics" and "symbolic issues" must specify what it is that is symbolized by political choices. To identify symbolic politics with status conflicts is to restrict too narrowly the range of referents of political symbols; debate over values does not necessarily reflect only distinctions of status.[6]

Issues can be symbolic of a given status order, and thus serve to protect or reinstate it. They can also symbolize historic allegiances and aspirations of social groups, and the values these allegiances represent. To be sure, these facets are likely to be confounded in concrete instances: as historical factors are important in forming groups which occupy different statuses, the cultural differences thus created are likely to give content to conflicts of status when they arise.

Nevertheless, issues can also become symbolic because of a group's attachment to values that these issues bring into focus, and conflicts over them can be due to the conviction of individuals as well as to status discrepancies suffered by the groups to which they belong. As Geertz (1964, pp. 62–64) points out, an ideology is a way of organizing perceptions and can become a motivating force independent of the social situation which gives rise to it. This fact must be considered in examining the response of a political ethos to symbolic issues.

[6]Hofstadter (1964a, pp. 99–103) himself points this out in a 1962 postscript to his 1955 article on pseudo-conservatism in which he refers to cultural politics (of which he offers prohibition as an example), and finds religious fundamentalism to be an important component of the politics of the radical right.

For example, the political controversy in the north over slavery cannot easily be reduced to a status conflict between subcultures within the north itself. Some have tried to explain it as an example of status politics (I deal with their arguments in more detail in Chapter 4), but the groups it polarized had status orders which were not very different and neither group practiced slavery; it would therefore not have been an appropriate symbol for any status conflict between them. For abolitionists, the possibility of abolishing slavery did not symbolize the assertion of their own place in the status order but rather the creation of a new social order in which the universal opportunity to achieve salvation was recognized and facilitated.

The endorsement of prohibition in revivalist communities in later generations symbolized an assertion of status. But status politics still does not constitute a sufficient explanation of their support for prohibition, for it does not explain how temperance came to be a symbol of social worth for them. A value will only be an effective symbol of social worth to a stratum to the extent that its members hold to the value strongly and sincerely. Prohibition was a positive value for voters in revivalist communities because it was part of their historical experience. The revivals had formed a culture with which they identified, and which distinguished them from those whom they believed to be achieving superiority over them.

Both abolition and prohibition were symbolic issues, albeit symbolic of different things, but both functioned as symbols because the communities that adopted them had experienced the revivals of the early nineteenth century which condemned both slavery and alcohol, and through which opposition to both became an element of their communities' culture.

When issues of this character become important, religious belief, directly or historically, is likely to have an effect on voting behavior. According to the authors who discuss symbolic or style issues, such issues emerge by default when class issues are unimportant, that is, generally in times of economic prosperity. "Position issues seem to have . . . strength because economic conditions call them forth with such cogency," according to Berelson et al. (1954, p. 185). Status hierarchies are likely to undergo readjustments when general prosperity brings about "a changed pattern in the distribution of deference and power," according to Hofstadter (1955, p. 135; cf. Hofstadter, 1964b, pp. 84–85). This study began with a similar hypothesis (even though symbolic issues are defined differently): that voters would look to their religion and the culture which grew out of it for standards when immediate interest offered no guidelines for electoral choice.

That hypothesis has not been confirmed. Since the Civil War, the points at which the revivalist ethos was most closely reflected in voting patterns were 1896 and the period 1926–1936; at both these times the nation's voting patterns were strongly affected by severe depressions, but for some voters their revivalist heritage was at least an equally important determinant of their vote.

The question of when the ethos will be salient, then, must be answered differently. It appears that specifically political conditions determine whether an issue affected by the ethos will be at stake in a campaign. Tautologically, the choice between candidates in a given election will be determined by the ethos when the candidates are distinguishable in its terms: one candidate must, either in his person or in his policies, hold out the promise that the "really real" world envisioned by the ethos will be realized. Further, for those influenced by the ethos, this dimension of choice must overwhelm other possible dimensions. The ethos is likely to become salient, then, either when the recognized bases for political decisions (traditional party affiliation and material interest, for example) do not clearly distinguish the available candidates, or when candidates, even though they are distinguished on these bases, show differences in terms of the injunctions of the ethos which appear overwhelmingly more important. The salience of a political ethos will be greatest, not when other dimensions are not necessary, but when they are not sufficient.

Whether voters' choices will be based on the revivalist ethos, then, depends on the choices that political parties make available. But it has been only occasionally that either of the major parties has presented a candidate to whose appeal the ethos responded. Rather, candidates who appealed to the values of the ethos have most often run on the tickets of one-issue minor parties. When revivalists have believed that neither major party represented their views sufficiently clearly, they have created new political vehicles to present candidates with unambiguous stands to which voters who shared the ethos could respond. Revivalists, acting with a strength based on conviction and out of proportion to their numbers, created abolitionist and prohibitionist parties, kept these organizations alive, and voted for them, even though they had no prospects of victory, because the parties clearly espoused positions with which the revivalists agreed.

The impact of abolitionism on American politics was much greater than the impact of the prohibition movement: it made slavery a major issue and forced a reorientation of the major parties' positions. A new party was formed which, though not abolitionist, was sufficiently strong in opposition to slavery to win most abolitionist votes and rise to major-party status. In contrast, prohibition had no such effect. The Prohibition party existed for several decades and consistently won a very small vote (and in New York, that vote came chiefly from revivalist communities). But although prohibition was achieved, it neither led to a realignment of the party system nor did it have much effect on politics in the long term.

The contrast between the effect of slavery and the effect of prohibition on national politics appears to demonstrate a limitation on political movements inspired by religious values, namely, that they are not by themselves sufficient to exert a major impact on the political system. They can have that impact only when their issues become identified with major economic or political interests. Slavery was a symbolic issue for the revivalists, for its continued existence symbolized the state of sin in which the country lay. For others it came to be the focus of intersectional economic and political conflict. Northern political leaders realized that the abolitionist constituency could be mobilized to support the expansion of a free-labor economy and to help defeat what they saw as the south's hegemony in national politics. Under these conditions, the distinct influence of the revivalists decreased, for they entered into a coalition with others who had different aims.

Prohibition, on the other hand, never came to be identified with a fundamental conflict of political interests. Even when it was most salient—in the periods just before the prohibition amendment was passed and just before it was repealed—it was regarded by many politicians as a distraction, an issue on which they were forced to take a stand to please a part of their constituencies but one which had nothing to do with their real political concerns.[7] Under these conditions the Prohibition party existed and won a steady but very small vote in revivalist communities for several decades. Prohibitionist candidates enjoyed spurts of strength when the major parties appeared to be changing positions on the issue (as when the New York Republican party officially withdrew its lukewarm support of the Prohibition amendment in 1930), but they never made much difference in state politics.

On one occasion, during the election of 1896, the revivalist ethos was an important determinant of voting behavior even though the revivalists themselves had little to do with shaping political choices. In that year the Democratic party presented a candidate who could not be evaluated on conventional bases, but could be evaluated in terms of the ethos. After an uprising of agrarian discontent, Populists cap-

---

[7]This impression, conveyed by historians (cf. Hofstadter, 1955, pp. 289–93), is also indirectly confirmed by a source sympathetic to the Anti-Saloon League (see Odegard, 1966, p. 129).

tured the Democratic party and nominated William Jennings Bryan. Bryan's image promised the triumph of virtue which the revivalist ethos demanded, although the revivalist constituency had no influence on his victory within the Democratic party. The Populist movement itself, though in some respects similar to the revivalist ethos, was fundamentally based on economic conditions. But the image Bryan projected nevertheless appealed to voters in revivalist communities in New York and won their votes when the rest of the state was voting overwhelmingly Republican.

In summary, symbolic issues become salient in much the same way as interest issues, even though they have a different cognitive character. They become politically important either because voters especially motivated by them create a new political vehicle to represent them explicitly or because a major party, in a state of transition, adopts the revivalist position in the hope of attracting a new constituency. When the choice presented to voters reflects distinctions which the ethos makes important, they respond in the manner which the ethos dictates.

I have argued that the nature of religion generally and the specific character of revivalism both suggest the possibility that a political ethos based on revivalist beliefs was responsible for the unique political behavior of revivalist communities. That is not, to be sure, the only possible explanation. An empirical relation between religious group membership and some form of secular behavior may have other causes. My argument that the effect of religious belief accounts for revivalist politics will be established by a detailed analysis of revival beliefs and practices, as well as an empirical examination of hypotheses derived from the religious-belief explanation contrasted to those derived from other possible explanations. Both the view of the nature of God and man which the revivalists taught and the behavior in daily life which they encouraged disposed believers to intervene politically to achieve their goals. Moreover, the empirical relation between the occurrence of revivals and subsequent voting patterns shows that it is less likely that the relation was due either to communal religious involvement or to accidentally associated factors than that it grew out of religious belief. It was by transforming belief systems that the revivals created a lasting political ethos.

3

The Revival Movement

The wave of revivals which spread from western New York in the 1820s and 1830s was primarily inspired by the preaching of Charles Grandison Finney. These revivals led to great increases in church membership, especially on the unchurched (and, according to those who supported the revival, irreligious) frontier (Cole, 1954, p. 13). Revivals have occurred intermittently in American Protestantism at least since Jonathan Edwards's preaching inspired the first Great Awakening, which began in western Massachusetts in 1734. In practically every generation, outpourings of revivalism led to increased fervency and increased church membership. Between waves, emotions calmed, backslidings occurred, and the churches settled into a complacency which then generated a new series of revivals.

But the revivals of the 1820s and 1830s were more widespread than any of their predecessors, at least in the areas where the Calvinist heritage was predominant. They were also of a new kind: Finney made revivals a human product rather than a gift of grace, and taught that God required men to promote them. The new belief implied that men must act both to save souls and to free the world of sin. And its political implications transformed the political loyalties and traditions of the areas where the revivals occurred, forming a political ethos whose influence persisted long after the revivals had ended.

Western New York, in which the revivals were concentrated, came to be known as the "Burned-Over District." The name originally meant "burnt-out," describing the barren state in which the area was left after its waves of enthusiasm subsided. It came to refer, however, to the frequent and intense outpourings of religious fervor themselves, in an analogy between fires of the forest and fires of the spirit. The Burned-Over District produced not only the Finneyite revival movement, but the Mormons, the Oneida Community, and many more millennial and utopian movements. It includes roughly the area of New York State west of the Adirondacks and Catskills (Barnes, 1964, p. 161; Cross, 1950, pp. 3–4). The area was also referred to, simply, as "the west," even though it extends to longitudes east of some of the "eastern" cities (such as Philadelphia, Wilmington, and Baltimore).

This part of New York, all the area beyond the Hudson and Mohawk Valleys, was virtually unsettled until the end of the eighteenth century. But once settlement began, the area filled up rapidly. Except for a small area along the Pennsylvania border, the majority of the settlers in western New York were migrants from New England. The Yankee settlers came principally from hill-country New England, the area that had been most affected by the Great Awakening and by the succession of revivals that occurred throughout the eighteenth century. Indeed, religious differences dating back to the Awakening were often part of the motive for migration (Barnes, 1964, p. 161; Cross, 1950, pp. 3–13; Mathews, 1909, pp. 153–69).

The Yankees who settled western New York formed communities with a culture different from that of the older communities of New York. The Hudson and Mohawk Valleys and most of what is now the New York metropolitan area were populated by Yorkers, descendants of the early Dutch and English settlers. As the middle years of the nineteenth century approached, they were joined by large numbers of newer immigrants who were in some ways closer in politics and culture to the Yorkers than were the Yankees (Benson, 1964, pp. 177–85; Fox, 1963).

The population of Ohio was also divided into two cultural groups. Ohio had a large Yankee population, but it was not so compactly settled. The first settlers of what is now Ohio were New Englanders who had sailed down the Ohio River to the Ohio Company's Purchase, founding Marietta in 1788. The Purchase continued to be a destination for migrants from New England. But most of Ohio's Yankees settled on the Western Reserve in the northeastern corner of the state. Many of them had not migrated directly from New England but had settled first in New York, or were the children of settlers who remained in New York (Chaddock, 1908, pp. 13–16; Mathews, 1909, pp. 173–81). Like the Burned-Over District from which so many of them had come, their territory was swept by revivalism in the 1820s. The southern portion of the state was settled largely from Virginia and Kentucky, and the eastern area between the Reserve and the

Ohio Company's Purchase was settled by Pennsylvanians, including Pennsylvania Germans and others whose Scotch–Irish ancestry resembled that of many of the Southerners (Chaddock, 1908, pp. 14–18, 30–37).

Church membership on the frontier in the early nineteenth century was quite small, and the revivals were an appropriate response to the unique combination of religious and social conditions which made it so. Denominationalism and the voluntary principle of church membership were inevitable conditions of American Protestantism. Many churches had been brought from Europe to America, and many more had been created. The multiplicity of churches precluded any establishment, so no denomination received state support (after the disestablishment of Congregationalism in New England), and none could claim the automatic adherence of all the residents of a territory. Territorial expansion meant that vast areas were settled where churches did not even exist. Revivals provided a mechanism for churches to establish themselves in new territories and to incorporate people who had no birthright membership in any church (Mead, 1963, pp. 107–27).

New congregations were first established by those settlers who had already been church members in their former homes. But they expanded through revivals. Revivalism differed from its twentieth-century descendant in that it was not separate from ordinary church life, but an integral part of it. The revivals did not introduce religion into an area, but built upon an already existing framework of institutions and beliefs (Mathews, 1969, p. 25). They almost always took place in the churches themselves or under the sponsorship of particular congregations.

It was not only the recency of settlement that made frontier church membership small and the revivals necessary to enlarge it. Church membership was not entered into casually, and there were many who, though they attended church regularly and held orthodox beliefs, did not regard themselves as converted. Conversion was a test for church membership, and was taken quite seriously: not having experienced a dramatic revelation which convinced him of his salvation, one might continue for years to believe that he was a sinner. Many such people hoped to be converted at some future revival (Cross, 1950, pp. 6–11). The majority of the people who were affected by revivals were in this category: not the profligate or the skeptical, but "sinners by courtesy only" (Barnes, 1964, p. 25).

Denominational affiliation on the frontier was not rigid. With churches few and far between, people attended the church that was available. The frequent revivals became community events which everyone attended. Revival preachers did not emphasize fine points of doctrine, both because their understanding of their mission did not require them to and because their usually limited theological education did not permit it.

Congregationalists and Presbyterians institutionalized inter-denominational cooperation in their 1801 Plan of Union. Under this plan the (national) General Assembly of the Presbyterian Church and the Connecticut General Association (Congregational) agreed that ministers of either denomination could be placed in churches of the other, and that new churches in New England would become Congregational while those to the west would become Presbyterian. The similar theologies of the two churches, despite their differences of polity, encouraged them to cooperate to face the dual problems of spreading Unitarianism and the difficulty of supplying clergymen to frontier areas (Cross, 1950, pp. 18–19).

The General Association had sent missionaries to the west as early as 1784, and eventually established the Connecticut Missionary Society. Its missionaries went to three areas: Vermont, western New York, and the Western Reserve of Ohio. Support followed settlement and gradually shifted westward, but half the number of missionaries were sent to the Burned-Over District for the first sixteen years. After 1801 the Society began sending its clergymen to Plan of Union churches, with the result that the Presbyterian Church grew rapidly through the provision of Congregational money, Congregationally trained clergy, and members who had come from Congregational antecedents. The Presbyterian Church grew larger than either the Baptist or the Methodist in the area, and it provided the auspices for the major revival movements of the period. As many Yankees migrated to northeastern Ohio after settling in New York, the development of the Presbyterian Church there followed a similar pattern (Davis, 1929, 481–82; Mathews, 1909, pp. 187–88; Presbyterian Church, 1941, pp. 90–91).

As early as the winter of 1799–1800, upstate New York was swept by what came to be known as the Great Revival, at the same time that a more boisterous revival occurred in Kentucky. There were smaller outbursts again in 1807–1808, 1815, 1819, and 1821 (Cross, 1950, pp. 9–12). So a tradition of revivals already existed in the area in which Charles G. Finney, who became the leading revivalist of the early nineteenth century, grew up.

Finney was born in Warren, Connecticut, in 1792, but he was taken west at the age of two. His family first settled in Oneida County, New York, and later on the shore of Lake Ontario. He received no college education, but taught school for a while and then went to Adams, New York, in 1818 to study law privately. Though he regularly attended the Presbyterian Church in Adams, he was unconverted, and his fiancée and his pastor, George Gale, prayed regularly for his conversion.

In the fall of 1821, he experienced a struggle with his conscience lasting three days until "it seemed as if I met the Lord Jesus Christ face to face." The next day he met the deacon of his church, whom he was to represent in court that day, and told him, "I have a retainer from the Lord Jesus Christ to plead his cause and I cannot plead yours." He abandoned his promising legal practice and began to study theology under Gale. Even in his early theological training he was unable to accept the strict Calvinism of the Westminster Confession. He found that Gale, who was considerably more orthodox, could offer him no proof of that creed that would be sustained in a court of law. After two years of study he was licensed to preach by the Presbytery of St. Lawrence in northern New York and a few months later he was appointed by an Oneida County female missionary society to preach in "the Northern parts of the County of Jefferson and such other destitute places in the vicinity as his discretion shall dictate" (Finney, 1876, pp. 4–61).

Finney conducted successful revivals in small towns in northern New York during 1824 and 1825. His revival in Western, New York, in September 1825, was the first to receive notice in eastern newspapers and his fame began to spread outside of the immediate area. From there he went on to conduct even more successful campaigns in the larger towns of Rome, Utica, Auburn, and Troy during the next two years. The increasing attention he received in the east brought with it a growing condemnation of what were regarded as the excesses of some of his methods (Finney, 1876, pp. 73–201).

During this time, Finney gathered around him a loosely organized group of followers who became known as "Finney's Holy Band." Some were already clergymen who were impressed with his success in revitalizing their churches (including his own former pastor and teacher, George Gale). Others were young men whom he converted and who decided to follow him into the revival ministry. Of these, the most impressive and important was Theodore Dwight Weld, a young New Yorker whom Finney converted while he was a student at Hamilton College (Cross, 1950, pp. 168, 202; Finney, 1876, pp. 184–88), who later became a leading abolitionist.

Although the people who heard Finney preach knew a long tradition of revivals, the ones in which they took part had a new character. The difference is illustrated by a subtle change of terminology which appeared at about this time. Even though the event was perceived as similar to the revivals of the previous century, the word "revival" acquired a different connotation. Originally used in the context "revival of religion," it now came to refer to "revival meetings." The emphasis thus came to be on the revival as a process rather than as a result.

Implicit in the distinction is the contrast between the belief that a revival occurred when God, in his infinite wisdom, saw fit to visit the church with it, and the belief that men, or a man, could deliberately stimulate a revival. According to Jonathan Edwards revivals were miracles which ministers "had no more agency in producing than they had in producing thunder or a storm of hail or an earthquake" (quoted in McLoughlin, 1959, p. 85). Finney explicitly disagreed with this view, saying that a revival "is a purely philosophical result of the right use of the constituted means." And by "philosophical," as McLoughlin notes, he meant "scientific" (Finney, 1960, pp. 13, 11n).

It is evident that a different theology, a different understanding of the relationship between God and man, underlay these two approaches to revivals. A part of the difference lay simply in the fact that in the first case, the relationship was defined by God's part in it, whereas in the second, at least relatively, man played a much greater part. Acceptance of the philosophy of constituted means also led to deliberate consideration of the measures that were permissible, appropriate, and effective in aiding the revivalist to bring his hearers to a conviction of their sinful state.

Believing that men could produce revivals, Finney clearly also believed that it was their obligation to do so. And believing that revivalism was a science, he devoted himself to discovering the methods of its application. During this period a whole new set of techniques, known as the New Measures, was developed to give the preacher more direct control of the course of a revival. The New Measures have been attributed wholesale to Finney, but he merely codified what others had already made common practice. Some of the measures were used by Jonathan Edwards, and perhaps earlier. Others were current in western New York before Finney. Daniel Nash in particular is known to have used some of the practices that came to be particularly identified with Finney. "Father" Nash was an upstate evangelist who began his mission before Finney did and taught him some of his methods (Cross, 1950, pp. 160–61, 179; Finney, 1876, pp. 70–71).

But codify the measures Finney undoubtedly did, and develop them to a fine point which he regarded as a science. His *Lectures on Revivals of Religion*, delivered in 1835, were an exposition not only of the measures but of his reasons for using them. They were all based on his principle that the winning of souls in a revival could be made scientific ("philosophical") by using methods that harmonized with the "laws of mind" (Finney, 1960, pp. 12–13).

The measures he advocated and practiced formed a comprehensive, coherent system of methods of persuasion. They encouraged public declarations of anxiety for one's soul and, when converted, of one's salvation. They enlisted allies in the family and community to pressure the potential convert. Above all, they involved dramatic, emotion-arousing preaching to remind listeners of the torments of hell and the joys of salvation.

Prayer was a central part of the revival. Formal prayer meetings occurred every evening during a revival season. These meetings were tense and emotional. Attenders were encouraged to give audible and physical vent to their emotions. To those who found groaning and bodily movement at religious services unseemly, Finney acknowledged that groaning should not be artificial. But he felt that refusing to groan might be a way of "resisting the Holy Ghost" (Finney, 1960, p. 105). All those present (including women) were encouraged to pray aloud. Vocal participation by women in religious meetings was not new to the frontier, but it was one of Finney's practices that most aroused his opponents (Cross, 1950, p. 177).

Finney not only encouraged more frequent prayer, especially during the revival season, but encouraged a qualitatively different style of prayer. Requests directed to God should not be vague, but for a precise object (usually the conversion of a particular person, mentioned by name). The prayer should be offered with the right motive, and with absolute faith that God would immediately intervene to fulfill the request (Finney, 1960, pp. 52–71). Prayers in Sunday meetings could thus be used as effectively as sermons, since the minister in his extemporaneous prayers reported to God on the behavior of his flock.

During the week, the revivalist and his lay supporters met regularly to pray for the salvation of the community. Small groups, most frequently composed of women, prayed by name for particular people (not the least their sinning husbands). These praying circles also provided monitorial assistants in public meetings to speak with those who had become anxious for salvation.

Pastoral visiting was also adopted to revival usage. In times past, the settled pastor usually called only on his own flock. The itinerant, however, would visit every home, often accompanied by a praying circle. He came not to socialize but to exhort. The prayer of faith was particularly used on these visits, as the minister and the converted members of the family knelt and recited the plight of the sinning relatives present. Later, when Finney preached in large cities, pastoral visiting by members of the congregation became an advertising technique, as they went from house to house in the neighborhood of the church carrying notices and inviting strangers to attend the meeting (Cross, 1950, pp. 179–180; McLoughlin, 1959, p. 98).

The devices mentioned so far were preparatory to the real work of revivals: they were directed toward arousing a community's anxiety over its members' spiritual state. They could be, and often were, used in anticipation of a revivalist's visit or in hope of creating the conditions that would demand the calling of a revivalist. But a revival was intended to win souls, and effective measures were also developed to that end. Once a person was aroused to an acute awareness of his own sinfulness and his need for repentance, special techniques were created to be applied unrelentingly to him. The inquiry meeting occurred after a regular revival meeting, as interested persons were invited to remain behind to receive counsel. The "anxious bench," introduced in the Rochester revival of 1830–1831, was a special pew in the front of the church to which those who had been aroused by the revivalist's preaching could come forward to receive prayers and special exhortation (Finney, 1876, pp. 288–89).

The "protracted meeting" was the village counterpart of the Kentucky camp meeting which had developed during the great revivals of the turn of the century. Since sermons specifically directed at the unconverted were the best means of bringing them to repentance, several days' preaching would be that much more effective than an hour's. Protracted meetings generally lasted about four days, with continuous meetings from morning to night. Merchants and businessmen closed their stores, farmers and housewives left their duties, and everyone concentrated intensely on the state of his soul. In large cities, where business could not so easily be brought to a halt, the protracted meeting was adapted to a three- or four-week period during which meetings were held every night (Finney, 1960, pp. 262–67; McLoughlin, 1959, pp. 92–94).

Originally, successive meetings were addressed by several different preachers in turn: the pastor, his assistants, and preachers who came from neighboring communities to help him when an unexpected season of revival had visited him. Finney altered this practice, believing that a single man should conduct all services. In a characteristic analogy, he argued that a sick person would not call in a different physician every day. The physician "would not know what the symptoms had been nor what was the course of the disease or the treatment nor what remedies had been tried nor what the patient could bear. Why he would certainly kill the Patient" (Finney, 1960, p. 245). Had he been familiar with modern medical practice he would undoubtedly have added that when a man was in particular pain over the state of his soul, he required a specialist.

As revivals made the itinerant specialist more important, the settled pastor became less so. The new measures encouraged dependence on revivals as the chosen time for soul-saving, which might be ignored at other times. They also encouraged a man who had theatrical talents to become a full-time revivalist and gave the itinerant an aura of glory that the settled pastor lacked.

The protracted meeting clearly required a special kind of preaching talent. Finney believed that preachers should be dramatic: handclapping, gesticulation, and sudden modulations of the voice would more vividly impress the hearers (Cross, 1950, pp. 173–75). Rhetorical techniques were well developed. Any unusual event could be interpreted as a sign of the coming millennium; the death of an unrepentant sinner became an example to the living, the revivalist describing his pain and torture vividly; prominent or skeptical members of the community were particular objects of exhortation, for their conversion could be turned to good effect as an example to others (Cross, 1950, p. 182).

More important than these rhetorical devices, however, was the revivalist's colloquial manner, exemplified by Finney's own style. He preached extemporaneously, so that he could take advantage of his audience's reactions. He rarely used notes, and when he did, they were mere outlines (he called them "skeletons") containing citations of Bible passages to incorporate in a sermon (Finney, 1876, p. 96). His preaching was direct, in short sentences and simple language. He was proud to report in his *Memoirs* the comment of one person who had heard him: "he don't preach; he only explains what other people preach" (p. 92). He made frequent use of analogies from agriculture, mechanics, and medicine, bringing his principles as close as he could to the experience of those who heard him, and exemplifying his conviction that the conversion of souls, like these other pursuits, was a science.

His sermons were not theological discourses, but direct statements to the sinner of the danger in which he stood if he did not repent and the joys that would be his if he did. He did not discuss sinners in the third person, but brought people into direct involvement by the use of "you." Every sermon was an exhortation to conversion. Even the *Lectures*, intended as an exposition of principles rather than a revival, were used as an occasion to win souls. (They were actually delivered as lectures, and the published version is based on a listener's notes.) Nearly every lecture closed with a demand that the hearers put into practice the principles they had just heard, by examining their own consciences, praying, and working for the conversion of others.

The new measures easily could, and did, lead to excess. Since Finney was more effective than any of his predecessors, he was also the man who brought notoriety to the measures, and he became the target of most of the opposition to them that developed with his growing renown. Opposition first arose in the Oneida Presbytery, where he conducted revivals between 1825 and 1827. The clergy there, close to the scene of Finney's work, were not so concerned about his practices as about those of some of his followers, who were especially enthusiastic in encouraging women to pray in public meetings and felt it their duty to invade the parishes of ministers opposed to revivals, denouncing them as enemies of God.

Such practices did not encourage traditional churchmen to be enthusiastic about the revivals. But the revivalists of this period were not schismatic; they did not form new denominations, and they did not regard themselves as independent of the existing churches. Some of Finney's more moderate supporters, hoping to preserve harmony, began to counsel him to check the reins of his most enthusiastic imitators (McLoughlin, 1959, pp. 20–30).

As revivalism flared throughout the area, some of Finney's opponents decided that they needed help from New England Congregational leaders to put an end to the excesses. A series of increasingly hostile exchanges between Finney and his followers, on the one hand, and his opponents and their New England supporters, on the other, led to a meeting between the two parties at New Lebanon, New York, in July 1827 (Beecher, 1961, vol. 2, pp. 74–76; Cross, 1950, pp. 30–37; Finney, 1876, pp. 211–17). The meeting was called by one of Finney's supporters in the hope of healing the breach.

Finney and several of his followers met for nine days of debate with the New England party led by Lyman Beecher of Boston and Asahel Nettleton, famed evangelist of the revival of 1800. Nettleton, more conservative now than he had been in his days as a revivalist, hoped to achieve a complete repudiation of Finney, but the outcome was inconclusive. The dispute was not over revivals themselves; the conferees unanimously adopted a resolution that "the idea that God ordinarily works independently of human instrumentality, or without reference to the adaption [sic] of means to ends, is unscriptural." The dispute was rather over the abuses of revival practices, but the obvious success of Finney's methods made it impossible for the New Englanders to repudiate him (Cross, 1950, p. 163; Opie, 1963, p. 330).

The dispute was not theological, because the more progressive thinkers of New England Congregationalism had long since abandoned strict Calvinism. The development of New England theology responded to the experiences gained by theologians in the revivals themselves (Opie, 1963). Under the leadership of Nathaniel Taylor, New Haven theologian and pioneer of the New Divinity, Congregational preachers were emphasizing the free will of men and their free agency in coming to God. This was understood by some as an assertion that a sinner could convert himself, and thus a denial of the old Calvinistic doctrine that a sinner could only be converted by the direct intervention of the Holy Spirit, but the Taylorites' reconciliations of their views with the Westminster Confession were ingenious. The acknowledgment of free will certainly made a strict acceptance of predestination impossible, but the drift toward Arminianism was a largely unconscious response to the success of revivals (Smith, 1957, pp. 88–89). Though Finney knew little of Taylorite theology, it was consistent with his own thought and practices.

Reports in the press of the New Lebanon conference pushed Finney even further into the limelight, and his successes grew. His ambition was to go to Boston, but his friends Gale and Weld, recognizing that his success was due at least in part to the peculiar susceptibility of westerners to his methods, counseled him to remain where the reception was better and the opposition smaller. He did move on, however, to Wilmington in 1827 and Philadelphia in 1828; in Philadelphia, site of the annual Presbyterian General Assembly meetings, he encountered considerable opposition from many of the leading Presbyterians of the city, but his revival was successful and he gained the support of some of the clergy. Excursions to New York in 1828 and 1829 further increased his fame, but his crowning achievement was the Rochester revival of 1830–1831.

The Rochester revival lasted for six months, from September to March, and during the period Finney preached three times on Sunday and three nights a week. He had the full cooperation of all the Presbyterian churches in the city, and members of other denominations also cooperated in the campaign. The revival marked several innovations in style. The anxious bench was used for the first time. He toned down his emotionalism considerably in order to appeal to the more sophisticated population of this city of 10,000, and made greater efforts to present a serious, logical argument. He also boasted that he was appealing to a new type of person: "the Lord was aiming at the conversion of the highest classes of society." For the first time he made temperance reform an integral part of conversion: this was an important step, for it marked the combination of personal religion with a reform crusade of a social nature. He used intemperance in his sermons as a symbol of the sinner's degradation, and the pledge to abstain became the sign of redemption (Finney, 1876, pp. 284–301; McLoughlin, 1959, pp. 54–58).

For many years thereafter, Finney remained a widely acclaimed and successful revivalist. His mission to Boston, from August 1831 to April 1832, marked his full acceptance by the New School theologians of New England. He spent the next three years as pastor of the Second Free Presbyterian Church in New York, where he was increasingly associated with the wealthy leaders of the "benevolent empire." In 1835, he went to Oberlin College as professor of theology and later became its president.

His later career will only concern us incidentally, however, for with the Rochester revival all the major themes of his work were evident; afterward, he appealed to a different constituency, already noted in Rochester. His methods grew more subdued, and soon the great wave of revivals he had inspired was over.

It was Finney's work in Rochester which inspired the greatest outburst of revivalism the area had ever seen, and had repercussions in many other parts of the nation as well. The 1831 report to the General Assembly of the Presbyterian Church declared that "the past year has been such a year of revivals and rejoicing in the church as never before was known in this land" (p. 205). The 1832 report was even more effusive:

> [In] sixty-eight presbyteries, . . . about seven hundred congregations are reported as having been . . . visited in rich mercy. In many of these places, thus refreshed by the showers of divine grace, the displays of the power of the Gospel have been glorious, almost beyond example. Several Presbyteries have had their whole territory pervaded by a heavenly influence, and every congregation has become a harvest-field for the ingathering of souls, to the fold of the good Shepherd. (p. 339)

These revivals, radiating from Rochester, spread through western New York and even reached the eastern parts of the state. The reports for 1831 and 1832 list presbyteries in which revivals extended to all or nearly all of the congregations, and others in which an unusual number occurred, although not to the same extent. All but one of New York's thirty presbyteries appeared on at least one of these lists.

These revivals were major community events, and even received notice in the newspapers of other communities. They were most likely to be reported in the religious press, of course, but religious journals had general circulation and were often a major source of news (Hamilton, 1964; Mathews, 1968, p. 9). Great events were reported in pastors' letters from far away, such as one from Mt. Pleasant, Ohio, published in the New York *Home Missionary* (October 1, 1830):

> But I must hasten to tell you what the Lord has done for us at Mount Pleas-
> ant. He has done great things, which rejoice the hearts of the people of God.
> According to previous appointment, a four days meeting was commenced
> here last Friday. . . . All our time, except what was necessary for taking refresh-
> ment and sleep, was taken up in praise, prayer, preaching and exhortation. All
> the exhortation and preaching was directed to the one point—repentance to-
> wards God, and faith towards Jesus Christ. . . . Christians prayed, Christians
> wept, and some sinners trembled, while others manifested the most determined
> opposition. . . . Fifteen people attended our inquiry meetings, eight of whom
> connected themselves with the people of God. (p. 120)

Another report told of a five days' meeting at New Carlisle, Ohio
(*New York Observer*, November 30, 1830):

> There were many displays of the gracious power of God in animating, com-
> forting and engaging God's people in the good work, for truly Zion did
> travail. . . . Sixty-three were received into the membership of the
> church. . . . The work was manifestly the Lord's.

Newspapers examined for the years between 1825 and 1835 contained reports of 1,343 revivals in New York, extending to every
county. Although the movement affected every part of the state to
some degree, its effect was greatest in rural areas of low population
density settled by Yankees. Table 3.1 shows the relation between several population characteristics and three measures of revivalism during the period 1825–1835: the number of revivals in each county, the
estimated proportion of the population of each county affected by revivals, and the index used in later chapters to measure revivalism in
New York (all the measures of revivalism for New York and Ohio are
described in Appendix B). The revivals were most intense in precisely
the upstate areas where Finney had preached early in his career: a
band from St. Lawrence County to Oneida County and the area
around Rochester were the two centers, with gradients of intensity
radiating from them. The area least affected was the Yorker area of
New York City and the lower Hudson River. As Table 3.1 shows, revivalist counties were Yankee counties of low population density; the
tendency for revivals to be more common in farm than in nonfarm
counties is slight.

While the three measures present much the same picture of the
type of county most likely to experience revivals, there is one difference worth noting between the first two. The first measures the
number of revivals; the second the estimated proportion of the population affected by them. The relation of population density to both is
negative, but it is larger in magnitude for the latter. In other words, a
higher proportion of the population was likely to be affected by the
revivals that occurred in low-density counties than in high-density

TABLE 3.1
Demographic Characteristics of Revival Areas, New York
(Multiple Regression)

| | Dependent variable | | | | | |
| | Number of revivals | | Proportion of population affected | | Revivalism index | |
Independent variable	0-order r	Beta weight[a]	0-order r	Beta weight[a]	0-order r	Beta weight[a]
Farms per capita, 1850	.163	.053	.161	−.026	.312	.177
% Yankee, 1855[b]	.235	.205	.304	.294	.406	.334
Population density, 1830	−.108	−.057	−.184	−.154	−.109	.012
Multiple R		.251		.337		.435

[a]The standardized partial regression coefficient, when all the other variables have been included in the equation.
[b]Percentage of population born in New England.

counties. Although the estimate of number of people affected must be regarded as very rough, these relationships appear to indicate that in counties of low density, revivals influenced a proportionately greater share of the population, where they were more often community events whose impact was more broadly felt.[1]

As the presbytery reports noted, the years of greatest activity were the middle years. An annual average of 107 events was reported for the years 1825–1828; 177 for 1829–1832; and 70 for 1833–1835. Table 3.2 shows the relation of demographic characteristics to the number of revivals reported during the early, middle, and later years of the decade. The changes over time were slight; the same kinds of areas were experiencing revivals at the end of the decade as at the beginning. There was a small relative decrease in the number of revivals in Yankee counties, and revivals became somewhat more concentrated in areas of low population density than they had been. The greatest relative increase over the decade was in the Yorker counties outside of New York City and its immediate surroundings. This was only a relative increase, however, for revivalism declined in level throughout the state.

[1]Although the estimates are rough, the consistency of the relationship between states and over time validates the finding: a greater proportion of the population was affected in low-density counties both in New York and in Ohio (see Table 3.3) and, although the data are not presented here, in each of the three periods into which the decade has been divided in Tables 3.2 and 3.4.

TABLE 3.2
Changing Distribution of Revivals, New York, 1825–1835

	Dependent variable: Number of revivals					
	1825–1828		1829–1832		1833–1835	
Independent variable	0-order r	Beta weight	0-order r	Beta weight	0-order r	Beta weight
Farms per capita, 1850	.165	.068	.122	.029	.169	.055
% Yankee, 1855	.236	.203	.193	.174	.202	.163
Population density, 1830	−.086	−.029	−.085	−.049	−.156	−.111
Multiple R	.248		.203		.244	

While the revival movement was not as intense in Ohio as in New York (Ohio's population was of course much smaller), it was probably more widespread there during the decade than in any other state; the Yankees settling northern Ohio from upstate New York brought their religious traditions with them. The newspapers examined reported 351 revivals in Ohio between 1825 and 1835.[2] The 1831 and 1832 annual reports to the Presbyterian General Assembly reported revivals in thirteen of Ohio's seventeen presbyteries (although there were large portions of the state, particularly in the northwest, where so little settlement had occurred that presbyteries were not organized). Revivals were most common in the northeastern corner of the state (the Western Reserve) and the counties immediately south of it; but there were many in the southern portions as well.

Table 3.3 shows the demographic correlates of revivalism in Ohio. The two measures of revivalism presented in Table 3.3 are the number of revivals reported in the county (which is the index used to measure revivalism in Ohio in later chapters) and the estimated proportion of the population affected. Revivalism was most common in Yankee counties (even somewhat more than in New York). Fewer revivals occurred in counties of southern than of nonsouthern settlement. The presence of farms had little or no effect on the occurrence of revivals. They occurred in more rather than less densely settled areas, but population density at this time had a different significance

---

[2] The number of reports was actually much larger, but (as explained in Appendix B) approximately 40% of the revivals were reported in towns whose counties could not be identified and therefore had to be ignored in this analysis.

than it had in New York. Few of the densely settled counties were urban; instead, they were fully settled areas with some towns. Sparse settlement did not characterize rural areas so much as areas that were just being opened to settlement, where institutional religion had not yet been established.

TABLE 3.3
Demographic Characteristics of Revival Areas, Ohio

	Dependent variable			
	Number of revivals		Proportion of population affected	
Independent variable	0-order r	Beta weight	0-order r	Beta weight
Farms per capita, 1850	−.078	.005	−.074	−.166
% Yankee, 1870[a]	.346	.349	.285	.214
% Southern, 1870[b]	−.244	−.115	−.205	−.186
Population density, 1830	.249	.320	.037	.009
Multiple R	.478		.334	

[a]Percentage of population born in New York.
[b]Percentage of population born in Virginia, West Virginia, and Kentucky.

In Ohio as in New York there is a difference between the effect of population density on the number of revivals and on the proportion of the population affected. In Ohio revivals occurred most frequently in counties of high density; but there was no tendency for a higher proportion of the population to be affected in high-density counties. Though revivals were fewer in low-density counties the same proportion of people (on the average) was affected by them or, in other words, each revival reached a higher share of the population than in high-density counties. As in New York, it was the more sparsely settled counties where revivals were more often community events reaching a large share of the population.

The temporal fluctuation of revivals in Ohio during the decade was similar to that in New York. The influence of the movement which originated in New York took some time to penetrate to Ohio, however, and did not decline quite as quickly: the average annual number of revivals was 17 between 1825 and 1828, 53 between 1829 and 1832, and 25 between 1833 and 1835. Revivals were most frequent in the Western Reserve, the northeastern corner of the state, and their distribution changed little over the decade. As Table 3.4 shows, revivals were slightly more frequent in nonsouthern-settled, high-density counties in about the same degree throughout the decade. They did become somewhat more concentrated in Yankee and nonfarm areas toward 1835.

TABLE 3.4

Changing Distribution of Revivals, Ohio, 1825–1835

Independent variable	Dependent variable: Number of revivals					
	1825–1828		1829–1832		1833–1835	
	0-order r	Beta weight	0-order r	Beta weight	0-order r	Beta weight
Farms per capita, 1850	−.073	.014	−.064	.025	−.100	−.064
% Yankee, 1870	.287	.293	.301	.306	.420	.413
% Southern, 1870	−.211	−.102	−.226	−.108	−.244	−.111
Population density, 1830	.246	.311	.247	.320	.179	.226
Multiple R	.425		.441		.497	

These revivals which reached such a large part of the two states also brought to them a new doctrine which abandoned some of the tenets of traditional Calvinism (innate depravity, predestination, and election by God's grace without any act of will on the part of the chosen). They were replaced by the belief that the individual was responsible for his own salvation. Revivals depended on the assumption that the individual was free to accept conversion, and revival doctrine therefore called for an active Christianity, one which led to activity of many kinds, religious and secular.

Finney's theology was almost entirely derived from his experiences as a revivalist and what he learned from them about the ways of the Lord. He frequently spoke of "experimental" religion (Finney, 1960, p. 141). By that he meant religious belief verified by immediate sensations and experience, but he might as well have intended a connotation more nearly like the modern one—practical, pragmatic.

Because of the relationship of his thought to his experience, his theology can best be approached by studying his understanding of revivals, set forth in the *Lectures*, which were delivered in 1835. He had written very little during his most active years (writing books, like the preparation of written sermons, took time away from the real work). It is of course impossible to know how his thought had developed during the preceding decade, but it appears that his revivals up to that time were based on the same theological ideas he presented there.

Since revivals were both the source and the goal of so much of his theology, his understanding of conversion is central to his understanding of the nature of man. An important sermon, preached in Boston in 1832, reveals much of its content in its title: "Sinners Bound to Change Their Own Hearts" (Finney, 1836, pp. 1–42). By a combination of Biblical and practical reasoning, Finney demonstrated what he regarded as the absurdity of the traditional Calvinist doctrines. His essential point was that God would not require man to do anything not within his power. "All holiness, in God, angels, or men, must be *voluntary*, or it is not holiness." Conversion amounted to a change of heart, after which men no longer sought self-interested ends, but "the glory of God and the interests of his kingdom"; the change was "from selfishness to benevolence" (Finney, 1836, pp. 7, 10).

Since conversion only required a change of heart, it was an act of will upon the part of man and fully within his power. True, God's intervention was necessary for the change of heart to be effective, but, he addressed his listeners, "God requires you to turn, and what he requires of you, he cannot do for you. It must be your own voluntary act" (Finney, 1836, p. 29).

Just as God would not require anything of which man was incapable, neither would he require anything not in man's best interest. "Certainly it is in accordance with right reason to prefer the glory of God, and the interest of his immense kingdom, to your own private interests. It is an infinitely greater good; therefore you, and God, and all his creatures, are bound to prefer it" (p. 19). God's dispositions conformed to the requirements of reason, as well as to the laws of nature, since he had established them.

In effect, Finney rendered unproblematical the perennial problem of Calvinism. The process of conversion by revival was designed to permit men the assurance that they were saved, an assurance which Calvin had denied them and for which Calvinists had for centuries been trying to find signs. Revival practices and revival preachers encouraged the belief that once brought to a point of anxiety that would persuade one to affirm that he was saved, one was saved: "the individual's expression of a new intent was identical with the miraculous inward change of sudden conversion" (Cross, 1950, p. 181).

Finney's theology formalized the assurance which the revivals provided in practice. Rejecting the doctrine of predestination, he argued that God's omnipotence and omniscience did not deprive the individual of the opportunity to make the act of will by which he would be saved. And if he was saved, he would know it, because God would not withhold such vital information from him. Finney's formal theology thus did away with the problem that the measures had, in large part, been designed to solve.

Finney's belief in free will not only made one responsible for his own conversion. It gave him a role in the salvation of the unsaved world. Finney's formal thought also followed his practice in emphasizing the role of the preacher. He believed that four agencies were at work in a revival: God, the sinner, other men, and the truth. While not denying the agency of God, he emphasized that "men are not mere *instruments* in the hands of God. . . . The preacher is a moral agent in the work; he acts" (Finney, 1960, p. 18); and that it was "impossible that [conversion] should take place without [the sinner's] agency, for it consists in *his* acting right" (p. 14).

Finney did not believe that his view of the agency of men and the predictability of revivals detracted in any way from the sovereignty of God. The means that he proposed would not work without the blessing of God; but conversion nevertheless occurred according to natural laws. God's blessing was equally necessary for a good harvest, but agricultural phenomena likewise followed natural laws. "The laws of nature . . . are nothing but the constituted manner of the operations of God." If farmers believed that a crop would grow only when it pleased God, and that it was wrong of them to plant in the expectation of receiving a crop, "why, they would starve the world to death" (Finney, 1960, p. 24).

"God has connected means with the end through all the departments of his government—in nature and in grace." Those who objected to direct efforts to promote a revival were not only unscientific, they were doing "the devil's work . . . effectually . . . by preaching the sovereignty of God, as a reason why we should not put forth efforts to produce a revival" (Finney, 1960, p. 21). This attitude Finney rejected as "cannot-ism" (pp. 379–80).

Finney's reliance on the responsibility of man for conversion gave his revivals an explicit justification which earlier revivals had lacked. The revivalists of the eighteenth century had believed their revivals were miraculous consequences of divine intervention. Jonathan Edwards, the initiator of the American revivalist tradition, believed he was a mere instrument in the hands of God. He shied away from the implications of revivalism; Finney willingly embraced them.

The practices of the two revivalists were similar in many respects. Edwards was as willing as Finney to play on the emotions of his audience. He responded at length to complaints about ministers' "addressing themselves, rather to the affections of their hearers, than to their understandings, and striving to raise their passions to the ut-most height," and concluded not only that the Bible supported the practice, but that intense, emotional preaching did more justice to the subject than coldness. He approved of ministers' "speaking terror to them, that are already under great terror, instead of comforting them" by saying that the message that sinners needed was indeed terrible and to comfort them too readily would be to withhold the truth from them (Edwards, 1868, vol. 3, pp. 334–39).

Some complained that during revivals too much time was spent in religious meetings and too little at work. But Edwards replied that it was "to the honor of God" that a people should regard their reli-gion as "the main business of life," and added with characteristic New England practicality that the time spent in religious activities would otherwise be spent in "frolicking and tavern haunting; idle-ness, unprofitable visits, vain talk, fruitless pastimes, and needless diversions." In terms very similar to Finney's he defended the out-cries and movements with which hearers often responded to emo-tional preaching, both as signs that the hearers were deeply affected and for the influence that they had on other attenders. Some objected to so much singing at religious meetings, especially of "hymns of human composure," to which Edwards (1868, vol. 3, pp. 340–49) re-plied that one could sing in words written by men as well as he could pray in those words.

But if their practices were similar, the two men understood them in entirely different ways. Edwards regarded groaning, uncontrolled bodily movement, and the dedication of all one's time to religion at the expense of earthly labor as acts of God and signs that his inter-vention was occurring. No action of the preacher was responsible for such behavior. For Finney, a revival was not a miraculous, incom-prehensible event, but a process in which "all the laws of matter and mind remain in force. They are neither suspended nor set aside in a revival" (Finney, 1960, p. 12). Because the laws of mind could be known, the preacher could—indeed, was obligated to—take advan-tage of them in conducting a revival that would promote the salvation of the greatest possible number of converts.

Though Edwards was aware that some religious practices were more likely to stimulate a revival than others, his attitude toward measures was consistent with his belief that revivals depended solely on God's intervention. His *Thoughts on the Revival of Religion* (Ed-wards, 1868) devoted a chapter to the courses of action that might be taken to promote the work, but most of them consisted in the fulfill-ment of religious duties rather than acts of persuasion. They include fasting and prayer, more frequent administration of the Lord's Supper, and attention to moral duties and acts of charity. The only one among them which might be interpreted as emphasizing human agency was his proposal that "a history . . . be published once a month, or once a fortnight, of the progress" of the work of revival, because "the tidings of remarkable effects of the power and grace of God in any place, tend greatly to awaken and engage the minds of persons, in other places" (pp. 416–25).

Edwards's "courses of action" were activities that man might undertake, not in the assurance that a revival would follow, but in humble hope that God would then decide to revive his church. For Finney, the "right use of means" meant the calculated creation of conditions for a revival and the exploitation of those conditions to win souls. In fact, if for Edwards the courses of action to be undertaken to promote revivals were relatively passive, for Finney even waiting was active. In a lecture entitled "When a Revival Is to be Expected," he discussed the signs that indicated a forthcoming revival. But most of these signs (that "Christians have a spirit of prayer for a revival," that "the attention of ministers is especially directed to this *particular object*, and . . . their preaching and other efforts are aimed particularly for the conversion of sinners," that "Christians begin to confess their sins to one another" and "are found willing to make the sacrifice necessary to carry the revival' on") are not visitations for which Christians must wait passively, but duties which they should fulfill (Finney, 1960, pp. 30–35). Finney, asserting the agency of the minister in a revival, regarded himself and other revivalists as practitioners of a science. Edwards, in contrast, believed he could no more produce a revival than a hailstorm or an earthquake.

Edwards's tone, unlike Finney's, was one of both caution and humility: caution lest the excesses of revivals offend some and that bickering among parties within the church detract from the great work, and humility lest ministers be filled with pride at their success (he included himself in this warning, as is evident from his writing). Edwards had, in the same degree that Finney lacked, concern for the possibility of what St. Paul called "scandal."

In his discussion of religious enthusiasm, Knox (1950, pp. 17–18) identifies lack of concern with scandal as a characteristic of most of the enthusiasts he discusses.[3] In Paul's epistles, any disrespect for the consciences of others can create a scandal or, as some modern translations of the Bible have it, a "stumbling block." Paul admonished the

---

[3]Knox's enthusiasts differed from the American revivalists in that most were concerned with the salvation of a select few rather than of the whole world.

Corinthians not to eat meat that had been sacrificed to idols. As Christians, they were at liberty to do so because pagan religious ceremonies were meaningless, but since it was offensive (scandalous) to some people, it became for them a stumbling block to accepting the faith (*I Corinthians*, Chapters 8–9). The enthusiast, Knox comments, is totally unconcerned about creating scandal (Knox, 1950):

> He is so sure of being in the right, that he would hold it an infidelity to countenance the scruples of those who disagree with him. If they are shocked by what he does, he can reply "Honi soit qui mal y pense"; he is acting under the direct inspiration of the Holy Ghost, and to criticize him is to betray a "carnal" mind. (p. 18)

Edwards's humility became evident when he patiently asked both supporters and opponents of the revivals to recognize their faults (Edwards, 1868, vol. 3, p. 405). Finney's self-assurance (not to say arrogance) only permitted him to recognize the faults of his opponents. He cited opposition to revivals as "the devil's most successful means of destroying souls" (Finney, 1960, pp. 14–15), and said that rejection of the new measures "*savors strongly of fanaticism*. And what is not a little singular, is that fanatics of this stamp are always the first to cry out 'fanaticism' " (p. 275).

For Edwards, God was at the center of all religion, and particularly of the revival phenomenon. For Finney, man was at the center. In his first lecture on revivals, he said, "*Religion is the work of man*. It is something for man to do," although he added, "It is true, God induces him to do it" (Finney, 1960, p. 9). Finney did not break abruptly with the prevailing theology of his day. Calvin's harsh doctrines had been undergoing a gradual modification almost since he asserted them, and Finney only continued a development that had been going on particularly in the century that intervened between him and Edwards. But his view was radically different from the predestination that Calvin had expounded and Edwards had continued to accept. The balance between God's part and man's part in salvation appeared to come down on the side of man. Finney's legacy transformed revivalism, to the point where revivals could be institutionalized, even programmed: Knox College in Illinois, founded by Finney's teacher, George Gale, had a revival every winter as part of the regular course (Tyler, 1944, p. 31).

The new emphasis on free will and the ability of man to do good led to a new emphasis on moral obligation, for a change of heart implied a change of conduct (Finney, 1836, p. 14). The demand for the fulfillment of moral obligations was more compelling because of the emphasis on free will, but it was of course not new. The doctrine of "disinterested benevolence," like the revival phenomenon, went back to Jonathan Edwards, and had been developed by the late eighteenth century theologian Samuel Hopkins, who argued that acts of benevolence could be signs that one was among the elect (Griffin, 1960, p. 6). For Edwards and Hopkins, acts of benevolence remained within the framework of the sovereignty of God, but with Finney's shift of emphasis they were more man-centered, and took on a utilitarian character. Finney (1836) stated more strongly Hopkins' assertion: the Christian showed that he was converted not only by "vivid emotions of love to God, repentance of sin, and faith in Christ," but also by "an habitual disposition to obey the requirements of God . . . [which] gives a right direction to all our conduct" (p. 62). Good works for Hopkins had been a fallible sign of an uncertain state of grace; now they became a necessary consequence of assured salvation.

Benevolence, like conversion, was not the pure work of God, but rather the voluntary act of the converted. The reasonable God who constituted the laws of nature and made it possible for man to learn and take advantage of them also made the decision to do good an eminently reasonable and practical choice. "Look at the *utility* of benevolence. It is a matter of human consciousness that the mind is so constituted that benevolent affections are the source of happiness, and malevolent ones the source of misery" (Finney, 1836, p. 55). Just as any reasonable man, properly instructed, could hardly help turning to God, so would he, after doing so, turn to working for the good of his neighbor—even though, as it often turned out, his neighbor might not define his good in the same way.

A final element in Finney's thought which contributed to his influence on social reform movements was millennialism. Conceptually not so closely related to the rest of his thought or distinct from that of his forebears, millennialism was very much a part of Finney's world, where Joseph Smith, William Miller, and John Humphrey Noyes founded movements that waited for the reign of God on earth during the same period. The expectation of the millennium was, of course, a part of traditional Christian doctrine, and even orthodox Calvinists took the success of revivals as a sign that the millennium might be approaching rapidly (Cross, 1950, p. 200). Further, the new emphasis on man's agency meant that acts of benevolence on the part of men might hasten the coming of the kingdom by spreading sinlessness and love. Millennialism led people to perceive society as dynamic and subject to change by human effort. If man could achieve his own salvation, and be influential in achieving that of others, he should go further and take whatever steps would contribute to hastening the salvation of the whole world.

Revivalists were optimistic about the reform of their country and the coming of the kingdom, but their optimism did not allow them to slacken their efforts. Finney did not believe that Christians should wait passively for the millennium any more than they should wait passively for a revival. Revivalists believed that they *would* achieve the kingdom, and they did not foresee the conflicts that would arise out of their struggle. But they knew it would be a struggle; they did not believe that progress was inevitable. If they were not as dour or pessimistic as earlier Calvinists, their optimism was nevertheless tempered by a sense of their own responsibility and by a belief that dangers lay ahead if they failed (Niebuhr, 1937, pp. 129–30).[4]

Quotations from Finney's writings and sermons reveal the simple and direct language, the colloquial tone, the metaphors drawn from everyday experience. Above all, he was concerned to create a theology which would be clear in its practical applications and accessible to the common man. He believed that obscurantism on the part of theologians held a large share of responsibility for sin, since it disaffected the common man from religion. In a sermon entitled "Traditions of the Elders," he preached from the text, "Thus have ye made the commandment of God of none effect, by your tradition" (Finney, 1836, pp. 67–90).

These, then, were the elements of revivalist thought and practice that contributed to the social reform movements that grew during the 1830s: a God who revealed the laws of nature to men that they might use them; a race of men who, by acts of their own will, might realize the will of God; a conviction that benevolent activity was the will of God, within the capabilities of men, and a sure sign of the salvation of those who undertook it; a disposition to use whatever means would be effective in achieving a chosen end, without regard for tradition; and the simultaneous belief that the triumphant kingdom of God on earth was hastening toward them, and that through their activity they might bring it on even faster.

These beliefs, taken together, demanded an activist orientation toward sin, and it was to be expected that, in Niebuhr's phrase, "the revival movement . . . produced a manifold activity, as its theory was certain it would do" (Niebuhr, 1937, p. 119). Revivals inspired both religious activity—the first duty of the converted was to pray, and to

[4]A complete consideration of Finney's theology would examine his doctrine of perfection, or "entire sanctification" (see McLoughlin, 1959, pp. 103–05; Opie, 1963, pp. 398–404). This is, however, a later development—the school of thought is sometimes called "Oberline perfectionism" since he elaborated it after he went to teach there in 1835. Although the idea that man can make himself perfect may be implicit in Finney's thought in the earlier period, it is not part of the set of doctrines that define the revivalism of that period, and is therefore not dealt with here.

promote revivals, for the conversion of others—and efforts to enact reforms in secular spheres. Some of the latter came to take on political relevance, and revivalists were in the forefront of efforts to promote them. In later years Finney listed the reforms with which a Christian ought to concern himself: "abolition of slavery, temperance, moral reform, politics, business principles, physiological and dietetic reform" (Cole, 1954, p. 77). The distinction between religious and secular reform, and likewise that between personal conversion and creation of a new social order, had no meaning in the world in which Finney and his converts lived.

Belief in man's ability to be saved and observation of the success of revivals did not lead the revivalists to any lessened perception of the widespread existence of sin in the world. Quite the contrary, it was all the more evident, and its extermination all the more urgent since man had the power. A facile leap from the ability to save oneself to the ability to save the world required no extensive consideration of possible differences in scale of the two operations or in the means that might be effective. "Preoccupation with sin served . . . for a sociology" (Cross, 1950, p. 207).

Moreover, organizational strategy received little consideration because a set of organizations dedicated to the revivalists' benevolent goals already existed and was used to full advantage by the new activists. The "benevolent empire" was a group of societies headquartered in New York, with interlocking directorates, engaged in several varieties of God's work. The revivals provided them with new members, new motives, and new resources. Their memberships overlapped, so that revival converts collaborated to enact reforms with a broad scope. During a single week in 1831, New York was the site of the annual meetings of the American Seamen's Friend Society, the General Union for Promoting the Observance of the Christian Sabbath, the Sunday School Union, the New York City Temperance Society, the American Tract Society, the American Peace Society, the American Home Missionary Society, the American Bible Society, and the American Education Society (Myers, 1960, p. 35).

The first duty of the newly converted Christian was, of course, to assist in the conversion of his neighbors. Finney believed that love for others was most properly expressed by desiring their conversions (Finney, 1960, pp. 452–53). He believed that the work of conversion—the work of the revival—should take precedence over all other benevolent activities, both for its own sake and because when all were converted the sins which the other activities attempted to eradicate would disappear. When many of his converts became more interested in abolitionism he grew impatient with them and urged them to return to the revival.

Through the praying circle and the Holy Band, Finney had already institutionalized the fulfillment of the duty to work for the conversion of others. But missionary societies made possible its fulfillment on a much larger scale. Missions had been the motive of the first of the benevolent societies, the Connecticut Missionary Society, founded in 1797. Bringing it and a number of other local societies into federation, the American Home Missionary Society was founded in 1826, and continued their work of supporting both itinerant evangelists and settled pastors in newly settled areas of the west (Griffin, 1960, p. 36). Persuasive literature could also contribute to converting sinners, and the American Bible Society, founded in 1816, and the American Tract Society, founded in 1825, were organized for that end. Coming eventually to operate their own presses, they filled frontier homes with the scriptures and pamphlets commenting upon them and upon the Christian life (Griffin, 1960, pp. 28–34).

The Christian life was also promoted by societies which converted secular reforms into Christian principles: the American Peace Society, though it never became as large or as influential as some of the others, hoped to convince Americans that warfare was a sin against Christ's peaceful preaching (Griffin, 1960, p. 39). The American Temperance Union carried on a work that had been pioneered by numerous local societies, and had been a concern of Christian preachers long before Finney introduced it into his Rochester revival.

Concern for the condition of enslaved blacks, which was to inspire the most important of the secular benevolent efforts, found first expression in the American Colonization Society. The Society was established in 1817 to promote the "return" of freed blacks to Africa. The ambiguity of such "benevolence" reflected the racist attitudes which many evangelicals shared with most other white Americans, despite their belief in principle that all men were equal under God. The colonization scheme's fundamental ambivalence was revealed by the society's rhetoric: in the north colonization was preached as an antislavery measure, but in the south it was presented as a measure to safeguard slavery by removing potentially disruptive free blacks (Barnes, 1964, p. 27; Sorin, 1972, pp. 39–43).

But at the same time that revivalism was transforming evangelical Christianity's benevolent impulse, slavery was becoming a more important national issue and forcing the attention of northerners generally. Revivalist belief in free will and personal responsibility, together with slavery's increasing national importance, led Finney's disciples to identify enslavement more clearly as a sin and insistently to demand its abolition. They were among the principal founders of the American Anti-Slavery Society in 1833 and leaders of the campaign for abolition that achieved increasing intensity in the succeeding decade.

The first society founded with an explicitly political purpose was the General Union for Promoting the Observance of the Christian Sabbath. It professed several goals: getting people to stop all work on Sunday, to boycott firms that operated on the Sabbath, and to stop all travel. But its principal purpose was to end the federal government's collusion in sin by eliminating Sunday mail. To this end, members flooded Congress with memorials and petitions. This was also the first benevolent society to arouse widespread and intense opposition from many who saw the move as a threat to the separation of church and state (Griffin, 1960, pp. 119–22; Wyatt-Brown, 1971).

Since most of the national societies emerged as federations of preexisting local societies, they existed both at the local and national levels and followed similar patterns of organization. At the national level, nearly all were headquartered in New York, and nearly all were interdenominational but dominated by Presbyterians and Congregationalists. The New York organizations were all supported by the same group of wealthy merchants and landowners, and on the rosters of their directorates the same names appeared over and over again: Stephen van Rensselaer, William Jay, Anson G. Phelps, and Gerrit Smith. But the name that appeared most often was Tappan.

Arthur and Lewis Tappan, born in Jonathan Edwards's Northampton, went to Boston as young men. Arthur was the first to move to New York, and he later invited his brother to join him. They ran a successful mercantile business which during the 1830s grossed over a million dollars a year. Though the business was hard hit by the depression of 1837, the Tappan brothers later founded the nation's first credit reference bureau, of which today's Dun and Bradstreet is the successor (Wyatt-Brown, 1969, pp. 1–2, 43–44, 127–34). They were involved in, and among the primary financial benefactors of, nearly all the benevolent organizations.

Their benevolent activity, especially Arthur's, predated their association with Finney. But they heard him on his first visit to New York in 1828, and in 1832 they bought the theater on Chatham Street which they turned into the Second Free Presbyterian Church (free because no pew rentals were charged), and invited Finney to become its pastor.

Memberships in the benevolent societies were overlapping because most members saw all of the activities as part of the same general crusade, even though some might devote particular attention to one reform rather than another. The consensus was not universal, however. Calvin Colton, an ardent defender of revivals, castigated the temperance drive as "Protestant Jesuitism," an effort to maintain ecclesiastical power over society (Cole, 1954, p. 124). Finney was, of course, among those who believed that all crusades for the betterment of men were ways of promoting the arrival of the kingdom, but he felt that all particular reform movements should be subordinated to the most important one, the revival itself. A general revival would bring all other reforms automatically in its wake, but without it there was no hope for the others (McLoughlin, 1959, pp. 111–12).

The scope of the societies can be inferred from the numbers of their local organizations and their budgets. The Bible Society claimed about 900 local auxiliaries, and the Tract Society over 3,000. The Sunday School Union had receipts of $72,500 in 1836, largely from the sale of texts to common schools and local Sunday schools. The Bible Society's receipts in the year 1835–1836 were over $117,000 (Griffin, 1960, pp. 83, 136, 139). Laymen were the prime organizers of the benevolent societies both at the local and national levels, although in many instances auxiliaries existed as appendages of congregations. The churches provided places to meet; many AHMS ministers were enthusiastic proponents of every crusade. Particularly those societies whose business was the distribution of literature depended on the local auxiliaries to report on needs and carry out distribution, and all societies received contributions from the auxiliaries (Barnes, 1964, p. 62; Griffin, 1960, pp. 85, 97–98).

The societies' activities at first were all based on the same premise: that the most effective means of promoting the reform of society was to convict individuals of the sinfulness of their ways and persuade them to change them. Their main activity, then, besides the distribution of literature, was the sponsorship of traveling agents who would visit towns and give persuasive lectures. These lectures were patterned after revival meetings; indeed, it can be fairly said, they *were* revival meetings. The lecturers concentrated in about equal measure on exposing the sinfulness of a particular evil, telling horror stories about those who had sinned, and telling of the good fortune that had come to those who had changed their ways. The temperance societies made much of "the pledge," whereby men agreed variously to abstain from hard liquor, from beer and cider as well, and in some cases from coffee and tea. Meetings often became as high-pitched as revivals themselves.

Revival practices provided a method for the benevolent activity which revivalist doctrine demanded. But the revivals contributed to the upsurge of benevolent activity in a more important way. The theology of revivalism was not especially different from that expounded at the time by academic theologians, but it was the revival movement, not the university, which produced active benevolence. The revivals had an effect not explained by their doctrine alone, because the ritual practice of the revival meeting strongly reinforced the converts' commitment.

Religious rituals, by providing a collective experience to validate the truth of the doctrines preached, strengthen believers' motivations to act on their beliefs. The ritual of the revivals was particularly well-suited to achieving this effect. Conversion was defined as a life-changing event. The revival was the occasion for a public declaration of that change, and the doctrine demanded that those who were thus publicly committed demonstrate their commitment with acts of benevolence in their public lives. Revival teachings not only provided a general orientation of ascetic activism but also defined appropriate activity in specific spheres. The simultaneous and widespread occurrence of revivals during this brief time period, affecting large numbers of people within a small and cohesive area, created a base of sentiments for later political action.

Kanter (1972) identifies the commitment mechanisms which served to maintain the allegiance of members to nineteenth-century utopian communities. A community requires the commitment of its members to continued membership, to group solidarity, and to the community's norms, and successful communities were accordingly found to have institutionalized mechanisms for instrumental commitment, for cohesion commitment, and for moral commitment. The commitment of revival converts was not of the same pervasive nature, for they continued to live in the family and community from which they came. Commitment was primarily to a doctrine and to the moral obligations it implied, and the explicit commitment mechanisms for which revival practice provided, as one would expect, were those Kanter identifies as moral commitment mechanisms: processes of mortification and transcendence (Kanter, 1972, pp. 102–23).

Mortification was achieved through public renunciation of a sinful past at the moment of conversion. Even before conversion, one identified oneself as a sinner hoping for salvation through displaying emotion and proceeding to the anxious bench. The revival also provided for transcendence through processes Kanter identifies as creating "institutionalized awe": the acceptance of an ideology and the opportunity to respond to the special religious leaders who conducted the revival.

According to Kanter (1972), these processes reinforce an individual's commitment to a utopian community because they "provide a new identity for the person that is based on the power and meaningfulness of group membership." (p. 103). Such mechanisms can, however, create an identity that is not necessarily oriented to group membership; when the processes are not explicitly identified with a community isolated from the rest of society, they can as well reinforce commitment to a more abstract set of ideals. This will be especially the case when moral commitment mechanisms are used to the near exclusion of mechanisms of instrumental and cohesion commitment.

Furthermore, the revival ritual, both in its explicit practice and in its motivating belief system, was a celebration of individuality. The change of heart was demanded of each individual as an individual, and after his change of heart he was expected as an individual to undertake benevolent actions. According to Weber, the Protestant ethic in earlier centuries was ambiguous in its demands. By calling for the rationalized pursuit of a vocation in the secular world, it did not make clear what kinds of activities were expected. Its consequences for economic behavior were therefore unanticipated. Nineteenth-century revivalism, however, made explicit demands for benevolent activities on the part of the converted, and the benevolent societies defined the kinds of activities that were expected.

And revival converts did undertake those activities. Though the extent to which revivals transformed the world-views of their converts and inspired them to activity is impossible to assess definitively, the evidence is strong that their effect was considerable. Contemporary reports testify to the beliefs of observers that this revival movement indeed reached more people than any previous one and that the measures were effective in converting the people reached. Leaders of the benevolent societies clearly associated their increased memberships with the revivals. And the succeeding chapters show that a lasting political ethos was created in areas that experienced revivals: when the electorate has been offered the opportunity to endorse specific policies related to issues raised by the revivals, revivalist counties have disproportionately supported them.

So revivalism provided both motive and method for reform. Claiming divine sanction for their goals, reformers felt free to use whatever means seemed effective to accomplish them. Claiming that one could tell, on the basis of secular action, whether or not a man was a Christian, they felt free to castigate any man who mocked them or hardened his heart against them. With such assurance of the rightness of their activities, it was perhaps inevitable that eventually they would turn to political means to enforce good behavior on the unregenerate.

Revival preaching, however, in no way explicitly justified the belief that the state might be used as an instrument for the reform of society. A generation earlier, revivals had been important in promoting the disestablishment of the Congregational Church: the union of church and society presumed that all citizens would also be church members, but revivalists demanded a converted membership (Niebuhr, 1937, p. 119). In the 1830s, too, many revivalists expressed a distrust of party politics: Horace Bushnell claimed that politics could not be made a means to reform because the social contract theories of government which he believed prevailed among politicians of his day "totally forbid the entrance of moral considerations" (Cole, 1954, p. 148).

Preachers generally saw the political system as itself an object of reform rather than an agent: Bushnell felt that the amorality of public life could be overcome through general repentance "with shame and fasting," the restoration of conscience to public matters, and a strict adherence to principle (Cole, 1954, pp. 147–49). Few went as far as Ezra Stiles Ely, a national Presbyterian leader, who on July 4, 1827, advocated a "Christian party in politics" (Blau, 1946), but most believed that politics itself could be reformed by electing better men. Finney's few remarks on the political participation of Christians referred to little more than the need to elect honest, upright men without regard for party (Finney, 1960, pp. 150, 297–98). He tended to regard politics as an unnecessary diversion from evangelism. On at least one occasion he feared "that the excitement of [election] day would greatly retard the work" (Finney, 1876, p. 230).

So neither revival doctrine nor revival practice expressly called for the use of political means to bring about the reform of society which the revivals envisioned and demanded. But Sabbatarians, teetotalers, and abolitionists were increasingly fervent in their convictions, and they ultimately decided that their morals must be imposed on others who could not be persuaded. Eventually they would enlist the state, the most authoritative mechanism available, in their campaigns.

As used in this book, the word "revivalism" refers to the complex of events, beliefs, and practices epitomized by Finney and characteristic of the revivals in the north during the decade 1825–1835. The meaning, the practice, and the theology of revivalism have changed many times. But the revivals inspired by Finney were crucial. They marked a decisive transition in revivalism itself,[5] making it the customary means by which the church renewed itself despite its denominational fragmentation and independence from secular authority. Moreover, they created a political ethos that has played a long-lived and significant role in American politics.

---

[5]That Finney marked a transition in revivalism is indicated by the fact that several major works on the history of revivals either begin or end with him: the works of Miller (esp. Miller, 1965), Sweet (1944), and Opie (1963) all trace the history of revivalism up to Finney (Sweet goes beyond to discuss the "wane" of revivalism). On the other hand, McLoughlin (1959) places Finney at the beginning of *Modern Revivalism*.

But the ethos was not yet a *political* ethos. It would only become political when revivalists took up the crusade to abolish slavery and applied their beliefs in conflicts on the political front. The ethos which Finney's revivals consolidated into a system and spread through much of the north was forged in the churches, and the beliefs were defined in the churches' terms: belief in man's ability to do right, a corresponding concern that he must be persuaded to, disrespect for traditional strictures and readiness to use whatever means might work, and the anticipation of the millennium. The fruits of these beliefs were missionary activities themselves, the distribution of the Bible, and the movements for moral reform, observance of the Sabbath, temperance, and abolition. But the greatest of these, in its effects on the life of the nation, was abolition.

4

The Rise of Political Abolitionism

During the 1830s and early 1840s the movement for the abolition of slavery in the United States, long dormant, was renewed. The newly-founded American Anti-Slavery Society and its network of state and local auxiliaries organized northern communities to oppose slavery and worked to improve the legal and social condition of free blacks in the north. In 1840 a faction of the movement founded the Liberty party to put forward abolitionist candidates for office and to agitate for the cause. Calling oneself an abolitionist implied believing in the doctrine of "immediate emancipation" (however one might interpret that elusive phrase) and working to bring it about. Although the abolitionists called their organizations Anti-Slavery Societies, they distinguished their movement from the antislavery politics which emerged in the middle 1840s and grew much faster than abolitionism had. Abolitionist politics was self-consciously benevolent: though nearly all of its activists were white (and this book is concerned only with white abolitionists[1]), its expressed aim was to free blacks and to improve their status. Antislavery politics, on the other hand, was based on a mixture of principles: opposition to slavery itself, growing intersectional hostility, and opposition to the extension of slavery out of a desire to reserve western territories for free whites.[2]

---

[1]The importance of black participation in the antislavery movement, which has generally been underrated, is described in Litwack (1961), Quarles (1969), Sorin (1971), and Wesley (1939).

[2]I follow this convention and use "abolitionism" to describe the movement before the founding of the Free Soil Party and "antislavery" thereafter. But I also use "antislavery" where a general term is necessary to describe all the parties and candidates presenting some form of opposition to slavery between 1840 and 1860, whether or not they were abolitionist.

Many of the founders and early activists of abolitionism had been influenced by the revivals and active in the benevolent movements they inspired. They were not the only abolitionists, but they were especially prominent in the wing of the movement which organized and supported an independent political party. The fact that so many who had experienced the revivals became active abolitionists was no coincidence: the revivals had prepared them by transforming their belief systems and by motivating them to energetic action for the freedom of the enslaved in accordance with their beliefs.

The inference from behavior to motivating belief is laden with ambiguity, as the historiography of abolitionism abundantly reveals.[3] My argument that religious revivalism, through its influence on its converts' belief systems, had a direct effect on abolitionist activities can be anticipated here briefly. After reviewing the history of abolitionism between 1833 and 1848, I will show that there was an empirical connection between events and behavior: those who experienced the revivals also voted abolitionist. How is that empirical connection to be explained? A number of hypotheses which contradict mine can be suggested: that abolitionism was the product of social structural conditions, political traditions, downward mobility, or identification with particular religious groups. One of these hypotheses may explain the relationship between revivalism and abolitionism: if so, then when appropriate variables are controlled, the statistical relation should vanish.

That relation does not vanish; it remains when any of these variables is controlled. Many other hypotheses might be suggested, so the test is not exhaustive. But it eliminates the most plausible counterhypotheses, leaving strong grounds for the inference that the connection between revivalism and abolitionism is not spurious but one of cause and effect.

To establish the connection, however, is not to explain it. I believe that the explanation lies in the political ethos which grew out of the beliefs disseminated by the revivals. Two aspects of revival thought in particular contributed to opposition to slavery: slavery was inconsistent with the revivalist doctrine of free will and therefore was regarded as sinful; and the revivals created the conviction that their converts should act vigorously and use all means available to exterminate sin. It is not that the revivals directly condemned slavery (they did, but it was only one of many anathematized practices) but that the revivals created an ethos embodying general principles which slavery violated.

Many abolitionist leaders acknowledged that they held those be-

---

[3]For an anthology of views on abolitionists, see Curry (1965).

liefs and that the religious conversion they experienced in the revivals had led them to their political activity. They articulated the revivalist ethos and its condemnation of slavery explicitly. Those who voted abolitionist also experienced the revivals. They may have perceived the same connection between their religious experiences and their opposition to slavery. On the other hand, it may be that they did not perceive the connection, but adopted abolitionism because it was consistent with dispositions the revivals had created; whether the consistency was consciously articulated cannot be known. In either case, however, the empirical relation between their revivalism and their voting is best explained by the conclusion that the revivals created a political ethos which they adopted.

The argument, then, contains two empirical parts and an intervening logical part. First, I demonstrate that there was a connection between revivalism and abolitionism which was not spurious, at least in the ways that commonly accepted explanations would imply. Second, I argue that there was a logical connection between the ideas of revivalism and both the ideas and the acts of abolitionism. Finally, I show that that connection was perceived at least by abolitionist leaders. In the absence of an empirically verifiable and more plausible alternative explanation for the connection at the mass level, it is most reasonable to accept that the same explanation which applies to the leaders also holds for their constituency.

Before the 1830s, the movement for abolition of slavery had almost died. As it grew in the north during the 1830s it immediately aroused hostility, opposition, and even violent attacks. The environment was unfriendly to the cause: racism was as pervasive in the north as it was in the south. All the original states had known slavery, and it was finally abolished in New York only in 1827. The Northwest Ordinance of 1787 had barred slavery from the territory north of the Ohio, but the census reported slaves in the state of Ohio as late as 1840, and some slaveowners in the southern counties kept slaves across the river but brought them to Ohio to work, while other landowners hired slaves from their Kentucky and Virginia owners (Bradford, 1947, p. 12; Litwack, 1961, p. 14).

Even where they were free, blacks suffered political and social discrimination which actually increased during the first half of the nineteenth century. Before 1821, white and black males in New York who met a property qualification were legally eligible to vote without discrimination; but the Constitution of 1821, which laid the groundwork for universal white male suffrage, placed a more stringent property qualification on blacks. A proposal for black suffrage had been defeated at the Ohio Constitutional Convention of 1802 by only one vote, but a proposal permitting limited slavery had been defeated in a committee of the Convention by the same slight margin (Chaddock, 1908, pp. 79–81; Fox, 1965, pp. 251–69). For many years Ohio had a "black code," the severest in the north. To limit the immigration of free blacks, the code required a bond and proof of freedom of all blacks settling in the state. Blacks were barred from testifying in a trial involving a white man (Chaddock, 1908, pp. 84–85; Foner, 1965a, p. 240; Litwack, 1961, pp. 69–74). Restrictions on social relations between the races, whether enacted into miscegenation and public accommodation laws or sanctioned only by custom, further limited their freedom. Tocqueville (1945) observed that "the prejudice of race appears to be stronger in the states that have abolished slavery than in those where it still exists; and nowhere is it so intolerant as in those states where servitude has never been known" (pp. 359–60).

Any movement for the abolition of slavery was bound to find such an environment uncongenial. Antislavery sentiment had existed for years, particularly immediately after the Revolution, but it was small and inconsequential. The condition of the slave and the free black had engaged the attention of the leaders of the benevolent societies: many of them had supported the American Colonization Society, and Arthur Tappan had promoted an abortive plan to found a black college at New Haven (Barnes, 1964, pp. 25–28, 35–36). But the revivals and the enlarged benevolent enterprise they inspired drew more urgent attention to the condition of blacks, and the success of emancipation in Britain was a further stimulus for the founding of the American Anti-Slavery Society dedicated to "immediate emancipation." The benevolent societies provided a method of organization and a network of people attuned both to the gospel and to the need to spread it. From the beginning, abolitionism was dedicated to securing rights for blacks in the north as much as to securing their freedom in the south.

The New England Anti-Slavery Society was founded by William Lloyd Garrison in 1832, and the New York City Society on October 2, 1833. The mob which attacked the New York group's founding meeting foreshadowed many violent attacks against abolitionists. The meeting had been announced for Clinton Hall, but upon learning that it might be attacked, the group changed plans and met at Finney's Chatham Street Chapel. They had barely enough time to elect Arthur Tappan president before the mob had found them and dispersed the meeting (Wyatt-Brown, 1969, pp. 104–06).

Both the New England and New York societies adopted the British slogan of "immediate emancipation," intending by it, in the words of the New York Society's address, "emphatically to mark our dissent from the project of gradual abolition." "Immediatism" did not imply an expectation that slavery would in fact be ended immediately, for any measure "promptly commenced with the honest determination of urging it on to its completion" would be immediate. Their program, they summarized, called for "immediate emancipation which is gradually accomplished." (Barnes, 1964, pp. 48–49).

The founders recognized that their use of "immediate" contrasted with ordinary usage. But the slogan did not represent a program so much as a new orientation toward reform. The call for immediate emancipation implicitly acknowledged a religious duty to work toward freedom of the slaves, in keeping with the revivalist belief that the saved must not countenance sin in any form but instead must act positively to see it eliminated. The call was both a statement of principle and a recognition of the necessity for action, but not a political demand. As Garrison explained, "We have never said that slavery would be overthrown by a single blow; that it ought to be, we shall always contend!" (Filler, 1960, p. 61n; Loveland, 1966).

The formation of a national society followed quickly. A convention called in Philadelphia on December 4, 1833, officially launched the society and elected Arthur Tappan its first president. Its constitution did not envision drastic measures to end slavery: it admitted the right of each state to legislate with regard to abolition, although it pledged that the society would attempt to convince all fellow citizens that "slave-holding is a heinous crime in the sight of God, and the duty, safety, and best interests of all concerned, require its *immediate abandonment*, without expatriation." The Society would endeavor, by constitutional means, to influence Congress to end the interstate slave trade, to forbid slavery in areas where it had jurisdiction (the District of Columbia and the territories), and to refuse to admit any new slave states. It further pledged to attempt to improve the status of "people of color" both by aiding them directly and by combatting prejudice. It explicitly opposed any efforts by slaves to free themselves by force (Kraditor, 1970, p. 5).

The society, while planning more diversified activities than most of the previous benevolent societies had undertaken, still followed their pattern, and expressed a fairly moderate program. It would principally undertake moral suasion and direct assistance to blacks. It recognized constitutional limitations on federal action to end slavery, and it condemned slave insurrections. Its members believed that their fellow Christians in the south could be brought to recognize, as they had, the sinful character of slavery.

The national society differed from other benevolent societies in that local organization generally followed, rather than preceded, its creation. An event at Lane Seminary in Cincinnati contributed many of the movement's most active early organizers. The seminary had been founded to train revivalists for the growing west. Lyman Beecher was president and Arthur Tappan a prime benefactor. In the first class, which entered in 1833, were Theodore Dwight Weld, Henry B. Stanton, and others of Finney's converts, as well as William T. Allan and James Thome, two southerners who later became active abolitionists. One of the first professors was Calvin Stowe, who would later marry the president's daughter Harriet.

Weld, Finney's Utica convert, was probably more responsible than any other person for the early spread of abolitionism, both among the benevolent leaders of New York and in the rural areas where it was to be strongest. Before his own conversion to immediate emancipation, he had served in the Holy Band and as a lecturer for the American Temperance Society. The rhetorical powers which later were put to use against slavery, and which Lyman Beecher (who was no ally) described as "logic on fire," were immediately evident. He was much in demand as a preacher throughout the west, and Lewis Tappan asked him to come to New York (Barnes, 1964, pp. 15–16).

He entered Lane Seminary instead. In its first academic year, the slavery issue had divided the school. In February 1834, Weld and other students organized an eighteen-day debate on abolition. Weld led the debate, and by its end the student body had unanimously endorsed immediate abolition. Many of these young men began working to educate and otherwise elevate the free blacks of Cincinnati; but the seminary's board of trustees determined to abolish the students' Anti-Slavery Society and censor their discussions. In protest, most of the students withdrew, and many took up regular abolitionist evangelizing. Several students transferred to the newly-founded Oberlin College, which agreed that they could name the faculty and the blacks would be admitted. Arthur Tappan transferred his benevolence to Oberlin and persuaded Finney to go there as professor of theology (Barnes, 1964, pp. 65–71, 74–76; Filler, 1957, p. 69).

Weld did not go to Oberlin, but was made an agent for the American Anti-Slavery Society. He recruited several of the Lane rebels to join him, and they set out to convert Ohio to abolitionism. During 1834 and 1835, Weld preached in the state. Almost invariably he encountered hostility, and occasionally dangerous mobs. But he turned the hostility to his advantage. He generally preached for several nights in a community. At the end of his lecture series he asked converts to immediate abolition to rise, and the numbers who stood up testified to his effectiveness. In April 1835, a convention at Putnam founded the Ohio Anti-Slavery Society, largely composed of local auxiliaries which Weld and his fellow students had organized (Barnes, 1964, pp. 81–82; Galbreath, 1928, vol. 2, pp. 206–07).

The same program was used to organize antislavery auxiliaries in New York. Beginning in 1833, the national society commissioned agents to work in upstate New York, and from their efforts a state society was founded. The founding convention at Utica, on October 21, 1835, was met by one of the more celebrated antiabolitionist riots. A notable effect of the Utica mob was the conversion of Gerrit Smith from colonization to immediatism. Disturbed at the violence, Smith invited the convention to adjourn to his home at Peterboro and joined them (Cross, 1950, p. 221; Myers, 1962, pp. 154–55; Richards, 1970, pp. 85–88).

Weld himself began lecturing in New York in February 1836, visiting the major upstate cities as well as several small towns. His success matched his earlier success in Ohio; in Rochester, for example, between 800 and 900 new members joined the male and female antislavery societies (Myers, 1962, pp. 173–76). An even greater contribution was the convention he organized in 1836 to train agents for the national society. Because the agents had been so successful, the 1836 annual meeting allocated $50,000 to expand the number of agents to seventy. Weld selected "the Seventy" and trained them, and their work within a year nearly doubled the number of existing auxiliaries. The presence of Angelina and Sarah Grimké at Weld's training session foreshadowed the debate over the position of women which within a few years would help to split the abolition movement (Barnes, 1964, p. 154; Myers, 1965, pp. 162–63; 1966, pp. 29–46).

The antislavery lecturers' activity was patterned after the revival. Each man usually lectured six times a week (including three times on Sunday) and stayed in the same place for several days, conducting a protracted meeting. The message was simple: "Insist principally on the SIN OF SLAVERY," the Society instructed Weld in his commission (Barnes & Dumond, 1970, vol. 1, p. 125). That is just what Weld and the other agents did, adding that subscription to the doctrine of emancipation was release from sin. Listeners were encouraged to make direct testimony and publicly proclaim that they were converted; and the effectiveness of the style rested largely on the fact that the preachers worked in areas where their hearers were accustomed to revivals. Their rhetoric was similar to that of the revivals and other reform movements: George Storrs, an antislavery agent, slightly altered a temperance address by the Methodist clergyman Wilbur Fisk and republished it as an antislavery document, to Fisk's great consternation. The style of preaching is perhaps best indicated by the frequency with which lecturers had to take furloughs to recover from their hoarseness (Barnes, 1964, p. 105; Myers, 1965, pp. 163–64, 169).

From the beginning, the societies were concerned not only with abolishing slavery; abolitionists condemned the harsh treatment of free blacks as well. Most of them strongly argued that blacks were not inferior to whites. Not all abolitionists would go so far, but those who did expressed a belief few white northerners would even consider at the time. Blacks were welcomed into the societies, and the Seventy included four agents assigned to work with blacks. Abolitionists worked to guarantee blacks the franchise and equal civil rights, and to defend them in legal difficulties. They demanded that their churches integrate seating arrangements and boycotted public accommodations that refused service to blacks. Their most important activity was providing education for blacks. Oberlin College was founded as an integrated school; one hundred women teaching at schools for blacks attended the 1837 Ohio Anti-Slavery Society meeting; and Prudence Crandall went to jail in Connecticut for having defied the law against opening a school for black children. The abolitionists emphasized education because they were convinced that blacks were as able to benefit from education as whites, and that the example of educated blacks would show whites, northerners and southerners alike, that their prejudices were wrong (Barnes & Dumond, 1970, vol. 1, p. 263; Filler, 1957, pp. 64–70; Myers, 1966, p. 38; Sorin, 1972, pp. 61–76).

The agents laid the groundwork for an effective network of local auxiliaries, especially in New York and Ohio (Filler, 1957, p. 67). Table 4.1 shows the relation of several demographic characteristics and of revivalism to county membership in Anti-Slavery Societies in those two states. The table shows both simple (or zero-order) correlation coefficients, which measure the extent to which each independent variable is related to membership, and regression coefficients (or beta weights), which measure the direct effect of each independent variable on membership.

TABLE 4.1
Determinants of Anti-Slavery Society Membership
(Multiple Regression)

Independent variable	Ohio		New York	
	0-order r	Beta weight	0-order r	Beta weight
% Yankee	.304	.217	.414	.214
% Southern, 1870 (Ohio only)	−.079	.088		
% Catholic, 1850	−.067	−.007	.204	.295
Farms per capita, 1850	−.090	−.035	.259	.220
Revivalism	.427	.371	.427	.264
Multiple R	.470		.564	

The zero-order correlation coefficient (designated as r) measures the strength of the relationship between two variables without regard for whether that relationship is explained by other variables. The zero-order correlation reveals whether two phenomena were common in the same areas. But it cannot be taken as a measure of the effect of one variable on another, because a large coefficient may arise when both variables are caused by some third variable. Multiple regression takes account of the relationships among independent variables. Consider the analysis of Anti-Slavery Society membership in Ohio shown in Table 4.1: the correlation coefficients of the percentage of Yankees and of revivalism are both large, showing that membership was much greater in Yankee and revivalist counties than in other counties.

But revivals were most common in Yankee counties too, and it might be that revivalist counties had large numbers of abolitionists only because Yankees tended to support both movements, rather than because there was a direct connection between them. Multiple regression tests for this possibility, revealing the relationship between a dependent and an independent variable when their common relationship to one or more other independent variables is controlled. If their common occurrence among Yankees explains the relationship between revivalism and abolitionism, the regression coefficient of revivalism will be zero (or close to it) when percent Yankee is controlled.

In both New York and Ohio, the regression coefficients for revivalism and the percentage of Yankees are smaller than their respective correlation coefficients, revealing that part of the relation of each independent variable to society membership is due to the other (and to the remaining independent variables). But the coefficients are still substantial, showing that each characteristic had an independent effect: that with comparable proportions of Yankees, the more revivalist counties had larger Anti-Slavery Societies, and similarly that of counties of equal revivalism, those with more Yankees had larger societies. In addition, the relative sizes of the regression coefficients tell which variable had the greater effect: revivalism was a more important determinant of Anti-Slavery Society membership in both states than was Yankee settlement.

Table 4.1 also shows that membership was a characteristic of rural areas in New York. In Ohio, rural areas were less abolitionist than urban areas, but only slightly.[4] The low absolute level of membership

---

[4]The fact that membership was high (and, as shown below, that the Liberty party was supported) in counties populated by southerners is surprising. In the next decade, however, as the next chapter relates, southerners voted against antislavery candidates and in favor of the Know-Nothing party which worked to prevent disunion.

should also be noted: despite what appeared to the society leaders to be overwhelming success, in only six counties in New York and three in Ohio could the societies claim as much as 2% of the population.

But these small numbers were well organized for antislavery agitation. During the next few years, as the American Anti-Slavery Society's constitution had envisioned, the societies began to pressure Congress to enforce what jurisdiction it had over slavery. The first efforts at political influence took two directions: petitions to Congress and questioning and endorsement of candidates. The petition campaign revealed that opposition to slavery was more widespread than membership figures indicated, but the response to endorsements revealed that willingness to act on it was limited.

The right of citizens to petition Congress was guaranteed by the Constitution. The petitions the societies circulated and submitted to Congress asked it to take the following actions within its power to limit the spread of slavery: to abolish it in the District of Columbia; to forbid it in the territories; to outlaw the interstate slave trade; and to refuse to annex Texas or to admit Florida to the union as a slave state (Barnes, 1964, p. 136).

The House responded to the flow of petitions in 1836 with the Pinckney gag rule, requiring that petitions on slavery or its abolition be tabled without action. Because the gag rule violated a constitutional right of northerners, many who had not been sympathetic to abolitionism were aroused. John Quincy Adams became a leading spokesman of abolitionists in Congress in the course of his eight-year fight against the gag. He never joined an antislavery society and never considered himself an abolitionist. He merely wished to defend the right of petition. But the two issues became closely identified in his mind and in many others, and the belief that southern Congressmen threatened the constitution won for abolition many more northern supporters. Adams, hoping to kill the rule by mocking it, engaged in a variety of subterfuges to present the forbidden petitions; and to do so he needed a continuing flow of petitions from the nation (Barnes, 1964, pp. 110–11, 122–29).

The Anti-Slavery Societies were happy to see that he got it. The depression of 1837 hurt many of the New York benevolent leaders badly. Since they had to reduce their contributions, the societies could no longer afford agents. But the agents had built up the auxiliaries to the point where their own work was less necessary. Individual members could easily collect signatures on the petitions the national society printed and submit them to friendly Congressmen whose names were circulated from New York. Women assumed an important role in local activities by circulating petitions among their neighbors, arousing the condemnation of antiabolitionist Congressmen and the press (Barnes, 1964, pp. 135–36).

The petition campaign contributed indirectly to the decline of the national society. Since the campaign depended on local activity, and, once begun, required little central direction, the auxiliaries did not depend on the national organization as they had when the burden of the work was borne by hired agents. Thus when factionalism broke open in the society in 1839 and 1840, its members were probably less concerned to keep it whole than they would have been five years before.

The response of their representatives to the petition campaign also made the abolitionists more concerned about the views these men held on slavery, and in many states the societies systematically questioned candidates for office and published their replies. Candidates for national office were questioned about their views on slavery in the District, on the gag rule, and on other questions of national jurisdiction. Candidates for state offices were questioned on issues pertinent to the state. In 1838, New York abolitionists asked candidates for state office for their views on trial by jury for accused fugitive slaves, the removal of all racial distinctions from the state constitution, and the state law which allowed slaveholders to come to the state and keep slaves there for up to nine months. William Seward, Whig candidate for governor, answered evasively while his running mate, Luther Bradish, responded to every question to the abolitionists' satisfaction.[5] The New York State Society had adopted resolutions formally binding its members to vote only for candidates supporting its stands, but the election outcome revealed that few abolitionists were yet ready to abandon their traditional parties, and that the votes of those who did were apparently balanced by an equal number of anti-abolitionist votes. In six of the eight senate districts, Seward's and Bradish's totals were practically identical; and while Bradish outran Seward by about a thousand votes in central New York, he fell behind by about the same margin in the New York City district (Benson, 1964, pp. 111–12; Sorin, 1971, p. 33).

In Ohio, on the other hand, it is likely that the abolitionist vote

---

[5]During the years that abolitionists were tentatively establishing their relation to the political system, politicians were equally tentative in defining their relation to abolition. In 1838 Seward dealt with the abolitionists evasively; in later years, though never an abolitionist, he became a leading antislavery figure. Millard Fillmore moved in the opposite direction: in 1838, running for Congress from Buffalo, he won the endorsement of the abolitionists by his replies to their questions, but in the 1850s he became the standard-bearer for northerners opposed to antislavery agitation (Rayback, 1959, pp. 100–01).

did affect the election of 1838, but the behavior of the elected legislators was disappointing. In 1833 the General Assembly had sent Thomas Morris, Democrat, to the Senate, where for six years he was the only senator to advocate abolition in the District of Columbia. Now that his term was to expire, many abolitionists endorsed and voted for Democratic state legislators in the hope that they would reelect him. Most abolitionists were Whigs, and their votes were widely credited with producing that year's Democratic increase in the legislative elections. But the new legislature replaced Morris with Benjamin Tappan, strengthened the Black Code, and passed resolutions condemning abolition (Smith, 1897, pp. 30–31).[6]

Further discouragement about the possibility of converting the major parties resulted from the apparent apostasy of Henry Clay. Though himself a slaveholder, Clay had long publicly deplored slavery and supported the colonization movement, and some abolitionists hoped that he would lead the Whig Party into stronger antislavery stands. But in 1839 he began to temper his position in an effort to win the support of the south for the 1840 nomination (Filler, 1957, p. 150).

Moral suasion and political efforts, therefore, did not appear to be bringing the end of slavery any nearer. The petition campaign was at best a symbolic victory: although sympathy for the movement grew in the north and the gag rule was eventually defeated, none of the petitions was ever granted. Endorsements revealed either that the abolitionists controlled very few votes or that the votes that they controlled did not control the representatives that they elected.

So despite adding a few more to their ranks and finding a few allies, the abolitionists grew increasingly dissatisfied with the major parties and began to discuss organizing an abolitionist party. Meanwhile, events within the societies themselves led to a widening split which also contributed to the decision to take independent political action. William Lloyd Garrison, editing the *Liberator* since 1831 in Boston, was the country's leading abolition journalist and recognized leader of the movement in New England. His understanding of slavery, to a much greater degree than that of the New York City and rural abolitionists, identified it as but one among many problems that must be eliminated in order to redeem American society. The reformation he envisioned included equal rights for women and the ultimate abolition of all government; their immediate corollaries required full participation by women in the antislavery societies and abstention

[6]Tappan was the free-thinking, Jacksonian brother of Arthur and Lewis, and at this time no foe of slavery. In 1848 he would abandon his party to support Van Buren and the Free Soil movement (Wyatt-Brown, 1969, p. 277; Holt, 1931, p. 331).

from voting or other participation in politics. His views also led him to an early rejection of religious orthodoxy, in which many evangelical abolitionists were to follow him, but not for many years.

Garrison's place in this book is small because he contributed little to the electoral wing of the antislavery movement, but he was indisputably a leading antislavery agitator during three decades. Because his positions were more extreme for their time than those of the evangelicals, however, he is more vulnerable than they to the charge that he hindered the movement by offending potential supporters. A literal interpretation must concede, with Kraditor, that Garrison wished to welcome adherents without regard for their views on other subjects, while his opponents attempted to drum him out of the movement in order to limit it to people with traditional views (on the woman question, for example). It is also true that Garrison never rejected on principle the right of other abolitionists to decide to engage in political activity, although he thought it both morally wrong and inexpedient.

But Kraditor's attempt to justify Garrison as proposing the "broad" platform for the antislavery societies, while the New York group supported the "narrow" platform, does not adequately respect the historical context (1970, pp. 8–9, 118). For, given the prevailing views of the day toward Garrison's positions on other issues, he could only alienate potential supporters by advocating them in *The Liberator*. The antislavery platform would be broadened not by expanding its issues to a general advocacy of human freedom, but by expanding the reasons for opposition to slavery.

In any event, the "woman question" came to a head at the national anniversaries of 1839 and 1840, as the New England Society sent women delegates and demanded for them a place on the meeting's committees. Women had been crucial to the gathering of petitions, and the Grimké sisters had raised issues and hackles by speaking to mixed audiences. New Yorkers opposed public activities by women on grounds of both public image and personal preference. When Lewis Tappan was nominated to a committee that included Abby Kelley at the 1840 anniversary meeting, he gave four reasons why it was immoral for a lady to sit behind closed doors with gentlemen, and walked out. Since Garrison had been more successful than Tappan and his allies at packing the meeting, women's rights to participate were vindicated, but at the cost of the unity of the society. The same day that Tappan walked out of the American Anti-Slavery Society anniversary, he met with thirty abolitionist leaders to form a competing organization. However, his American and Foreign Anti-Slavery Society, which explicitly denied women the right to vote, never really took hold (Wyatt-Brown, 1969, pp. 197–98).

The split had been expected for some time, and the issue of women's participation may only have hastened a decline that decentralization and competition for funds between the national and state societies had already made likely (Barnes, 1964, pp. 148–52). The desire to maintain an active national campaign, the poor results of petitions and endorsements, and the New York leaders' desire to keep abolitionism "respectable" by distinguishing their views from Garrison's all suggested the course of action which was pursued next: an independent abolitionist political party. Hostility to Garrison particularly affected the evangelicals and those in the benevolent-society tradition, and it was this group that led the movement into politics.

The executive committee of the national society, then still in the hands of the Tappans, called a convention which met in Albany in July 1839 to discuss possibilities for political action. Myron Holley, there and at a series of conventions he organized in New York and Ohio in the next several months, was the most vigorous early advocate of a new party, and at Warsaw, New York, a convention resolved to run abolitionist candidates and nominated James Gillespie Birney for president. Birney, who had gone from slaveholder to colonizationist to abolitionist largely under Weld's influence, had been secretary of the American Anti-Slavery Society since 1837. He declined the nomination, but privately indicated his willingness to run if he could be shown that the time for third-party action was ripe (Fladeland, 1955, pp. 181–83).

The decision to form an independent party was hardly unanimous among abolitionists, even those who were thoroughly convinced of the propriety of some form of political action. A variety of arguments was arrayed against the proposed step.[7] Some opposed it on principle, even if they did not go as far as Garrison did in renouncing all connections with the government. They nonetheless shared the distrust of most evangelicals toward politics, and believed that in a political party expediency and the need to compromise would soon force them to sacrifice their "sacred regard for duty," in Birney's words (in 1836). To engage in politics directly was to confess that "moral means" had failed, and that the way to victory was not through the winning of hearts but the winning of power. Some felt that whatever respect abolitionists enjoyed in their communities was due to general recognition that they had nothing to gain personally from their activity, but that the formation of a party implied a quest for independent political power (Fladeland, 1955, p. 176; Kraditor, 1970, p. 119).

[7]The views of most abolitionists on forms of political action changed frequently and rapidly during the 1840s. The following statements should therefore be taken as typical positions and justifications of those positions, rather than the unchanging attitudes of the men quoted.

In addition there were several tactical objections to the formation of a third party. Some joined Birney in claiming (in 1839) that "the great Anti-Slavery enterprise can never succeed without independent nominations," but that care must be taken to discuss the subject fully among abolitionists and unite them behind the proposal before it was carried into action (Fladeland, 1955, p. 180).

Those who accepted the "municipal theory" of slavery, that it was subject to the exclusive jurisdiction of the states but that Congress could legislate on matters respecting the territories and the interstate slave trade, thought that a national abolitionist party had no reason to exist. Gamaliel Bailey, editor of the abolitionist Cincinnati *Philanthropist*, argued that an abolitionist party was improper, since it required candidates to endorse a position which they would have no power to enforce if elected, and that the implied threat to southern institutions would keep moderate northerners out of the party (Rayback, 1948, pp. 165–66).

But the most important arguments had to do with the abolitionists' potential effect on the major parties. Most people, even abolitionists, would be unwilling to desert their parties for a new one with small chance of success. They had joined other parties because of those parties' stands on other issues, and they would not forsake their earlier affiliations at the cost of losing any influence they might have in spheres unrelated to abolition. William Goodell argued that abolitionists would become divided against themselves if they attempted to exert influence on other subjects. William Jay argued, further, that a third party which drew reformers from the major parties would eliminate the one influence that kept the parties from complete corruption. Some antislavery politicians had been elected with the endorsement of major parties. These men, not at all unnaturally, were thoroughly opposed to the third-party idea, and many abolitionists saw growing possibilities of influencing the major parties (Filler, 1957, pp. 162–63; Holt, 1931, pp. 188–89; Kraditor, 1970, pp. 145–47; Stewart, 1970, pp. 55–56).

On the opposite side, abolitionists argued for a third party saying that it was the duty of abolitionists to elect only men who were dedicated to bringing slavery to an end. For many years antislavery societies had passed resolutions calling on their members to vote only for abolitionists, and the major parties were not nominating them. Yes, politics was corrupt, said William Goodell, but this was only because moral men left it to the politicians; if disinterested men entered politics, they would be able to reform it (Fladeland, 1955, p. 180; Kraditor, 1970, pp. 120, 145).

The major parties were both unredeemable servants of the slave

power, according to a theme that was to be heard with increasing frequency during the next two decades. Gerrit Smith wrote that no national party could be an antislavery party, for the south would never
vote for it; past history showed that both major parties were dedicated to silencing the enemies of slavery. Thus he considered it a
positive duty of the abolitionists to organize their own party
(Kraditor, 1970, pp. 145–46).

Finally, it must be admitted that unrealistic expectations of the
growth of abolitionism, shared by abolitionists and their opponents,
led the third-party men to believe that they could take over the nation
within a decade. In 1838 Francis Granger, New York Whig, feared
that the abolitionists would have one quarter of his state's votes by
1840 (Rayback, 1959, p. 101).

Whatever their ambivalence, a group of abolitionists decided to
go ahead with the plan for a third party. The 1840 election offered
them the choice between Martin Van Buren, who had pledged in 1836
to veto any bill abolishing slavery in the District of Columbia, and
William Henry Harrison, who specifically disavowed the support he
received from some abolitionists, so the moment seemed propitious to
woo abolitionists away from the Whigs and Democrats (Filler, 1957, p.
154; Holt, 1931, p. 43). A new convention met in Albany in April
1840, formally established the Liberty party, and adopted a platform
which committed it absolutely to the abolition of slavery. Birney was
again nominated for president, and this time he wrote a letter of acceptance which invoked the slave-power specter to convince his fellow abolitionists of the need for an independent political organization.
He reviewed the failures of political activity in the two-party context
and recited the history of northern concessions to the south in the national government (Fladeland, 1955, p. 187–88).

Once the step was taken a number of abolitionists who had opposed it nonetheless supported Birney; Bailey raised the ticket on the
masthead of the *Philanthropist*. Others, such as Lewis Tappan, while
not openly identifying with the party, voted for its candidates. The
Ohio Anti-Slavery Society, however, declined to endorse the third
party, and while the party essentially took over the activities of the
New York Society, the two remained separate in Ohio. This difference
persisted, making the New York party more a creature of pure
abolitionism. Ohio Liberty men, on the other hand, were already
working toward a major-party coalition (Rayback, 1948, pp. 168–69;
Sorin, 1971, pp. 18–19; Wyatt-Brown, 1969, pp. 198–99).[8]

[8]In 1842, Gerrit Smith wrote Salmon Chase that "in this section, a Liberty party convention is an abolition convention" (Foner, 1970, p. 81).

The different relations between the Anti-Slavery Societies and the Liberty party organizations of the two states are reflected in the fact that votes for the Liberty party were much more concentrated in the same areas as society membership in New York than in Ohio. The correlations of society membership with the 1840, 1842 (gubernatorial), and 1844 votes in Ohio were .44, .40, and .44, respectively; in New York, they were .61, .51, and .63, respectively. However, with the formation of an abolitionist party and the division into factions of the American Anti-Slavery Society, the societies declined in influence. In both New York and Ohio most of the organized abolitionist activity during the next several years occurred within the party (Griffin, 1960, p. 152).

The Liberty campaign of 1840 can be called a campaign only by courtesy. Birney himself left in May for the World Anti-Slavery Convention in London, and did not return until after the election. Nor was the outcome encouraging for the prospects of independent political action. He received barely 7,000 votes, drawing as much as 1% only in Massachusetts and getting the votes of no more than an estimated 10% of the eligible voters among the members of antislavery societies (Fladeland, 1955, p. 188; Smith, 1897, p. 46).

But the party had been brought into existence, and if it was to continue it had to resolve in different form the same issues that had arisen over its creation. The two questions that were crucial were coalition and the scope of the platform. Opponents of coalition felt that, having organized as an abolitionist party, they could not nominate or endorse any man, however friendly to the cause, who was not himself an abolitionist. Advocates believed that the party could bring Whigs and Democrats to work for the end of slavery by supporting major-party candidates who were sympathetic, and by nominating candidates who would win wider support than any pure abolitionist could. The issue divided the party into eastern and western wings, with New Yorkers leading the fight for purity while Ohioans were the main advocates of coalition.

On coalitions, at least the issue was clear. On the platform, there were several divergent views. Some believed that the party had to be a one-idea party, ready to disband once it had accomplished its single objective. The address of the 1841 Liberty convention, written by William Goodell, announced that the party would take no stands on issues other than advocacy of emancipation; because slavery was the cause of most of the other national ills, the others would disappear once it was cured (Fladeland, 1955, p. 211–12).

To others it was equally evident that since slavery was related to all other political issues, their opposition required them to express their views on those issues. Their claim that government actions proved the dominance of the slave power implied that they would have taken different actions, and they felt that these positions should be spelled out. The desire to attract a wider following was also a motive for expanding the platform: Goodell later argued that "the masses of men who feel that they have wrongs of their own to be redressed . . . could have no confidence in a Liberty party not committed to universal equality and impartial justice to all." The problem, of course, was to define the stands on which abolitionists could agree, but many of the men who had attempted to expel Garrison for mixing abolition with other issues now went on to try to make the Liberty party a party of universal reform. Disagreements on issues extraneous to slavery, in Kraditor's (1970) words, "had been an argument first against the organization of a third party and later for one-ideaism, [and] had become a strong motive for abandoning the latter policy" (pp. 152, 154).

Yet a third position was that opposition to slavery should be moderated for the sake of a wider following which would bring about a major-party coalition. Salmon P. Chase even suggested that the party publicly renounce the label abolitionist, justifying his stand by differentiating between moral and political antislavery action. "Abolition seeks to abolish slavery everywhere. The means which it employs . . . are of a moral nature." Abolition, he said, was not a proper objective of political power, but antislavery, which aimed at the separation of the federal government from slavery, was. Antislavery would broaden the party's appeal because both abolitionists and nonabolitionists would endorse it (Foner, 1970, p. 80).

Without ever resolving these differences, the party worked for the next four years to build state and local organizations and run local candidates. As early as May 1841, it held a new nominating convention. Delegates from all free states except Michigan and Illinois attended and renominated Birney for the 1844 race (Fladeland, 1955, p. 211).

Organizing a third party in the mid-nineteenth century was no easy task, not only because of the tenaciousness of party loyalties but also because of the balloting procedure. The states made no provision for the printing of ballots, and candidates depended on their local party organizations to print and distribute their tickets to the voters (Bass, 1961, p. 254). So to get any votes at all a party required at least a rudimentary local organization.

Nonetheless, votes for the Liberty party showed small but steady gains. The 1842 gubernatorial vote was two and one-half times the 1840 vote in New York, and six times as great in Ohio (although in both states it was only about 2% in 1842). The Ohio faction actively worked for the nomination of a more "available" candidate for 1844, and Birney expressed his willingness to withdraw. Birney's image of the candidate for whom he would withdraw, however, was a widely respected man known for his abolitionism, such as William Jay, while Chase and Bailey hoped to persuade a prominent antislavery politician such as John Quincy Adams or William Seward. But when overtures to all potential candidates were rejected, the 1843 convention reaffirmed the nomination of Birney. Accepting the nomination, Birney indirectly criticized the Ohioans for their attempt to make a nomination of expediency from the ranks of nonabolitionists (Fladeland, 1955, pp. 224–26; Rayback, 1948, pp. 171–72).

The 1844 campaign was a serious effort, and though the vote was still small it showed the strategic significance of the party. Liberty men attempted to copy some of the practices that had made the Log Cabin campaign of 1840 so notorious: Birney made an extensive eastern tour, and large rallies were held throughout the north. Liberty men met in East Aurora, New York, for an Independence Day rally, at which toasts were drunk in "pure, cold water" (Fladeland, 1955, pp. 227–28; Roach, 1938, p. 162).

But the improved position of the Liberty party in 1844 was not due to its own efforts nearly as much as it was due to national political developments during Tyler's presidency. One of the major issues of the campaign was the annexation of Texas as new slave territory, which would restore slavery to an area where the Mexican government had previously abolished it. Polk, the Democratic standard-bearer, was committed to annexation. Clay, nominated by the Whigs, had once been the hope of some of the antislavery forces, but he had disappointed them in 1839, and in 1844 his deliberate equivocation on Texas further alienated them (Fladeland, 1955, pp. 234–36; Holt, 1931, pp. 202–05).

In both New York and Ohio (as elsewhere) the Liberty party made gains over its 1842 total. It suffered slight losses from 1843 in New York in the areas where it was strongest, and Benson argues that its losses prove that Texas was not an important issue in 1844 (Benson, 1964, pp. 261–62). But the percentage decline (from 4.5 to 3.1%) was in part due to the much higher turnout in the later election; the Liberty total declined by only 185 votes. It is possible (though it cannot be known) that the relative share of the Liberty party declined while its absolute number of votes remained constant because nearly all its constituency had voted in 1843, but that the major parties were more able to mobilize voters for the presidential election. Committed ideologues are much more likely to be activists than other voters and to vote in a higher proportion in off-year elections. But in any case, losses between an election in local constituencies and a national election do not necessarily represent a decline of strength, since abolitionists outside of the party would be more likely to support it when its candidates appeared to have a chance of winning (it did not in fact win any offices in New York in 1843; its best county, Madison, gave it 26%). The revivalist ethos was not the only force acting upon voters' decisions. Even where it was strong, it competed with other factors (for example, the 1846 referendum on black suffrage discussed below won far more votes than any Liberty candidate, apparently because abolitionists were able to support it without sacrificing traditional party loyalties).

Though the Liberty party received only 3% of New York's presidential vote, it took enough votes from Clay to throw New York's electoral votes, and with them the presidency, to the Democrats. In an election that was close throughout the nation, the Liberty vote in New York was accused by contemporaries, and has been acknowledged by historians, as one of the major factors in Polk's victory (Alexander, 1969, vol. 2, pp. 82–83; Roach, 1938, p. 171; Sellers, 1966, pp. 160–61).

At best, though, Liberty men had prevented the election of a moderate and assured the election of a southerner, a man who supported the annexation of Texas and the extension of slavery. It was evident to Chase and other Ohioans that for the party to take advantage of its possession of the balance of power, it would have to work out an accommodation with antislavery men in the major parties. Accordingly, Chase called a Southern and Western Convention of the Friends of Universal Liberty for June 1845, in Cincinnati. It succeeded in attracting some Democrats and Whigs, and approved a platform which did not mention immediate abolition but called for a "union of all sincere friends of Liberty and Free Labor" (Foner, 1970, pp. 80–81; Rayback, 1948, pp. 173–74).

But the party was unable to use its balance of power effectively. As Chase moved further from abolitionist principles and closer to union with antislavery elements in the major parties, Birney, Goodell, and Gerrit Smith were moving toward a platform of universal reform. An 1847 convention in Macedon Lock, New York, reaffirmed an absolute commitment to abolition and declared that the Constitution implicitly outlawed slavery in the United States, but the platform also included a number of other planks, among them free trade, the distribution of the public lands in small parcels, and opposition to all monopolies. Birney, having been seriously injured in a fall from a horse, could not accept another nomination for president. The new group, calling itself the Liberty League, nominated Gerrit Smith (Fladeland, 1955, p. 262–63).

The Liberty party was falling apart. In the 1846 Ohio election, it did better than it had ever done before, but its vote fell off in 1847 (Holt, 1931, p. 290). In New York the group was so demoralized that it did not even run a candidate for governor in 1846.

The defection of the universal reformers left Chase free to proceed toward coalition: the most absolute proponents of abolitionism in the party had left it, and others who were alienated by the move to expand the party's program (in a remarkably Democratic direction) were more receptive to coalition. At the same time, the Mexican War and the fight over the Wilmot proviso were pushing the slavery question into the center of national politics, and many members of both parties were becoming more receptive to an antislavery party (Rayback, 1948, p. 174).[9]

The national Liberty convention was scheduled for the fall of 1847. Chase wanted to postpone it until after the major parties had met the next year, expecting that their nominations would repel the antislavery men in their ranks. He was overruled, and the convention met in Buffalo in October. But delegates were ready to make some concessions to expand their following. Their platform reaffirmed the party's demands for nonextension, for abolition where Congress had jurisdiction, and for repeal of the fugitive slave law. But it did not call for immediate abolition. The nomination was given to John P. Hale, whose election to the Senate from New Hampshire the year before by Liberty men and antislavery Whigs and Democrats made him a symbol of coalition. Birney, noting with disappointment that Hale was neither a Liberty man nor an abolitionist, condemned the party for having sacrificed principle to expediency (Fladeland, 1955, p. 265; Rayback, 1948, pp. 176–78).

But the worst was yet to come. Antislavery Whigs and the radical Barnburner Democrats of New York were defeated at their parties' conventions the next year and were ready to bolt. They joined the Liberty men at a Free Soil Convention at Buffalo in August 1848. By an explicit exchange, the Liberty men wrote the platform and the Barnburners nominated Van Buren for the presidency. Hale withdrew as the Liberty candidate and the party was absorbed in the new Free Soil party (Smith, 1897, pp. 138–43).

With the 1848 Free Soil convention, abolitionist politics as an independent force disappeared and was replaced by antislavery politics. Van Buren, former foe during the petition war and opponent of aboli-

---

[9]National events between 1846 and 1848 are discussed more fully in the next chapter.

tion in the District of Columbia, was hard for the abolitionists to take. The 1848 platform, largely written by Chase, called for complete separation of the federal government from slavery, nonextension into new territory and abolition in the District of Columbia, together with a number of reforms unrelated to slavery (a homestead act, retrenchment in government expenses, and cheap postage, among others). But there was no call for immediate emancipation, and there was another, equally significant omission: there was no mention of the franchise or equal rights for blacks. This omission, probably necessary to guarantee the support of the Barnburners and certainly necessary to broaden the antislavery appeal, nevertheless meant the abandonment of a principle for which the Liberty party had stood ever since its founding and which it had reiterated in every platform (Foner, 1965b, pp. 319–20; Holt, 1931, p. 328). The fear that had been expressed by some abolitionists at every stage of increasing political activity, that it would lead to a dilution of principle, seemed unequivocally confirmed.

Thus recounted, the passage from moral suasion and abolition revivals to majority-bent politics assumes an air of inevitability. The petition campaign seemed no more than a justifiable use of constitutional rights to expose to the nation its greatest evil. The petition campaign led naturally to the search for representatives who would receive and exploit the petitions, and when few were found, it seemed equally advisable to establish a new party which would nominate candidates who could be trusted. The development of a party and the acquisition of some minor political strength made it seem but a small step to major strength, even if some principles had to be sacrificed to popularity.

But if it was inevitable, it was only so because of the direction that had been given to the early abolition campaign by its origins. Without the religious impetus, an antislavery campaign might have been political from the start, or might not have begun at all. Without the specific orientation of the revivalist ethos, a religious antislavery campaign might have remained restricted to moral suasion.

In discussing the relation between religion and political behavior, I described three general theories, each of which can be applied to revivalism and abolitionism. According to the theory that the relation is spurious, revivalism and abolitionism might be related only because they are caused by similar conditions of social structure, or because the true causes of abolitionism are related to revivalism. The theory of communal involvement implies that the revivalists adopted abolitionism, not because of their distinct beliefs, but because of their common membership in, and identification with, religious organizations. Only the theory of religious belief implies a direct relation between the two.

To show that there was a direct relation I must rule out the first two theories. If either of them is correct, the relationship between revivalism and abolitionism will vanish when appropriate variables are controlled. The religious belief explanation is supported if the relationship does not vanish under controls.

Some of the social conditions which produced revivalism are known. If revivalism and abolitionism were related because they sprang from common causes—if, for example, those involved in them had similar geographic origins or occupations—those causes should explain the observed relationship. But they do not: Table 4.1 shows that revivalism has a strong effect on membership in Anti-Slavery Societies even when the population's cultural composition (Yankee, Catholic, and for Ohio, southern) and concentration on farms are controlled.

TABLE 4.2
Determinants of Liberty Party Votes, Ohio
(Multiple Regression)

Independent variable	1840		1844		1846	
	0-order r	Beta weight	0-order r	Beta weight	0-order r	Beta weight
% Yankee	.539	.597	.521	.551	.374	.431
% Southern	−.064	.280	−.005	.354	.107	.422
% Catholic	−.074	.049	−.284	−.125	−.286	−.108
Farms per capita	−.059	.045	.030	.176	−.008	.177
Revivalism	.317	.185	.421	.321	.371	.331
Multiple R	.597		.679		.599	

The analysis of abolitionist votes provides further confirmation. Table 4.2 shows the effect of several variables on the 1840, 1844, and 1846 Liberty votes in Ohio, and Table 4.3 presents a similar analysis for the 1840, 1842, and 1844 votes in New York and the vote in the 1846 referendum to grant equal suffrage to blacks. The effect of revivalism on the 1840 vote in Ohio was relatively small because abolitionists who were already organized into the Ohio Anti-Slavery Society did not cooperate with the Liberty party. But in subsequent years abolitionists who had been influenced by revivalism came to support the Liberty party in Ohio as they did from its inception in New York, and revivalism had a strong effect in all elections after

1840. With two exceptions in New York (in 1840 and 1842), the effect of New England origins is greater in both states, but nevertheless the coefficient of revivalism shows that its relationship to abolitionism is not explained by their common occurrence among Yankees.[10] (Similar evidence is presented in the next chapter for votes for antislavery candidates in the following decade.) This evidence supports the argument of the effect of religious belief.

TABLE 4.3

Determinants of Liberty Party Vote and Support for Black Suffrage, New York (Multiple Regression)

Independent variable	Liberty, 1840		Liberty, 1842		Liberty, 1844		Suffrage, 1846	
	0-order r	Beta weight	0-order r	Beta weight	0-order r	Beta weight	0-order r	Beta weight
% Yankee, 1855	.349	.180	.419	.157	.521	.333	.637	.509
% Catholic, 1850	−.079	−.061	.041	.131	−.121	−.040	.056	.055
Farms per capita, 1850	.276	.063	.361	.225	.435	.196	.300	.018
Revivalism	.443	.352	.551	.414	.456	.261	.512	.298
Multiple R	.491		.617		.618		.697	

But it does not dispose of all the grounds for arguing that the relationship is spurious. If the relationship is not explained by their common antecedents, it may be that abolitionism is caused by some other variable with which revivalism is correlated. If it is, the relationship will vanish when that other variable is controlled. It could be that abolitionist politics was caused by some prior political tradition; if revivalism had an effect, the voting behavior of revival areas must in fact have changed when abolitionism arose. If the vote for abolitionists can be explained by the earlier voting behavior of revival counties, the effect of revivalism will vanish when one controls for the vote in some earlier election.

[10]The effects of revivalism and Yankee origins are actually more complex, and these tables, by not telling the full story, underestimate the effects of revivalism somewhat. Revivalism and Yankee origins actually intensified each other's effects; revivals among Yankees were much more likely to produce abolitionists than were revivals among non-Yankees. In technical terms, this means that the product term of Yankee origins and revivalism has a large coefficient when it is added to almost all of the regressions presented in the preceding tables, especially those for Ohio, and in several cases contributes a statistically significant increase in explained variance. The regressions with interaction terms are omitted because they would needlessly complicate the presentation of the data.

Donald (1966) has proposed that abolitionism was determined by a particular set of social structural conditions: he argues that people became abolitionists in reaction to a decline in their social status. He cites Cross's *The Burned-Over District* as saying that "antislavery was strongest in those counties which had once been economically dominant but which by the 1830's, though prosperous, had relatively fallen behind their more advantageously situated neighbors" (p. 28).[11] He finds that the abolitionists were descendants of "old and socially dominant Northeastern families," and implies that they experienced downward intergenerational mobility. He is surprised that men of such benevolence were unconcerned with the plight of the urban poor and the factory laborer. He concludes that the abolitionists were a displaced stratum, victims of a status revolution which was transferring social and economic leadership "from the country to the city, from the farmer to the manufacturer, from the preacher to the corporation lawyer" (Donald, 1966, p. 33).

Though Donald does not use the phrase "symbolic issues," he argues that people declining in status adopted abolitionism as an assertion of their moral superiority. But he provides no plausible explanation of why the slavery question was chosen, or why slaveholders were their target, when other issues, such as temperance or rural values, would have more appropriately symbolized their conflict with the new, industrial northern elite which was allegedly displacing them.

In any case, his thesis has been strikingly refuted on empirical grounds. He infers abolitionists' inability to adjust to an increasingly urban world from the fact that only 12% were born in principal cities; but Skotheim (1965, p. 52) shows that only 6% of the country's population lived in cities larger than 5,000 in 1810, after almost all the abolitionists in Donald's sample were born. They were therefore an unusually urban group for their time.

Abolitionists were not downwardly mobile: most of them were indeed from old northeastern families, but except for a few like Adams (not an abolitionist, but Donald may have classified him as one) and Jay, their families were average in status rather than prominent. Sorin identifies the hundred leading abolitionists of New York. Of the thirty whose fathers' occupations could be determined, 46.5%

---

[11]Donald does not give a page reference, and my reading of Cross (1950) reveals only the following description of counties where abolitionism (support for the Liberty party) was strong: counties of "Yankee derivation, social maturity, superior education, and at least average prosperity" (p. 226).

had the same status as their fathers and 40% had higher status. "More important," Sorin (1971) adds, "[the fathers] were generally missing from the pages of biographical dictionaries and of their respective counties' histories. . . . This is a relatively strong, if impressionistic, indication that the fathers had, at least, no more prestige, were no richer, and received no more deference than their abolitionist sons" (pp. 107–08). A contemporary chronicler, a Democrat, noted that "in proportion to its numbers, [the Liberty party] probably contains more men of wealth, of talents, and personal worth, than any party in the state" (Hammond, 1848, vol. 3, p. 479).

Most importantly, Donald seems to be reading late nineteenth and early twentieth century history onto that of the 1830s. While he asserts that this was the age of the city, the manufacturer, and the corporation lawyer, the enterprise that he implies did not come into existence until after the Civil War. If the abolitionists were unconcerned with the plight of the factory laborer, it was because they still envisioned the possibility that every man could be a free laborer, and believed that they lived in "a dynamic, expanding capitalist society, whose achievements and destiny were almost wholly the result of the dignity and opportunities which it afforded the average laboring man" (Foner, 1970, p. 11).[12] The status revolution Donald describes is essentially the same as the status revolution that has been invoked as the explanation of the rise of Progressivism in the early twentieth century (Hofstadter, 1955, pp. 134–38), an age which seems at face value to come much closer to having the characteristics he imputes to the 1830s.

Donald's argument is about abolitionist leaders, and therefore data about the behavior of the electorate are not entirely relevant. But they can be used to test at least one hypothesis suggested by his work. According to his theory, the abolitionists should have come from areas that were declining in population, at least relative to nonabolitionist areas. If population decline explains the relation between revivalism and abolitionism, Donald's theory is confirmed in preference to the theory that abolitionists were motivated by religious beliefs.

Tests of the proposition that the relation between revivalism and abolitionism is spurious are fairly easy to propose and carry out. It is harder to distinguish empirically between the argument that com-

---

[12]Foner is talking here about the typical Republican, rather than the abolitionist, but he demonstrates the importance of the free-labor ideology as a basis for Republican antislavery.

munal involvement in a religious or cultural group determined voting behavior and the theory that the salient distinguishing characteristic of the group was its religious belief. If differences between religious groups in their behavior are not due to religious belief but to in-group association, however, such differences should be explained by cultural origins or denominational affiliation.

The theory of communal involvement requires that I test for the effects of these variables before accepting that the revivals had an effect on political behavior through their impact on religious belief.[13] Denominational membership does not fully distinguish between the communal-involvement and religious-belief theories, for denominations may be communities of belief as well as social communities, so behavioral differences between denominations might be due to either of these differences. If it is not denominational composition but the revivals themselves that account for differences in county voting behavior, however, there are strong grounds for concluding that it was belief that made the difference, for the incidence of revivals is evidence of a heightened degree of religious involvement, and the doctrine preached by the revivals was particularly hostile to slavery.

The political tradition argument implies that abolitionism (at least, abolitionist voting) should be concentrated among voters who shared a party tradition before antislavery parties arose; the status revolution theory implies that abolitionism should have been greatest in economically declining areas; and the communal-involvement theory implies that denominational membership should explain the effect of revivalism. These theories can be tested, then, by analyzing the effect of the Whig presidential vote in 1840, the proportion of the population belonging to the Methodist and Presbyterian Churches,[14] and popula-

[13]Cultural origin variables are already included in the model because they are also regarded as causes of revivalism itself. The fact that tests of these relations (like the relations between antislavery and rurality) are required by more than one alternative theory does not create redundancy, since my interest is not in choosing between these theories but determining whether hypotheses derived from any of them disconfirm the religious-belief theory.

[14]Data on denominational membership, however, are from 1850, and are based not on a census of religious membership but on the seating capacities of churches of each denomination. Presbyterian Church membership is estimated by the combined seating capacities of Presbyterian and Congregational Churches because these two together represent the strength of the Presbyterian Church before the abrogation of the Plan of Union in 1837.

As noted below, the fact that the earliest available church membership data are from 1850 means that they may reflect increases due to the revivals. If controlling for membership reduces the effect of revivalism, therefore, the effect of revivalism may not be spurious but indirect.

tion growth (as an indicator of economic growth). If the relationship between revivalism and abolitionism is explained by any of these theories, it should vanish when these variables are controlled.

But one cannot simply examine the joint effect of revivalism and any one of those variables; the test must also examine the effects of the variables previously analyzed. The relationship might be spurious because part of it is explained by the variables already examined and another part by the variables now to be incorporated into the analysis. The straightforward test would be to include all the hypothesized independent variables in a single multiple-regression equation. This test would be indecisive, however, because the large number and intercorrelations of independent variables and the small number of cases would subject all the derived estimates to considerable random error.

Instead, I have tested the effects of the variables included in the previous analyses together with each of the variables suggested by the political-tradition, status-revolution, and denominational-affiliation theories, adding only one of these latter variables at a time. There are thus four additional tests: one for prior voting tradition, one for population decline, and one for each of the two denominations. Tables 4.4 (for Ohio) and 4.5 (for New York) summarize the results of each of these four tests.

These tables[15] summarize five distinct regression analyses for each abolition variable: the one already presented and four extensions, each of which adds only one variable to the first. For each of these regressions, the coefficient of the added variable, the coefficient of revivalism, and the multiple correlation coefficient are shown. The procedure is not a conventional stepwise regression, but differs from it in two respects: first, at no point are all independent variables included in the same regression. Second, the order of entry of variables is determined not by a criterion of additional explained variance, but rather by the theoretical relevance of an additional variable, so that the initial model and the model with an additional variable can be compared to test a theory.[16]

[15] Because revivalism had a relatively small effect on the 1840 vote in Ohio, it has been omitted from Table 4.4. The 1840 vote in New York is omitted from Table 4.5 simply for want of space, but the effect of revivalism on it is not explained by any of the additional variables.

[16] For want of space, I have not presented the full set of coefficients for each variation of the basic model. The coefficients of the other independent variables differ only slightly from their coefficients in Tables 4.1 through 4.3.

TABLE 4.4
Determinants of Abolitionism, Ohio
(Extended Multiple Regression)

Added variable	Anti-Slavery Societies			Liberty, 1844			Liberty, 1846		
	Beta weight added variable	Beta weight revivalism	Multiple R	Beta weight added variable	Beta weight revivalism	Multiple R	Beta weight added variable	Beta weight revivalism	Multiple R
Original model (no added variable)	—	.371	.470	—	.321	.679	—	.331	.599
Population increase, 1830–1840	-.101	.348	.478	-.270	.261	.716	-.206	.285	.623
% Congregational and Presbyterian, 1850	.188	.302	.500	.279	.219	.725	.131	.283	.611
% Methodist, 1850	.212	.337	.509	.161	.295	.695	.067	.320	.602
% Whig, 1840	.147	.373	.480	.186	.324	.691	.294	.335	.631

The tables show that by these tests the religious belief explanation is strongly supported. In every case the coefficient of revivalism is large and stable (it actually increases in some cases when the additional control variable is added) and the increment in explained variance due to the added variable is minimal. Neither prior party tradition, denomination, nor population change can explain the relationship between revivalism and abolitionist politics.

So none of the competing theories discussed above explains away the effect of revivalism. That the coefficients of some of the control variables are large is immaterial. The religious-belief theory does not necessarily imply that any relation between them and political behavior will vanish; they may themselves exert an independent influence. The sizes of their coefficients, moreover, provide tests of their own adequacy as contributors to the explanation of abolitionism.

The vote for the Whig party had some effect on abolitionism. In New York, in fact, when the effect of Whig voting is tested, the coefficient of revivalism generally declines more than it does with other control variables. But it is larger than the coefficient of the Whig vote. Abolitionism was evidently more prevalent among Whigs than among Democrats, but it still required the impetus of the revivals to emerge.

To the extent that economic growth is measured by population increase, it had relatively little effect on abolitionism. In New York, contrary to the prediction implied by Donald, it was the most rapidly growing counties that were most abolitionist. In Ohio, the opposite is true, as the status-revolution theory would predict. But the greatest population growth between 1830 and 1840 occurred in areas that were almost empty in 1830; it did not represent urbanization, as is shown by the negative correlation ($r = -.37$) between population growth and population density in 1840. The entire northwestern part of the state was newly-opened frontier; it was not an area of abolitionism, but neither was it an area of urban growth or increasing industrial and mercantile activity.

The effect of Methodist Church membership is generally quite small and in some cases negative. So is the effect of Presbyterian Church membership in New York. In Ohio, its effect is larger; in one case (the 1844 vote) it is larger than the effect of revivalism. This no doubt reflects multicollinearity due to the Presbyterian Church's position as the major representative of the Calvinist tradition and the main locus of the revivals. However, denomination comes nowhere near explaining the effect of revivalism. Moreover, since the revivals contributed to church membership (the statistics are for 1850), the relatively large size of the coefficient of Presbyterianism may in part re-

TABLE 4.5
Determinants of Abolitionism, New York
(Extended Multiple Regression)

Added variable	Anti-Slavery Societies			Liberty, 1842			Liberty, 1844			Suffrage, 1846		
	Beta weight added variable	Beta weight revivalism	Multiple R	Beta weight added variable	Beta weight revivalism	Multiple R	Beta weight added variable	Beta weight revivalism	Multiple R	Beta weight added variable	Beta weight revivalism	Multiple R
Original model (no added variable)	—	.264	.564	—	.414	.617	—	.261	.618	—	.298	.697
Population increase, 1830–1840	.138	.290	.575	.112	.435	.623	.133	.286	.627	.040	.305	.697
% Congregational and Presbyterian, 1850	−.071	.284	.568	.105	.383	.624	−.149	.304	.633	−.085	.322	.701
% Methodist, 1850	−.151	.274	.581	.019	.412	.617	−.165	.272	.636	−.238	.314	.729
% Whig, 1840	.153	.237	.579	.136	.390	.627	.005	.260	.618	.216	.260	.720

flect the growth of these churches due to the revivals. In any case, these data do not provide much support for the theory of communal involvement. Only one of four possibilities (two denominations in two states) offers even limited support.

By each test, then, I have shown that the relationship between revivalism and political behavior cannot be explained by an alternative theory which declares it to be spurious or due to communal involvement in a religious group. No matter which controls are applied, the relationship remains strong. The inability to explain the relationship by other variables offers strong confirmation of the theory that it was the revivals themselves which created a political obligation fulfilled by support for abolition of slavery. The failure to confirm the theory of communal involvement is particularly important. Abolitionism is explained by a set of events—the revivals—rather than by more enduring characteristics such as denominational affiliation. This constitutes strong warrant for concluding that a consequence of those events was a changed consciousness, and that that changed consciousness was what changed political behavior.

The relationship between revivalism and support for black suffrage in New York is also important, both for assessing the revivalists' motives and for understanding the relationship of third-party politics to traditional-party politics. Abolitionists combined opposition to slavery with concern for the rights of free blacks within their own state. The outcome of the vote in the 1846 referendum was correlated not only with revivalism but also with membership in Anti-Slavery Societies and votes for Liberty candidates (the correlation of the referendum with society membership is .52; with the 1844 vote, .73). This consistency is important in regard to the status-revolution theory, for it contradicts the claim that abolitionists attacked slavery in the south as a means of striking out irrationally at a world they could not control. Whatever the motives for their sympathy with the deprivation of blacks, they were at least consistent in applying it to those in the north as well as in the south.

The suffrage vote was much higher (28% of the electorate favored it) than any previous vote for a Liberty candidate, and the vote by counties ranged from a low of 2% in New York County to a high of 73% in Clinton County. In several counties the overwhelming majority voted in favor. This, together with its high correlations with Liberty votes and its relationship with revivalism, is important in demonstrating that there was a pervasive political ethos in revival areas. Although party loyalties were quite strong and most voters never voted for the Liberty party, they nevertheless endorsed abolitionist principles when they could do so without changing party.[17]

Why should there have been such a direct connection between revivalism and abolitionism? Throughout history many forms of behavior have been defined as sinful or otherwise immoral, and the holding of other human beings in bondage has only in recent centuries borne that stigma. Why, at this particular time and in response to these events, did its definition as sin come to be so compelling? And why did opposition to it take the forms that it did?

One reason for the revivalists' insistent attention to slavery had little to do with revivalism itself. The importance of slavery in the nation's economy and politics was increasingly evident. It had expanded into the states of the New South, and was the basis of the region's economy. If in the eighteenth century it had been possible to assume that the institution would die a natural death, it was no longer possible in the nineteenth century.

But slavery was particularly a sin to the revival convert because of his new understanding of the nature of man. If man was inherently depraved, totally dependent on God for justification, he could not complain about the station in life to which he was assigned. But God had given man free will, through which he might win his own salvation, and to enslave him deprived him of the possibility of exercising that free will.

There is no direct evidence of the connection between religious beliefs and abolitionism for the average voter, for it is only the leaders whose writings have been preserved. But abolitionist leaders attested that they derived their opposition to slavery from religious conviction. "All a man's powers are God's gift to HIM. All else that belongs to

---

[17]No analogous evidence is available for Ohio. A referendum on the same issue was held in 1867, and the result shows some correlation with revivalism. But it correlates so closely with the Republican vote in the same year ($r = .97$) that one must interpret the referendum as a party vote which was not necessarily a valid measure of opposition to discrimination.

Fox (1917) claims that the New York referendum itself was "as straight a party question as one finds" (p. 272) with Whigs supporting it and Democrats opposed. It is true, as Table 4.3 shows, that a Whig voting tradition had a greater effect on the referendum vote than on the vote for Liberty candidates, but the correlation of the referendum with the 1846 Whig gubernatorial vote is not high ($r = .31$), and while the Whigs received 51% of the vote in 1846, suffrage was opposed by 72% of the voters. Stanley (1969) shows that while the Democrats were close to unanimous against it, and Whig leaders endorsed it, many Whigs voted against it. Support was correlated with support for earlier abolitionist candidates. Two later referenda on the same question (1860 and 1869) were quite closely correlated with Republican votes in those years, and less closely correlated with earlier indicators of abolitionism. These two referenda, like the one in Ohio, probably did represent the partisan identification of the issue more than opposition to discrimination.

man is acquired by the *use* of these powers. . . . Slavery robs of both" (Weld, 1864, p. 20). Because God had made every man *"a free moral agent,"* the slaveowner "tramples upon rights, subverts justice, outrages humanity, unsettles the foundations of human safety, and sacrilegiously assumes the prerogative of God" (Barnes & Dumond, 1970, vol. 1, p. 98).[18] To the revival convert, no one could validly claim that God sanctioned the total dependence of one man on another. "It was not," says Staiger (1949), "that dependence upon God was 'inconsistent with human liberty,' . . . but rather that lack of liberty was inconsistent with [belief in free will and other] tenets of New School theology" (p. 393).

The belief that slavery was wrong did not originate with the revivals. It had been condemned officially, if mildly, by the Methodist Church as early as 1780 and by the Presbyterian Church in 1818. Even the particular cast revival doctrine gave to abolitionism was not new. Arminianism, which rejected the belief that man was totally corrupt, had been gaining strength among Christian evangelicals throughout the eighteenth century, particularly in England. On that basis they increasingly claimed that slavery meant dehumanization (Davis, 1966, pp. 291–390; Mathews, 1965, p. 8; Murray, 1966, p. 26). But that recognition had not taken hold on the American continent. Despite lukewarm condemnations of slavery by some churches, only a few small religious groups like the Quakers actively espoused its abolition, and they had not been inspired to start a movement which attempted to affect national life.

Revivalism did inspire a movement. The belief that slavery was a sin, spread by the faith which revivalism made popular, had a compelling urgency which earlier denunciations of slavery did not have. The urgency was heightened by revivalism's claim that wherever sin existed in the world, the saved must act immediately to exterminate it.

Not all revivalists acted on revivalism's abolitionist implications with equal steadfastness. Finney himself was never more than a reluctant abolitionist. Though he had condemned slavery in the *Lectures on Revivals* (Finney, 1960, pp. 288, 298), and though he was active in the New York and Ohio Anti-Slavery Societies,[19] he expressed a some-

---

[18]The same argument was used by feminist abolitionists to oppose the servitude of wives to their husbands. It was couched in nearly identical language, undoubtedly to embarrass men into treating blacks and women consistently (see the letter of Angelina Grimké in Barnes & Dumond, 1970, vol. 1, p. 416).

[19]The New York Society was founded at his Chatham Street Chapel, and the Ohio Society elected him vice president at its founding convention and, later, chairman of its fourth anniversary meeting (see Cole, 1954, pp. 205, 209; Fletcher, 1943, vol. 1, p. 238; McLoughlin, 1960, p. liv).

what condescending attitude to abolitionism in his *Memoirs* (1876):

> When I first went to New York, I had made up my mind on the question of slavery, and was exceedingly anxious to arouse public attention to the subject. I did not, however, turn aside to make it a hobby, or divert the attention of the people from the work of converting souls. (p. 324)

Not only did he not divert the attention of people from the revival, he attempted to divert many in the opposite direction. He discouraged Oberlin students, including some of the former Lane rebels, from leaving the school to take antislavery agencies (Barnes & Dumond, 1970, vol. 1, pp. 323–29). He even discouraged Weld from devoting all his attention to the campaign, arguing that the conversion of the nation was not only a necessary prerequisite to abolition, but that abolition would follow in its wake:

> Br[other] Weld is it not true, at least do you not fear it is, that we are in our present course going fast into a civil war? Will not our present movements in abolition result in that? Shall we not ere long be obligated to take refuge in a military despotism? . . . The church and the world, ecclesiastical and state leaders, will become embroiled in one common infernal squabble that will roll a wave of blood over the land. The causes now operating are in my view as certain to lead to this result as cause is to produce its effect, unless the publick mind can be engrossed with the subject of salvation and make abolition an appendage, just as we made temperance an appendage of the revival in Rochester. . . . We can now, with you and my theological class, bring enough laborers into the field to, under God, move the whole land in 2 years. (Barnes & Dumond, 1970, vol. 1, pp. 318–319)

While condemning slavery in the *Lectures* (Finney, 1960), he urgently warned that "great care should be taken to avoid a censorious spirit on both sides. . . . A denunciatory spirit, impeaching each other's motives, is unchristian, calculated to grieve the Spirit of God, and to put down revivals, and is alike injurious to the church, and to the slaves themselves" (pp. 298–99). Moreover, he was unwilling to treat blacks equally in practice: he refused to abolish segregated seating in the Chatham Street Chapel and wanted to institute it at Oberlin (McLoughlin, 1959, p. 110).

Finney's own ambivalence, however, does not invalidate the thesis that the revivalist ethos influenced abolitionism. Not all the content of the revivalist ethos was contained in revival doctrines; its political consequences were due to their implications as much as to their overt content.

By the accounts of many abolitionists, moreover, revivalism was an important motivating force for them, especially for those who were in the anti-Garrison wing of the movement and led in the founding of the Liberty party. The most striking fact that Sorin discovers about the hundred leading abolitionists of New York is that a high proportion were actively religious: at least 68% were ministers, deacons, elders, or otherwise involved in evangelical activity, and 89% lived in the revival district between 1826 and 1833. Of the men Sorin identifies as the ten leading white abolitionists of New York, only one is known to have been converted by a revival (Henry B. Stanton was converted during Finney's Rochester revival of 1830–1831). Of the other nine, three for whom full-length biographies are available (Birney, Lewis Tappan, and Gerrit Smith) experienced conversion outside of the revivals (Fladeland, 1955, pp. 30–32; Harlow, 1939, pp. 51–52; Sorin, 1971, pp. 64, 112–13; Wyatt-Brown, 1969, pp. 28–30, 33–34). But all three fell into the orbit of Finney or of his disciples, and all supported the revivals or took part in the benevolent movement that grew out of them.

For the leaders, then, there is clear evidence that their abolitionism was due in some measure to revivalism. They experienced the revivals, and their own testimony demonstrates that they perceived a connection between the religious beliefs they held and the obligation to free the slaves.

There is no direct evidence that the revivalist ethos was part of the belief system of abolitionists in the electorate as a whole. But the way they voted is consistent with the hypothesis that their politics was influenced by new religious beliefs, for there was a direct connection between the revivals and their voting. Other explanations for their abolitionism, moreover, do not empirically explain its relation to revivalism. Since that connection is not empirically explained by other factors, it is likely that they, too, were influenced by the revivalist ethos.

It was the crusade against slavery which made the revivalist ethos a *political* ethos. Opposition to slavery grew out of revivalists' religious beliefs, but it became the most important of their many concerns because its importance and its extent made it appear to them to be the most abominable manifestation of sin in the land. The importance of slavery in the life of the nation, moreover, was what made their struggle so difficult, because the possibility of abolition directly threatened many Americans. The opposition revivalists encountered when they brought the conflict into the political arena reinforced their beliefs and made them embrace the ethos even more strongly. Revivalism did not explicitly call for a political struggle against slavery, nor did the founders of abolitionism envision that the struggle would become a political one. But the revivalist ethos made the entry into politics likely because its attitude toward measures to eliminate sin was pragmatic: if the (ready-made) measures of revivalism did not work, others which appeared practicable should be tried.

There are several reasons why politics was more possible for the adherents of revivalism in the nineteenth century than it had been in the past. When the church had been established in New England, efforts to reform it had often implied opposition to public authority. With disestablishment, however, the state was at worst a neutral force in revivalism's primary concern, which was to reform church life. So revivalists did not have the initial hostility to state-enforced measures that their predecessors might have had.

Because the nineteenth-century revivalists were optimistic about man's abilities, they did not depend on the state to maintain order through repression. Earlier Calvinists had believed that men needed the state to protect themselves from the consequences of their own sinfulness (Walzer, 1969, pp. 31–45). The later revivalists thought that they could use political power to save men not from the consequences of sin but from sin itself. In their view the state could become another mechanism of persuasion.

The benevolent impulse led to concrete reform programs outside of religious institutions. The adoption of goals like Sabbath observance, temperance, and abolition of slavery necessarily brought their campaigns into public life. If secular behavior was sinful, the state was complicitous in sin and would have to be fought on its own grounds.

But it was the revivalists' pragmatic view of measures which enabled them to overcome their considerable reluctance to use political means to exterminate sin. Initially the newly converted abolitionists followed the pattern set by the benevolent societies. Spread the faith and spread information, and the country could not help but recognize its sin and renounce it. When this did not provide the immediate results hoped for, revivalism implicitly provided a further guideline: use whatever means will contribute to the result. In a universe governed by discoverable laws, in which effective means are correct means, one must naturally continue the search for effective means when those previously tried have failed.

This attention to means, which had been characteristic of the revival movement, led the abolitionists gropingly into politics. They were not sure of the appropriate scope or form of political activity, but they were sure of their goal, and sure that when one set of means failed another must be tried. The volatile opinions of men such as Birney and Goodell on the policy decisions that confronted the Liberty party—whether to create a party at all, whether to limit the platform to "one idea" or expand it to encompass the general reform of society—indicate that they were uncertain of how they ought to engage in politics. In stark contrast, Garrison was certain that government and political parties were coercive and therefore evil, and he consistently governed his behavior accordingly. The Liberty men, though at odds each internally and among themselves, only agreed that they could disagree with Garrison and take advantage of the government as they found it. As a revival preacher had said without a trace of irony, "why should a good man stop, who knows certainly that he is right exactly, and that all men are wrong in proportion as they differ from him?" (Cross, 1955, p. 205). Finney's reasonable God would not have created a world in which, as Weber (1958a, p. 120) concluded, political activity was incompatible with an ethic of ultimate ends.

5
The Antislavery Realignment

A complete partisan realignment and political reorientation occurred in New York and Ohio, and in most of the north, between 1848 and 1860. The slavery controversy was taken out of the hands of the small band of religiously inspired abolitionists and fought between members and factions of the major parties. With the death of the Whig party, the brief success of the Know-Nothings, and the rise of the Republicans, party organization and voter loyalties changed dramatically. The revivalist ethos played a major role in stimulating that realignment by making slavery a critical political issue, but revivalists did not achieve their goals. Political debate was not over the abolition of slavery: opposition to slavery came to encompass a much larger segment of the northern electorate, and was represented by the demand for containment rather than abolition. The protection of the interests of white northerners came to be the principal motive of antislavery, and benevolence toward blacks became distinctly secondary.

So on its own terms the political ethos of revivalism failed. It did not achieve the reform of society it envisioned. The revivals had not only preached the belief that slavery must be abolished because it was a sin; they had also taught that blacks were equal to whites in the sight of God and equally capable of salvation, and that in recognition of that status all forms of discrimination against them should be done away with. But while opposition to slavery spread, its corollaries were not adopted.

The spread of antislavery and its place in the politics of the 1850s involved a complicated interplay of competing political factions. Each of those factions was forced to define its relation to slavery, and its political fortunes largely depended on the stand it adopted. The available positions were not simply support or opposition. The degree of support or opposition and the protections or limitations to slavery which any given faction advocated had to be carefully defined to make clear to constituents the interests it intended to serve.

Once slavery had become a major issue, politicians could adopt antislavery stands while expressly refusing to call for outright abolition. Some opponents of slavery presented the moral grounds for their case, but the concrete measures they supported were attempts to contain slavery, not to end it. They were working for the interests of the nonslavery northern economy even if they adopted some abolitionist rhetoric. The support of abolitionists was no longer crucial to any important major-party faction, because abolitionists represented the extreme wing of the antislavery bloc. Abolitionists, therefore, played a relatively unimportant part in the debates of the 1850s. Independent abolitionist politics was superseded by antislavery politics, and there was no room in the party system for an effective independent abolitionist force.

The story of the antislavery realignment is therefore not centrally related to the history of the revivalist ethos. It must nevertheless be told in some detail, because it illustrates several important points about the nature and limits of the effect of the revivalist ethos on politics.

First, political debate in the 1850s was, more and more exclusively, about slavery, and slavery was the issue which determined the realignment. Even though the terms of the ensuing debate became unacceptable to revivalists, it was they who largely inspired it in the first place.

Second, one of the competing factions of considerable importance was the Know-Nothing party. The Know-Nothing party was the most important political manifestation of nativism that the United States had seen until that time, and many historians have asserted that nativism grew out of revivalism in the same way and for the same reasons about abolitionism did. I will show, however, that despite its platform the Know-Nothing party represented opposition to antislavery more than it represented nativism. Moreover, it was not supported by voters in revivalist areas. The argument that nativism and abolitionism had the same religious roots is not borne out by the analysis of the Know-Nothing vote.

Third, the account demonstrates that the effect of revivalism on politics was in fact very limited after 1848. Not only were the issues defined differently, but revivalism was not a major influence on voting behavior in the 1850s, particularly after the Republican party superseded the explicitly antislavery (though even then not abolitionist) Free Soil party.

Finally, the political successes and failures of other political factions illuminate the failure of abolitionists. Social structure and political constitution dictate that the American political system is a system of two dominant parties; third parties have been important in times of uncertainty and rapid political change. Abolitionism could not succeed politically unless its demands were incorporated into a major-party coalition. To some extent its leaders and issues became part of the Republican Party, but the original goals of abolitionism were abandoned. The Know-Nothing party died; its nativism was not sufficiently important and its opposition to antislavery ran contrary to the preferences and interests of too many northerners for it to succeed. The Free Soil party also died, but its leaders, far more than the abolitionists, joined the Republican party, together with many Whigs and some Democrats who were willing to take public stands against the extension of slavery. The story of factional competition in the 1850s is important even though revivalism played a minor part, because it illustrates the fate of political minorities in the American system and thus helps to explain the fate of revivalism.

The struggle over slavery became a struggle between competing economic interests. Slavery became a major issue not because revivalists urged that the divinely ordained freedom of blacks must be recognized, but rather because of the struggle between the slave labor system and the capitalist free labor system for control of western expansion and national politics. Abolitionism was sufficiently congruent with the interests of the capitalists for them to adopt some of its rhetoric and some of its demands; but they subverted the premises out of which it grew. The relation of revivalism to national politics in the 1850s thus illustrates that the political system incorporates a moral demand only when it corresponds to the interests of some economic group, and that in such cases (as was the case with the abolitionists) the needs of economic groups will very likely require that the moral basis of the demand be relegated to a secondary position. Revivalism brought a major issue into politics, but when that issue was coopted, the debate did not confront the immorality of the denial of freedom which made revivalists oppose slavery.

Slavery and the growth of parties which in some sense opposed it were nevertheless central to the realignment. An electoral realignment is a "change in the effective constituencies of competing political parties brought about by a lasting alteration in the distribution of party loyalties in an electorate" (Hammond, 1976, p. 65). Such a change often appears in what Key (1955) identifies as a "critical election," which he defines as an election in which

> voters are . . . unusually deeply concerned, in which the extent of electoral involvement is relatively quite high, and in which the decisive results of voting reveal a sharp alteration of the pre-existing cleavage within the electorate. . . . The realignment made manifest in the voting in such elections seems to persist for several succeeding elections. (p. 4)

The emergence of new issues important to a large segment of the population, which crosscut traditional party loyalties, or the occurrence of a major crisis with which the existing parties and their policies seem incompetent to deal, are the typical occasions for a critical realignment. Third-party activity often foreshadows realignments, and third parties act as "halfway houses"[1] for those who ultimately change political allegiance. A realignment usually both transforms and benefits the party that happens to be out of power. But it can lead to a reorientation of the party system generally, effecting a vast change in the agenda of politics (Burnham, 1970b, p. 9; Pomper, 1970, pp. 180–82; Schattschneider, 1960, p. 88).[2]

Even when large numbers of voters change party at the same time, the causes of their change are not self-evident. Although political leaders often pay a great deal of attention to new political issues at the same time as realignments occur, it cannot be assumed that voters attribute the same importance to those issues. Electoral realignments must therefore be studied in a way which leaves open, but permits one to address, the question of their causes. The method must allow one to examine, for example, whether and how the slavery issue (and other issues) affected the change in voter loyalties which occurred in the 1850s. The method used here to study electoral realignments is direct factor analysis. While its statistical properties are described elsewhere,[3] I will briefly review its interpretation.

---

[1]The phrase is used by MacRae and Meldrum (1960, p. 669), Pomper (1971, p. 196), and Sellers (1971, p. 161). See also Burnham (1970b, pp. 27–28), Hammond (1976, pp. 63–64), and Mazmanian (1974).

[2]The words "realignment" and "reorientation" are often used interchangeably. As used here, however, a "realignment" is a change in the party loyalties of the electorate, while a "reorientation" is a change in the organized parties' policy orientations and orientations to particular groups in the electorate, as demonstrated by legislation proposed and supported, platform positions, groups appealed to by particularistic characteristics of candidates nominated, etc. The relation between realignment and reorientation must be established empirically.

[3]Direct factor analysis was first applied to electoral realignments by MacRae and Meldrum (1960, 1969). I have used an extension of their method which permits the analysis of more than one party at a time; it is presented in Hammond (1976). The mathematics of factor extraction is described in MacRae (1970, pp. 91–171).

In any year the percentage supporting a given party may rise or fall, but if the relative degrees of support in each county remain similar to previous years, the change does not represent a realignment. Controlling for such year-to-year fluctuations, factor analysis as used here defines a hypothetical measure of the quality which best explains long-term changes in stable patterns of party support. Each county and the vote for each party in each election is assigned a value measuring the extent to which the county, or the party vote, possesses that quality (the county values are referred to as factor scores, and the party values are referred to as factor loadings).

The temporal sequence of factor loadings can conveniently be presented in a time-series graph. If a realignment occurred, the loadings will exhibit the following pattern: a period during which the loadings for one of the major parties are approximately equal will be followed by a transition period (which may be abrupt or gradual) and then by a period in which the loadings are again approximately equal, but opposite in sign to the loadings of the earlier period. If the sequence demonstrates the occurrence of a realignment, the county factor scores can then be examined to determine its causes. The counties where most voters changed in one direction will have high positive scores; the counties where most voters changed in the opposite direction will have high negative scores. These scores can be correlated with presumed determinants of the realignment, such as demographic characteristics and measures of sentiment on important issues. If they were in fact the determinants, they will have high correlations with the factor scores, and their correlations will not vanish when other variables are controlled.

Figures 5.1 and 5.2 show the time series of factor loadings from an analysis of the elections spanning the mid-nineteenth century in New York and Ohio. They show that a realignment occurred in both states, and that in both the transition period lasted approximately from 1848 to 1860. The two figures are similar, because national influences were most important in effecting party realignment. In both states, the most important year was 1856, in which patterns of party support reversed. In both states, the realignment was presaged by the antislavery Liberty and Free Soil parties; the figures show graphically "a cloud no bigger than a man's hand" appearing in 1840 in the form of the first Liberty candidates, growing bigger through the 1840s, subsiding slightly during the compromise years of the early 1850s, and reappearing with the Republican party. In both states, the Whigs considerably more than the Democrats were pulled in opposite directions by the antislavery parties and the nativist Know-Nothing party.

The two figures show that the dissolution of the second party system was forecast as early as 1848, when the presidential election revealed a shift in voting toward the pattern that was to prevail for several decades after 1856. The second party system was still governing the country, for the antislavery parties were never large enough to achieve effective representation (although for a time the Free Soil party held a decisive balance of power in the Ohio state legislature). But slavery was of increasing importance to voters, and the Whig and Democratic parties continued to take ambiguous positions on slavery-related issues. So the second party system was dissolving gradually, and the electorate was responding to a fluid, multiparty system. The erratic fluctuations of party loyalties during the long transition period suggest that the idea of a party system is a construct that has more reality for its most active members, officeholders and party officials, than for the populace at large. Voters' loyalties appear more changeable, affected from year to year by current issues.[4]

Because of the overriding importance of national politics to the realignment, similarities between the two figures are more important than their differences. But there are important differences, due to the simultaneous effects of the prior political geography of the two states and their differing reactions to events during the period. Some of these differences are evident immediately from the time series graphs, while others are shown by the relations of voting patterns with other variables. In general, the time series is smoother in Ohio; the fluctuations in the loadings of the two major parties and of the Free Soil party in New York between 1848 and 1854 are not matched in Ohio. Furthermore, the realignment affected the Democratic party very little in Ohio, and the factor has a correspondingly smaller magnitude than in New York. The greater stability in Ohio reflects a more stable pattern of support for antislavery politics.

One might assume from the time series in the figures that the realignment was due to opposition to slavery. Taking Figure 5.1 for New York as an example, the Free Soil vote of 1848 and the Republican vote of 1856 have the greatest positive loadings. At the opposite extreme (leaving the Know-Nothing vote aside for the moment) the Whig vote of 1848 and the Democratic votes of 1856–1868 have the greatest negative loadings.

In most of these cases, slavery appears to have been a defining

---

[4]Sorauf (1967, pp. 37–38) reaches a similar conclusion. MacRae and Meldrum (1960, pp. 673–78) show that a long transition period preceded the New Deal realignment in Illinois; in the next chapter I present a similar finding for the New Deal in New York.

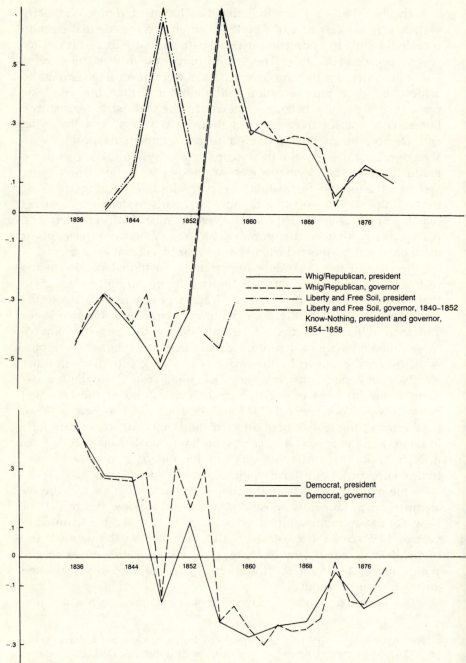

Figure 5.1 The pre-Civil War political realignment in New York (factor loadings from the first principal component of election returns, 1836–1880).

issue (and even Grant's candidacy in 1868 may have aroused the same response). The positive loadings would represent opposition to slavery, and the negative loadings support (or at least neutrality). One might then infer that the realignment came about because slavery became increasingly salient both to parties and to voters, and that voters changed loyalties because the opposing party's attitude to slavery was more congenial to them.

But that conclusion requires the assumption that voters changed their party loyalties because they were influenced by the parties' positions on slavery. That assumption can be tested directly by analyzing the correlations of the factor scores with demographic and political characteristics of their counties. To explain the pre-Civil War realignment, one must examine not only events during the critical period but also the composition of the counties that shifted in each direction.

In relating the events of the period to the time series shown in the figures, I will call the factor for each state (somewhat loosely) an "antislavery" factor, and suggest that the size of the loading for any given party and year reflects the salience of antislavery to those who voted for it. However, I will also show that the relationship between antislavery and the vote is a complex one, and the sense in which these factors can be called antislavery factors will be clarified after I have traced the course of political events to 1860.[5]

Slavery, while not the dominant issue during the entire period,[6] had a more or less continuous place in national politics from the time of the petition campaign onward. The annexation of Texas was a national issue in the 1844 election, and differences over slavery became identified with two factions of the Democratic party in New York in a split which was to have important consequences for antislavery politics.

The "Hunker" and "Barnburner" factions of the New York Democrats, originally divided over the question of canal construction in the late 1830s (although the names were not generally applied until the next decade). The Hunkers, or Conservatives, agreed with the Whigs that the state's canal system should be expanded, even at the expense of depleting the state's general fund. The Barnburners, or Radicals, advocated the end of canal construction and the elimination

[5]This book does not attempt to analyze the causes of the Civil War, but any discussion of the northern electoral realignment has implications for that topic. Recent treatments of Civil War historiography which focus on partisan politics include Fehrenbacher (1962), Foner (1974), and Silbey (1964).
[6]Silbey (1967a) argues that party loyalty rather than intersectional conflict governed the behavior of most members of Congress during the 1840s. But, as mentioned above, this may have been more true for Congressmen than for voters.

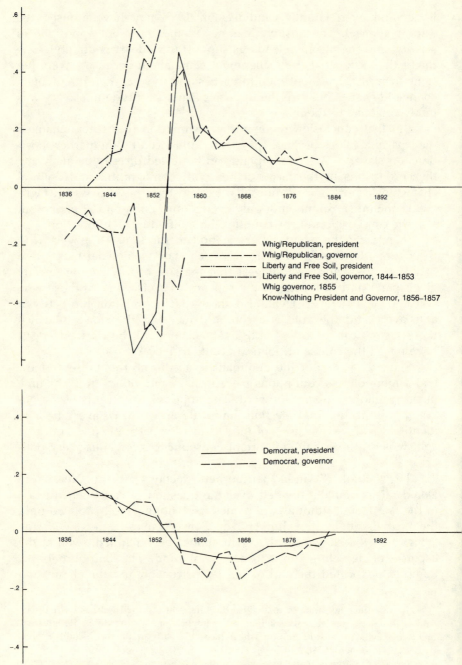

Figure 5.2 The pre-Civil War political realignment in Ohio (factor loadings from the first principal component of election returns, 1836–1884).

of the state debt (Donovan, 1925, pp. 14–24). The breach was broadened with the nomination and election of Polk in 1844. Martin Van Buren, leader of the Barnburners, hoped to be nominated for president. But his opposition to the annexation of Texas made him unacceptable to the southern Democrats. A majority of the delegates to the Democratic national convention had been pledged to Van Buren by the conventions appointing them, but his opponents forced the readoption of a two-thirds rule. After several indecisive ballots Van Buren's supporters threw their votes to James K. Polk, who thereby became the nation's first dark-horse candidate for the presidency (Donovan, 1925, pp. 54–56; Hammond, 1848, vol. 3, pp. 449–65; Holt, 1969, pp. 195–96).

Van Buren's defeat at the 1844 convention signaled the widening rift between the northern and southern wings of the party. The Barnburners' disgruntlement was more than "merely the normal complaints of political losers," for they were convinced that intrigue had sacrificed Van Buren to the interests of slavery (Foner, 1970, p. 151). The Barnburners were further offended after the election when Polk appointed some Hunkers but no Barnburners to cabinet and administrative posts (Donovan, 1925, pp. 63–64).

After the election the issue of Texas had become thoroughly identified with slavery; what may have arisen as a dispute merely over local issues and federal patronage came to be identified by the partisans with the struggle between north and south to control the Democratic party, and the intraparty struggle in turn was identified with the two sections' socioeconomic systems. Thus, though Barnburners were not abolitionists, they frequently opposed slavery or its extension as a means of opposing the southern Democrats' hegemony in their party.

Polk's presidency brought the Mexican War, and with it the Wilmot proviso. The proviso decreed that any newly annexed land would be closed to slavery. On the whole, the Barnburners and other northern radical Democrats supported the Mexican War, but opposed the introduction of slavery into newly acquired territories. Whigs, on the other hand, took advantage of the war to stir partisan hostility after they won control of the Congress in the 1846 election (Van Deusen, 1959, pp. 240–41). Northern expansionist Whigs contrasted Polk's willingness to compromise on Oregon with his going to war over Texas as clear evidence of his subservience to the slave power. Northern Whigs and radical Democrats united with antislavery Congressmen to pass the proviso in the House, but it was defeated in the Senate. All but one of New York's Democratic Congressmen supported it (Donovan, 1925, pp. 84–85; Van Deusen, 1959, pp. 242–43).

The New York State Democratic convention of 1847 completed the split between the Hunkers and Barnburners when the convention refused to consider a resolution endorsing the Wilmot proviso. The factions held separate conventions in 1848 and nominated competing delegations to the national convention. When the Barnburner delegation refused to pledge itself in advance to the convention's nominee, the Hunker delegation was admitted. The convention nominated Lewis Cass, a "northern man with southern principles," and the Barnburners seceded to form their own party. Their convention, held in Utica in June, adopted a platform supporting the Wilmot proviso and calling for the limitation of slave territory (Donovan, 1925, pp. 93–94, 99–104).

The Whig national convention also rejected the appeals of its antislavery advocates. To oppose Cass, the Whigs nominated the slaveholding Mexican war hero, Zachary Taylor. The Barnburners and other antislavery Democrats and Whigs were now ready to bolt. They and the Liberty party united at the Buffalo Free Soil convention (Bradford, 1947, p. 74; Holt, 1931, pp. 306–07, 331).

The outcome of the Buffalo convention and its significance for abolitionist politics have already been discussed. The 1848 election, however, was of wider significance for what now became antislavery politics. In Ohio, Van Buren won 11% of the vote, more than doubling the best previous poll of the Liberty party. He did best in the Western Reserve and, to a lesser extent, the newly settled northwestern section, the Ohio Company's Purchase, and Clinton County in the southwestern part of the state. This was Whig country, and Van Buren won most of his votes from Taylor. The Free Soil party did not nominate a candidate for governor, and Ford, the Whig, maintained the support of the Free Soilers by refusing to endorse Taylor and by advocating repeal of the Black Code (Holt, 1931, pp. 337, 343). From the almost perfect correlation between the votes for Cass and the Democratic gubernatorial candidate ($r = .99$), it can be assumed that most of Van Buren's votes came from Whigs. The few prominent Democrats (such as Benjamin Tappan and Congressman Jacob Brinkerhoff) who supported Van Buren did not carry their party with them. Figure 5.2 shows that with respect to the eventual realignment, the 1848 Democratic vote did not differ particularly from previous elections. But the Whig presidential and gubernatorial votes diverged remarkably, the former reaching its lowest point with respect to the realignment, and the latter diverging slightly from previous years in a direction that foreshadowed the later rise of the Republican party.

Many Ohio Free Soilers had opposed the nomination of Van Buren, and were convinced that any other candidate would have done better (Bradford, 1947, pp. 74–76; Holt, 1931, pp. 315–17; Stewart, 1970, p. 156). Nevertheless, they determined the outcome of the election: Ford won the governorship, but Taylor lost to Cass.

The Free Soil vote, though twice as large as the 1844 Liberty vote, came from the same areas ($r = .88$). The Ohio party leaders were primarily Liberty men, and its supporters were largely abolitionists, or at least from areas where abolition sentiment was strong. The party in Ohio was firmly based on opposition to slavery, as it was not in New York. Its ideological unity enabled it to remain together and exert an important force in the state during the next several years.

The 1848 and 1850 elections gave Free Soilers the balance of power in the legislature; they cooperated with the Democrats in 1849 and with the Whigs in 1851 to send Chase and Benjamin Wade to the Senate, where they became two of that house's strongest opponents of slavery. Two Free Soilers also supported the Democrats in a complicated dispute over the contested election of delegates to the legislature in 1849, and in return the Democratic legislators accepted the repeal of the Black Code (Bradford, 1947, p. 109; Holt, 1931, pp. 393–94).

Despite the relative quiescence of the slavery issue after the 1848 defeat and the Compromise of 1850, the Free Soil party steadily improved its position in Ohio, winning 5% of the vote in the gubernatorial election of 1850, doing better in 1851 and 1852, and reaching a high of 18% of the gubernatorial vote in 1853. In these elections, the issues for which the Free Soil party stood evidently remained important to Ohio voters, and the party's strength continued to augur for the eventual realignment (Figure 5.2).

In New York the Free Soilers also determined the outcome of the 1848 election, but in the opposite direction. Either the native son or his platform was so popular with the New York Democrats that he won 26% of the vote to Cass's 25%. As had happened in 1844, the third-party vote determined the winner of New York's electoral votes, and those electoral votes gave Taylor the presidency.

Figure 5.1 shows that the previous electoral coalitions of both major parties were disrupted in the 1848 election. Because many Democrats and Whigs voted Free Soil, the distribution of both major parties' votes differed from the past. The election of 1848 was a clear harbinger of the realignment to come. The Democratic vote, considerably more affected than the Whig vote, was distributed much as it would be after the realignment when many antislavery Democrats would become Republicans; the Whig vote was as different from the subsequent Republican vote as it would ever be; and the Free Soil vote closely resembled the Republican vote in later years.

The distribution of the Free Soil vote was not as similar to previous Liberty votes as it was in Ohio (with 1844, $r = .60$), nor was it closely related to Anti-Slavery Society membership ($r = .29$). Of the counties with the largest Anti-Slavery Societies, only one (Herkimer) also had a particularly high Free Soil vote, and several counties that had no societies, or very small ones (St. Lawrence, Delaware, and the counties at the southeastern corner of Lake Ontario), gave 40% or more of their vote to Van Buren. Finally, the relationship of the 1846 suffrage referendum to the 1848 Free Soil vote was much lower ($r = .46$) than to the Liberty vote in previous years.

Clearly, the Free Soil vote did not depend in any strong degree on previously expressed abolitionism. None of the party's leaders from the Barnburner faction was an abolitionist. Thirteen men who later became Free Soil leaders had been delegates to the 1846 state constitutional convention, and none of them had supported Negro suffrage. Many of them loudly proclaimed that their support of the Wilmot proviso did not stem from love for blacks but from a desire to protect the free white laborer in the territories. Wilmot himself told his House colleagues, "I would preserve to free white labor a fair country, a rich inheritance, where the sons of toil, of my own race and own color, can live without the disgrace which association with negro slavery brings" (Berwanger, 1967, p. 125; Foner, 1965b, pp. 314–15).

So the style of the 1848 Free Soil campaign in New York, a forerunner of the realignment of the next decade, was set by the compromise of the Buffalo convention. Deemphasize the end of slavery, deemphasize rights for blacks, and the party could have a much wider appeal. Abolitionists were a minority of those who voted for Van Buren in 1848.

This heterogeneous Free Soil coalition did not remain united. The elections of 1850 and 1852 essentially represented a return to the status quo of before 1848; the party was not organized to contest the 1850 gubernatorial election, and its vote in 1852 fell to 5%, almost as low as the 1844 level. It lost the support of most of the Barnburners, who rejoined the Democratic party after a tortuous series of negotiations (Donovan, 1925, pp. 113–16). Many of them remained there even after 1856.

The leadership of antislavery politics in New York passed to Seward and his faction of the Whig party. Seward had remained with his party and supported Taylor in 1848, and in a northern campaign tour argued that the Whigs were the antislavery party. The 1848 Democratic split gave the Whigs an overwhelming state victory, and Seward's manager, Thurlow Weed, used it to elect Seward to the Senate. But the Whigs, like the Democrats, were seriously divided. Seward and Weed's radical antislavery faction, known as the "Wooly Heads," was opposed by the anti-antislavery "Silver-Grays," led by Millard Fillmore and Francis Granger. The radicals were not abolitionist, but wanted to prevent the further extension of slavery. Neither were the moderates proslavery, but they opposed any actions by the north that might lead the south to secede.

Fillmore was elected to the vice-presidency with Taylor and became president upon his death in 1850. His accession exacerbated the split between the radicals and the Silver-Grays: he used federal patronage to gain temporary advantage over the radicals, but they enjoyed the support of the majority of Whig voters and were able to recapture the party machinery (Alexander, 1969, vol. 2, pp. 142–43, 147; Curran, 1963, pp. 34–35). Opposition over slavery reinforced opposition over patronage. Fillmore gave his full support to the Compromise of 1850, while Seward opposed it strongly by invoking "a higher law than the Constitution." But the mood of the Congress favored national harmony, however bleak its prospects might be. The Compromise passed, organizing the Mexican cession as a territory with no stipulation as to slavery, and strengthening the fugitive slave law (Alexander, 1969, vol. 2, pp. 151–52; Smith, 1906, pp. 8–9, 17–18). It was touted as providing "finality" to the slavery question.

But the opposition between factions became more intense. At the 1850 state convention, Fillmore's allies, Daniel Ullman and Francis Granger, called for the endorsement of Fillmore and the Compromise. When, instead, the delegates endorsed the principles of the Wilmot proviso and commended Seward, Fillmore's supporters walked out. Victories by the antislavery factions in New York and other states enabled them to nominate their candidate, Winfield Scott, for president in 1852. But the divisions were tearing the Whigs apart. Scott carried only four states and lost the election to Franklin Pierce (Ellis, Frost, Syrett, & Carman, 1967, p. 229).[3]

Though the Compromise attempted to impose "finality" on discussion of the slavery issue, and the mood of the nation, expressed in the 1852 election, seemed to accept it, antislavery agitation was kept alive in the north by a series of cases growing out of the new fugitive slave law. The new law created special federal commissioners who had sole discretion to determine whether an alleged slave was a fugitive. The accused was denied the right to present testimony in his own defense, and penalties were prescribed for those aiding in the escape of a fugitive. The commissioner's fee was set at $10.00 for de-

[3]The last years of the Whig party, especially in New York, are discussed by Carman and Luthin (1943) and by Donald (1961).

claring the accused a fugitive and returning him, and $5.00 for releasing him (Smith, 1906, p. 15).

The fugitive slave law, rather than the possibility of slavery in New Mexico, was what most disturbed the north about the Compromise. The conditions of return of an accused fugitive clearly made it possible that free blacks might be consigned to slavery. Perhaps worse, the legislation allowed the federal government to intrude in the states, and many northerners were upset at the invasion of the north by slavehunters. Opposition to the law made it virtually unenforceable in antislavery areas. Several states passed personal liberty laws whose effect was to annul the fugitive slave law. Ohio's laws, enacted by the Republican legislature elected in 1855, prohibited the confinement of accused fugitives in state jails; protected blacks from being carried out of the state without being declared fugitives by federal officials; and established punishments for seizing or arresting persons on claims that they were fugitives (Litwack, 1961, pp. 249–50; Porter, 1906, pp. 20–21).

In a number of celebrated rescue cases, northerners banded together to free accused slaves who had been captured in their communities. In at least one instance, a slavehunter was killed. A white and a black man were sentenced in federal court for their part in the 1858 Oberlin-Wellington rescue, and when the State Supreme Court rejected an appeal which claimed that the fugitive slave law was unconstitutional, the case and opposition to the law contributed to the Republican victory in the 1859 election (Filler, 1960, pp. 202–03; Porter, 1906, pp. 23–26). In the later 1850s, political issues were increasingly defined by the slavery question.

But in the first years of the decade, the Compromise alleviated the conflict over slavery. A new issue, nativism, arose and for a time appeared predominant. Maine passed a prohibition law in 1851, and temperance advocates in other states began calling for Maine laws in their own states. Whig State Senator Myron Clark introduced a prohibition statute into the New York Legislature in 1853; it was passed, only to be vetoed by Democratic Governor Horatio Seymour. In the Ohio gubernatorial election of 1853, the Free Soil candidate endorsed the Maine law, while neither the Whigs nor the Democrats did. He received the largest vote cast in the state for a candidate of an antislavery party up to that time (Bradford, 1947, p. 115; Curran, 1963, p. 115; Ellis et al., 1967, p. 230).

Nativism and antinativism had been intermittently influential in the politics of the eastern states since the 1830s. More Whigs than Democrats sympathized with nativism, but not all Whigs approved of it. Seward, as governor of New York in 1840, had supported appropriations for parochial schools (Curran, 1963, pp. 49–63; Pratt, 1961, p. 354).

But in the early 1850s the nativists organized a distinct political force. A nativist secret society, the Order of the Star Spangled Banner, was founded in 1850 in New York City, and lodges sprang up rapidly in the rest of the state and elsewhere. In 1853 its offshoot, the Know-Nothing party, adopted a platform calling for restricted naturalization, a free nonsectarian school system, Bible reading in public schools, and nonclerical control of church property (Curran, 1963, pp. 86–88; Scisco, 1901, p. 85).

From the beginning, the party attracted supporters with a confused variety of political goals: in New York City it could be taken as a reform movement against the Democratic machine's corrupt exploitation of the immigrant vote. It was also supported by Maine law advocates, and by some antislavery men who thought the party's very newness would allow them to use it as an antislavery vehicle. In contrast, it also attracted many who had actively attempted to force the Whig Party to abandon antislavery because it threatened the preservation of the union, and who now saw in the Know-Nothing platform an agenda for politics that would distract the nation from the questions that threatened to divide north and south. In particular it attracted the New York Whig leaders allied with Fillmore and Granger. When Fillmore was denied renomination in 1852, Silver-Grays who recognized that they had lost control of the Whig Party left to join the Know-Nothings (Curran, 1963, pp. 101–03). They hoped to build up the new party to undercut Seward and Weed.

If the Compromise of 1850 had created even the possibility of a final solution to the problem of slavery, it was completely eliminated by Stephen Douglas's introduction of the Kansas–Nebraska act to the Senate early in 1854. The act provided that slavery might be introduced into any newly organized territory where a majority of the settlers wanted it. The act's supporters defended it on grounds of popular sovereignty; its opponents rejoined that it repealed the Missouri compromise. After a debate of more than a month, the Senate passed the bill in a vote which divided nearly all Democrats and southern Whigs against northern Whigs and Free Soilers. By a much closer margin, in which many northern Democrats joined the opposition, the bill passed the House in May (Smith, 1906, pp. 95–103, 107). To northern opponents of slavery, the bill represented the complete capitulation of Congress to the Slave Power.

Even before the bill had passed the Senate, anti-Nebraska meetings were organized in the winter throughout the northwest. At first, anti-Nebraska Whigs and Democrats tended to call separate meetings.

However, a fusion convention in Ohio in July named candidates for a state Supreme Court judgeship and the Superintendent of Public Works, the only state offices to be contested in the fall; the candidates were a Whig and a Democrat who had voted for Van Buren in 1848. The Know-Nothing movement joined the fusion forces, which won an overwhelming victory in 1854 (Bradford, 1947, pp. 136–43; Roseboom & Weisenburger, 1934, pp. 241–42). It seemed evident that the Whig party in Ohio was dead, but the forces temporarily united by the Kansas–Nebraska Act made a confusing array.

In New York, the situation was still more complex. The Know-Nothings were developing a large following, especially among the resentful Silver-Grays. At the same time, the factional center of gravity in the Democratic party had shifted. The Hunkers had split into Hardshells and Softshells over the issue of welcoming the Barnburners back into the party (the latter, who thought no conditions should be placed on the Barnburners' reincorporation, were called Softshells because they "had no backbone"). Led by Horatio Seymour, the Softshells gained the support of the Barnburners and by 1853 had become the strongest faction in the state's Democratic party (Chalmers, 1967, pp. 38–40).

Few antislavery Whigs in the east were yet ready to abandon their party for the new one that was growing in the west. They vainly hoped to remain strong enough to benefit from growing anti-Nebraska sentiment without allies. Seward especially wanted to hold the Whig party together: his Senate term expired in 1855, and he wanted to guarantee a legislature favorable to his reelection. But he had to control the party's convention first. The Wooly-Heads' candidate for governor was Myron Clark, who firmly supported Seward and opposed the Kansas–Nebraska Act, while Daniel Ullman, the candidate of the Silver-Grays, was a long-time ally of Fillmore and in 1850 had led a group of conservative Whigs in calling a convention to support Clay's Compromise (Curran, 1963, pp. 124–28; Foner, 1941, pp. 55–59; Sundquist, 1973, p. 66).

Clark was a temperance advocate and a member of the Know-Nothing Order, however, and hoped to attract the votes of the nativists. Ullman, on the other hand, declared his opposition to the Kansas–Nebraska Act, hoping to appeal to antislavery voters. So the distinction between the two men was more of faction than of personal position, but the factional distinction was important: Clark, by accepting the support of the radicals, implicitly declared his solidarity with those adamantly opposed to the extension of slavery. Ullman, on the contrary, was known as a moderate for whom the preservation of the union justified any necessary compromise on slavery.

The 1854 state convention followed Weed's leadership and nominated Clark. He sought the endorsement of the Know-Nothing Order as well, but it was largely dominated by old Silver-Grays. They managed to discover an irregularity in his membership, for which he was expelled.[8] They then gave their nomination to Ullman, the Silver-Gray the Whigs had rejected (Berger, 1973, p. 59; Curran, 1963, pp. 122–28).

The refusal to endorse Clark despite his position on temperance was important. The Know-Nothings had not previously nominated candidates of their own, but a New York Know-Nothing paper (the *Standard*) justified the decision by saying that

AN ENTIRE REPUDIATION OF EVERYTHING LIKE ABOLITIONISM was necessary to preserve [the Know-Nothing Order's national] integrity and unity. THIS INDEPENDENT NOMINATION, THEREFORE, IS A GUARANTEE TO OUR SOUTHERN FRIENDS that, whatever the parties of the north may do, the patriotism of the masses knows no distinction between north and south.

The declaration was quoted by Thurlow Weed's paper in full agreement that it accurately explained Ullman's candidacy (*Albany Evening Journal*, October 24, 1854).

In discussing the significance of the contest, neither man's partisans spoke much of nativism. While many correspondents demanded to know Ullman's position on temperance (he lukewarmly declared that he would not oppose a prohibition law if the legislature presented him with one[9]) and his nativity,[10] little or no discussion of immigration or naturalization laws appeared. Slavery, the union, and the role of the Know-Nothings with respect to those issues, on the other hand, were frequent topics.

The small anti-Nebraska group in the state did not name its own candidate, but supported Clark. When the Hardshells refused to support Seymour and named their own candidate, the race became four-sided and was hard fought. Clark won a narrow victory, but the size

---

[8]J. P. Faurot to Ullman, September 27, 1854. Ullman Papers, New York Historical Society.

[9]Ullman to D. Andrews, September 16, 1854; copy in Ullman papers, New York Historical Society.

[10]The 1854 Campaign was noteworthy for producing one of the most ingenious political slanders of the nineteenth century: Ullman, the candidate of the nativist party, was accused of being a "Hindoo" (Curran, 1963, pp. 136–37). Many correspondents asked Ullman to respond to the accusation, but most professed not to be concerned with the issue themselves but rather to fear its effect on others (e.g., Charles S. Olmstead to Ullman, October 11, 1854; Francis Granger to Ullman, October 17, 1854; Ullman papers, New York Historical Society). The epithet "Hindoos" came to be applied to the Know-Nothings generally.

of the Know-Nothing vote was astounding (Curran, 1963, p. 129; Ellis et al., pp. 231–32; Smith, 1906, p. 113).[11] Its local candidates (endorsed by Whigs or Democrats in several districts) won nineteen of the state's 33 Congressional seats, and their strength in the legislature was sufficient to elect a Senator if they could reach an agreement with the Hardshells (Curran, 1963, pp. 141–42).

The returns from the election demonstrate that both Whig factions' perceptions of the principal issue of the campaign were shared by the voters, for Clark and Ullman divided the old Whig constituency into its antislavery and unionist components. The correlation of the Whig vote of 1852 and that of 1854 is strikingly low ($r = .09$); indeed, the correlation of the 1852 Whig vote with the 1854 Know-Nothing vote is higher ($r = .24$). A large share of those who had voted Whig in 1852 evidently switched to the Know-Nothings in urban counties populated by non-Yankee natives, while the Whigs won strongly in Yankee counties and did better in rural than in urban areas (Table 5.1).

TABLE 5.1

Determinants of Whig and Know-Nothing Gubernatorial Vote,
New York, 1854
(Multiple Regression)

Independent variable	Whig		Know-Nothing	
	0-order r	Beta weight	0-order r	Beta weight
% Yankee, 1855	.547	.458	−.259	−.231
% Catholic, 1850	−.283	−.207	.092	.058
Farms per capita, 1850	.472	.173	−.196	−.076
Revivalism	.277	.042	−.106	.010
Multiple R	.635		.282	

Most of the counties where the Know-Nothings did well had opposed antislavery. The party had attracted many men who hoped to make it a vehicle for opposition to slavery, and some western counties which had demonstrated relatively strong antislavery sentiment were among Ullman's best counties (Curran, 1963, p. 170). However, the lowest Know-Nothing totals were recorded in the strongest antislavery counties (Cortland, Lewis, Madison, and Oneida, where Anti-

[11]Clark defeated Seymour by only 309 votes, each candidate receiving a third of the total; Ullman received 26%, and the Hardshell 7%.

Slavery Society membership had been greatest and where the Liberty party had won most of its votes). Thus the Know-Nothing vote in 1854 was moderately (though distinctly) anti-antislavery. Table 5.2 shows that its correlations are negative with all indicators of antislavery sentiment, whether Anti-Slavery Society membership, the referendum on black suffrage, or the vote for abolitionist candidates. The converse is true of the Whig vote. It was greatest in the Burned-Over District, and its correlations with antislavery indicators are quite large. The high correlation of the 1854 Whig vote and the 1852 Free Soil vote ($r = .51$) shows that the Whig party, having evicted its Silver-Gray faction, was able to attract virtually all the previous antislavery constituency.

So the Whigs had divided into antislavery and anti-antislavery factions; the Know-Nothing organization represented the latter rather than its nativist platform. Nevertheless, it had attracted some antislavery people upstate, and for several of those who were sent to the legislature, the slavery issue was more important than their loyalty to their new party. Granger and Ullman were determined to use the party's success to prevent Seward from returning to the Senate; but when the Whigs promised support for the Maine law, enough of the Know-Nothing legislators supported Seward to reelect him. When the order expelled those it accused of being Sewardites (all who refused to swear that they had voted a straight party ticket in 1854), several lodges seceded (Curran, 1963, pp. 146–49, 160).

Popular sovereignty had created a volatile situation in Kansas, and with the new year it became the focus of attention for supporters and opponents of slavery alike. While events there may not have corresponded to the image presented in the east, it was of course the image that affected the eastern vote, and "antislavery groups in other sections of the nation equated every quarrel among the settlers in the territory with the slavery expansion issue." It was commonly accepted in the free states that "border ruffians" had moved in from Missouri, held fraudulent elections, and presented a proslavery constitution to Congress (Berwanger, 1967, p. 97; Smith, 1906, pp. 126–33).

Kansas was the dominant issue in free-state politics in 1855 and 1856. Fusion between the Know-Nothings and the anti-Nebraskans continued into 1855 in Ohio: together they nominated the state's first Republican ticket. They named Chase for governor, and backed him with a state ticket composed entirely of Know-Nothings. Conservative Whigs who refused to support Chase nominated former governor Allen Trimble. They named no ticket for other offices; their sole intention was to defeat Chase. Chase won a minority victory, while the rest of the Republican ticket won by a large margin (Bradford, 1947,

TABLE 5.2

Correlations among Political Indicators, New York

	Whig President, 1852	Know-Nothing Governor, 1854	Know-Nothing Sec. of State, 1855	Know-Nothing President, 1856	Know-Nothing Governor, 1858	Whig Governor, 1854	Republican Sec. State, 1855	Republican President, 1856	Republican President, 1860
Revivalism	0.237	−0.106	−0.330	−0.505	−0.331	0.277	0.457	0.486	0.516
Anti-Slavery Societies	0.199	−0.059	−0.164	−0.313	−0.168	0.250	0.351	0.345	0.384
Liberty Governor, 1842	0.141	−0.152	−0.351	−0.573	−0.319	0.433	0.617	0.635	0.604
Liberty President, 1844	−0.015	−0.280	−0.288	−0.635	−0.396	0.516	0.580	0.691	0.643
Black Suffrage, 1846	0.245	−0.184	0.003	−0.499	−0.248	0.513	0.351	0.587	0.685
Free Soil President, 1848	−0.117	−0.292	−0.261	−0.491	−0.342	0.555	0.605	0.687	0.690
Free Soil President, 1852	−0.008	−0.168	−0.265	−0.632	−0.356	0.512	0.672	0.746	0.710
Whig President, 1852	1.000	0.238	0.243	0.120	0.234	0.088	0.184	0.118	0.281

pp. 146–50; Roseboom & Weisenburger, 1934, p. 243). As Figure 5.2 shows, the distribution of the vote in 1855 represented the realigned party composition almost as clearly as did the presidential election of the next year.

Know-Nothings cooperated with the Republican party, but they did not vote for Chase. The relatively high correlation of the 1855 Whig vote with the Know-Nothing presidential vote the following year ($r = .75$) and their similar magnitudes (8 and 7%, respectively) indicate that many Know-Nothings voted for Trimble. Moreover, the nativist vote came from areas not at all marked by prior opposition to slavery. Table 5.3 shows the correlations of the 1855 Whig vote and the Know-Nothing vote in the next two years with previous antislavery votes. All are very small; most are negative. The Know-Nothings, though they played a role in the Republican party's founding in Ohio, evidently did not share its antislavery intentions.

The Republican party formally organized in New York for the 1855 election. Seward and his followers joined it, as did many of the old Barnburner faction, who had walked out of the Soft Democrats' convention the year before when it had tabled a resolution opposing repeal of the Missouri Compromise. The Republicans nominated Barnburner leader Preston King as their candidate for Secretary of State in the 1855 election (Berger, 1973, pp. 47, 80–81).

The Secretary of State was the highest office voted on in 1855, but the election turned on the parties' positions on national issues. The Whigs, decimated by the defections of the Sewardites and by previous losses to the Know-Nothings, failed to nominate a separate state ticket. But a convention of "Straight-Out Whigs" made its sympathies plain by passing a resolution condemning "a Northern party on geographical boundaries" (*Albany Evening Journal*, October 24, 1855).

The Know-Nothings narrowly defeated King, and the election revealed the increasing polarization of the state. The Know-Nothings did well in a few northern counties which had previously been antislavery, but they lost the strong support they had enjoyed in western New York (except for Erie County [Buffalo]), and their best showing was in the east. Their overall vote, even more than that of 1854, came from counties which had previously rejected antislavery (correlations with antislavery indicators, shown in Table 5.2, are negative and larger than those for 1854). On the other hand, the correlations of the Republican vote with antislavery indicators are positive and larger than those of the previous year. The difference between the two parties was once again interpreted in terms of slavery, and little mention was made of nativism. A few days after the election, the *Tribune* complained that the Know-Nothings had campaigned on a platform call-

TABLE 5.3

Correlations among Political Indicators, Ohio

	Whig President, 1852	Whig Governor, 1855	Know-Nothing President, 1856	Know-Nothing Governor, 1857	Republican Governor, 1855	Republican President, 1856	Republican President, 1860
Revivalism	-0.226	-0.042	-0.157	-0.118	0.136	0.277	0.295
Anti-Slavery Societies	-0.085	-0.021	-0.065	-0.121	0.254	0.272	0.304
Liberty President, 1844	-0.099	0.011	-0.149	-0.194	0.464	0.576	0.625
Liberty Governor, 1846	-0.045	0.049	-0.144	-0.188	0.433	0.560	0.610
Free Soil President, 1848	-0.190	-0.080	-0.209	-0.225	0.558	0.652	0.735
Free Soil President, 1852	-0.205	-0.071	-0.187	-0.200	0.544	0.622	0.703
Free Soil Governor, 1853	-0.225	-0.057	-0.206	-0.199	0.431	0.551	0.560
Whig President, 1852	1.000	0.521	0.447	0.348	-0.003	0.013	0.340

ing for changes in naturalization laws, but were now claiming that their victory was a verdict against "Black Republicanism" (New York *Daily Tribune*, November 15, 1855).

By 1856 Kansas had become "bleeding Kansas," as the struggle between free-state and slave-state factions turned to violence in Lawrence. The first Republican national convention met in Pittsburgh, adopted a platform calling for the abolition of slavery in the territories and the admission of Kansas under the free-state constitution, and nominated the relatively unknown ex-Democrat Fremont for president. None of the major figures of the party was sufficiently "available," such figures as Chase and Seward being unacceptable to at least one faction of the newly founded party (Smith, 1906, pp. 156, 163–64).

The internal divisions within the Know-Nothing party over slavery reflected those in the nation as a whole. The party was dominated by its unionist elements, who still hoped that Know-Nothingism might preserve the union by diverting attention from slavery. The Know-Nothing national council had adopted a Union oath in 1854, enabling the party to attract conservative northern Whigs as well as almost all of southern Whiggery (Curran, 1963, pp. 197–201; Smith, 1906, p. 137).

Yet many had joined the party hoping it would take a strong antislavery stand, and a large share of the delegates came to its 1856 national convention in Philadelphia demanding resolute opposition to slavery extension. The convention split over the issue: it reversed the party's previous stand by denouncing the repeal of the Missouri Compromise, but also indirectly demanded that Congress not interfere with slavery in the territories. At that the antislavery elements left the convention. The unionist remnant nominated Fillmore for president. The signer of the Compromise of 1850 had joined the Order in 1855, and his nomination symbolized the party's desire for national reconciliation (Crandall, 1960, pp. 137–38; Curran, 1963, pp. 207–09; Holt, 1931, p. 177).

The nation was not to be reconciled, however, as the outcome of the 1856 election showed. The election was fought largely over the slavery issue, with Kansas as the focus. Rumors abounded that the south would secede if Fremont was elected. For many northern Whigs who now recognized that their party was dead, the division into Republican and Know-Nothing successors represented the necessity of a choice between "liberty and union" (Foner, 1970, pp. 139–40; Smith, 1906, pp. 169–70).

But if that was the choice, more northern voters chose liberty. The electoral votes were nearly geographically polarized, with all of the south voting Democratic, most of the north voting Republican, and only border Maryland supporting the candidate of national unity. The Republicans won in Ohio and New York, and both victories were brought about through a new distribution of the vote; the division manifested the full force of the realignment (Figures 5.1 and 5.2).

Despite the peak reached by the realignment factor in Ohio in 1856, the effect on the Democratic vote was slight; although its distribution changed, the change was a relatively small one (with 1852, $r = .91$). It was the Republican vote which was remarkably different from its Whig predecessor, as many Ohio Whigs of southern antecedents voted for Fillmore. Table 5.4 shows the composition of support for Know-Nothings and Republicans in Ohio in 1856. The Know-Nothings were supported overwhelmingly in counties populated by people of southern origin. The population of the southern part of the state had strong cultural and commercial ties to the south. Though some southerners had voted antislavery in the previous decade, they no longer did. One can infer that their support for the Know-Nothing Party represented for them the possibility of preserving the union. (The vote, incidentally, correlates .38 with the vote for Henry Clay in 1824.) The composition of the Republican vote was not very different from that of previous antislavery candidates. The main difference is that it was more noticeably rural; but Yankee origins was the major factor, and revivalism still had an effect, if a smaller one.

TABLE 5.4

Determinants of Republican and Know-Nothing Vote,
Ohio, 1856
(Multiple Regression)

Independent variable	Republican		Know-Nothing	
	0-order r	Beta weight	0-order r	Beta weight
% Yankee, 1870	.534	.434	−.275	.000
% Southern, 1870	−.370	−.092	.684	.550
% Catholic, 1850	−.169	−.169	−.151	.014
Farms per capita, 1850	.318	.254	−.529	−.286
Revivalism	.277	.112	−.157	−.044
Multiple R	.637		.730	

The realignment factor reached a peak in New York in 1856 as well. The most striking fact about the New York realignment was the accession to the Republicans of a large share of the Barnburners. Pierce's treatment of the Kansas question had finally alienated the antisouthern, antislavery elements of his own party, and several counties that had been strong in support of Van Buren in 1848 were now won by the Republicans, as they were for many years afterward. The 1848 Free Soil vote and the 1856 Republican vote were quite similarly distributed ($r = .69$).

Figure 5.1 shows the development of the Republican coalition in New York. The increase in Democratic loadings from 1852 to 1854 was due to the fact that the Barnburners in 1854 had supported the regular Democratic candidate, while a large share of the Hunkers had supported the Hardshell candidate. The precipitous decline between 1854 and 1856 is explained by the return of the Hardshells and the loss of the Barnburners. The 1856 Democratic vote displayed the distribution that was to remain stable for many decades after the Civil War.

The rise in Whig/Republican loadings from 1852 to 1856 occurred in two approximately equal parts. The interval from 1852 to 1854 saw the union of many Whigs and the remaining Free Soilers, together with the defection of the Know-Nothings. The interval from 1854 to 1856 brought the Barnburners into the Republican coalition. The Republicans remained strong in the areas they had won in 1855 (the correlation between the two years' vote is .91), while heavy gains in Barnburner counties offset the losses sustained the year before in some eastern Whig counties.[12]

The Know-Nothing vote, on the whole, was also highest in the same counties as the year before ($r = .69$), but heavily concentrated in the area around New York City and the Hudson Valley. The demographic determinants of the votes for each party are shown in Table 5.5. Voters in rural, Yankee, revivalist counties strongly rejected the Know-Nothings.[13] It was from these same areas that the Republicans

[12]Though the leaders of the Barnburner faction had joined the Republican party in 1855, many voters only followed them in 1856. The 1855 election statistics are not included in the factor analysis of the realignment (and therefore not included in Figure 5.1) because 1855 is the only year for which votes for Secretary of State have been analyzed.

[13]The Know-Nothing vote in 1856 and 1855 was also concentrated in counties with large numbers of immigrants. This does not mean that the foreign-born voted for the party that intended to proscribe them. It is a good example of what has been called an "ecological fallacy," but also illustrates Hammond's point (1973, pp. 770–71) that differences between individual-level and aggregate-level relations can often be explained as the result of a contextual effect: in this case, native voters were more likely to vote Know-Nothing in counties with large numbers of immigrants than in those with few immigrants, so at the aggregate level the relation between the two variables is larger than at the individual level. The multiple regression analyses in Table 5.5 show that when other variables are controlled, the effect of percentage foreign on the Know-Nothing vote is reduced. Data from smaller units confirm the point: Curran's analysis (1963, p. 105) of ward data from the 1855 election in four New York cities shows that wards with foreign-born populations voted against the Know-Nothings (for New York City, $r = -.77$; for Syracuse, Utica, and Rochester, each separately, $r = -.6$).

drew most of their support. The effect of revivalism was not as important in determining the Republican vote as it had been for the antislavery parties. Revival areas voted Republican (and were even stronger in rejecting the Know-Nothings than in endorsing the Republicans). But their place in the composition of the Republican vote was smaller than it had generally been for antislavery third parties. Parallel findings for the Democrats are not shown, but Democratic strength was greatest in urban, foreign-settled, non-Yankee areas, to an even greater degree than it had been before the realignment.

TABLE 5.5

Determinants of Republican and Know-Nothing Vote,
New York, 1856
(Multiple Regression)

Independent variable	Republican		Know-Nothing	
	0-order r	Beta weight	0-order r	Beta weight
% Yankee, 1855	.560	.304	−.501	−.291
% Foreign, 1850	−.517	−.259	.331	.201
Farms per capita, 1850	.712	.316	−.511	−.137
Revivalism	.486	.257	−.505	−.339
Multiple R	.809		.673	

Events from 1856 to 1860 complete the story of the progressive deterioration of relations between north and south. The debate over the competing Kansas governments continued. The Dred Scott decision shocked the north: it presented the possibility, however remote, that slavery might be introduced into the free states. John Brown's raid on Harper's Ferry, while applauded by very few northerners until after secession itself, nonetheless convinced southerners that unless they could control the north there was no place for them in the union. And the election of Lincoln persuaded them that they could not control the north (Filler, 1960, pp. 251–53, 267–73; Smith, 1906, p. 214).

The election of 1857 in Ohio, occurring shortly after the Dred Scott decision was handed down, continued to reflect the salience of slavery, as its high loading implies. The Know-Nothing vote fell to half its 1856 level, but voters who left it apparently divided between the Democrats and the Republicans. By 1859 the party had vanished, and most of its remaining adherents had been absorbed into the Republican party.

The 1860 election in Ohio was a four-sided contest; the state elections in October revealed that Lincoln's opponents would have no hope of defeating him unless they united, but efforts for unity were unsuccessful. Lincoln won a clear majority, and Bell and Breckinridge each received less than 3% of the vote. The sources of the Republican vote are shown in Table 5.6 (together with the analogous findings for New York). The 1860 vote, unlike the vote for Fremont in 1856 (shown in Table 5.4), was no longer rural, and (controlling for other variables) southern-settled counties contributed positively to the Republicans. Many Know-Nothings had evidently voted for Lincoln (Bradford, 1947, p. 217). But probably an equal number voted for Bell (the correlation between the Constitutional Union vote and the 1856 Know-Nothing vote is .76). Whether or not the Republicans benefited from the Know-Nothings' demise, however, the latter party had never been particularly strong in Ohio.

TABLE 5.6

Determinants of Republican Vote, Ohio and New York,
1860 (Multiple Regression)

Independent variable	Ohio		New York	
	0-order r	Beta weight	0-order r	Beta weight
% Yankee	.569	.685	.732	.486
% Southern (Ohio only)	.077	.410		
% Catholic	−.322	−.155	−.239	−.068
Farms per capita	−.050	.099	.691	.395
Revivalism	.295	.154	.516	.197
Multiple R		.715		.864

In New York, where it had been strong, it held on somewhat longer. An attempted fusion between Know-Nothings and Republicans in 1858 had failed for several reasons. The Republican platform contained a strong antislavery resolution, and the Republicans named a full state ticket. Weed had actively worked against a possible fusion, because he wanted to maintain control of the party and prevent Know-Nothing influence from hurting Seward's chances for the presidency. There were, however, successful fusions in most congressional campaigns and for other local offices (Curran, 1963, pp. 271–74). The vote for the Know-Nothing candidate for governor fell to half Fillmore's 1856 vote. Apparently a large portion of 1856 Know-Nothing voters voted Republican in 1858, for the decrease in the Republican loading for that year indicates a decline in the salience of antislavery.

The party ceased to exist after 1858, but that portion of its membership which refused to unite with the Republicans organized the state's short-lived Constitutional Union party. The New York delegate to the Constitutional Union convention in 1860 had been a Know-Nothing, and when the state party held its convention at Utica almost all those in attendance were former Know-Nothings. The party fused with the Democrats in New York in the 1860 election, but there, too, Lincoln won a majority. Fillmore's 1856 supporters divided evenly between Lincoln and Douglas (Curran, 1963, pp. 287, 291–92);[14] but the distribution of the Democratic vote was virtually unchanged, while the distribution of the Republican vote was markedly affected. Democratic gains from Know-Nothings in 1860 were in areas where Democrats were already strong, so factor loadings changed little after 1856, even though Douglas's vote increased by thirteen percentage points over Buchanan's. But Republican gains from the Know-Nothings occurred in areas where Republicans were relatively weak, and represent what might be called a second realignment (ideological and geographical) of the Republican vote.

Overall Republican support was still negatively correlated with previous Know-Nothing strength (between Know-Nothing, 1856, and Republican, 1860, $r = .63$). The demographic sources of Republican support in 1860 (shown in Table 5.6) were not particularly different from those of 1856, although the influence of Yankee origins was a good deal greater, and the party did better than it had four years earlier in foreign-settled counties (this is probably due to winning the vote of Know-Nothings rather than of the foreign-born themselves).

The place of nativism in the rise of the Republican party continues to be an issue among historians. It has been argued that the ideological impulses of the Republican party were abolition or containment of slavery, temperance, and hostility to foreigners and Catholics,[15] all of which went together because they shared the same evangelical roots. Nativists perceived the harmony between Republican principles and their own, and Republican and Know-Nothing leaders carefully fostered a coalition to accommodate these voters.[16] Silbey concludes that since the Democrats were avowedly the party of the immigrants, nativists "had no place to go now [after the Know-Nothing party died] except to the Republicans. The Republicans did not hesitate to woo the nativist-oriented groups either" (Silbey, 1967b, p. 14).

[14]For detailed evidence that Know-Nothing voters divided between Republicans and Democrats, see Kantrowitz (1965, pp. 125–30) and Hammond (1972, p. 201).

[15]This argument is presented by Formisano (1971, p. 239), Hays (1967, p. 158), and Kleppner (1966, p. 189).

[16]As Holt (1969, p. 8 et passim) has demonstrated for Pittsburgh.

Foner's interpretation has it that, on the contrary, the principles of the early Republican party were hostile to nativism: their desire for economic expansion and free-state control of the western territories required the continued settlement of large numbers of immigrants. Accordingly, the state Republican organizations dissociated themselves from ethnic issues soon after their founding, and the 1856 and 1860 national platforms strongly opposed the proscription of immigration and abridgment of the rights of naturalized citizens (Foner, 1970, pp. 232–36, 248–49, 257). Foner does not question the assumption that the bulk of the nativists eventually joined the Republican party, but argues that it was not because the party espoused nativism.

Both sides of the debate, then, accept the assumptions that there was a large bloc of nativist voters in the 1850s; that the Know-Nothing party succeeded in capturing this segment of the electorate for a short while, and that they were then receptive to the appeals made to them by the Republican party.

But though the Republicans won part of the Know-Nothing vote, they by no means captured it all. The Republican share of the vote in Ohio increased by less than four percentage points between 1856 and 1860. The Know-Nothings had won 7% in 1856, and the remaining 3% evidently voted Constitutional Union. In New York, the Know-Nothings had won 21% of the vote in 1856; in the 1860 election, the Republican total increased by 8% (from 46 to 54%) while the Democratic total increased by 13% (from 33 to 46%). Fewer than half the Know-Nothings apparently voted Republican.

Know-Nothing voters, therefore, did not move disproportionately into the Republican party. More importantly, they adhered to the Know-Nothing party in the first place not because they were nativists but because they were opposed to antislavery agitation. That was clearly the case for the Silver-Gray Whigs who formed the leadership of the party in New York. I have made the same claim about Know-Nothing voters, and that claim must be considered in more detail. In retrospect it is impossible to make any conclusive demonstration of the issue-motivations of Know-Nothing voters, especially since there is no direct electoral measure of nativism; were there, for example, a referendum on a nativist issue,[17] one could use its correlation with the Know-Nothing vote to gauge the extent to which the vote was based on nativism.

But voters could recognize its appeal to anti-antislavery senti-

[17]There was such a referendum in Massachusetts, where voters in 1859 approved an amendment denying naturalized citizens the right to vote until two years after naturalization (Foner, 1970, pp. 250–252).

ments. The party was certainly inconsistent in its attachment to nativism: it attempted to appeal to foreign Protestants in the north and to native Catholics in Maryland and Louisiana (Curran, 1963, p. 231; Scisco, 1901, pp. 165–66). Much of its rhetoric about the need for national unity referred to unity between sections of the country rather than unity against any foreign threat. The party's electoral weakness in antislavery areas and its strength in nonantislavery areas strongly suggest that voters responded to the appeal in the same terms.

The Republicans and the Know-Nothings were heirs to Whig electoral support. But the Whigs who became Know-Nothings had been unionist, while those who became Republicans had been antislavery. In Ohio, the correlation of the Know-Nothing vote with previous antislavery votes, though relatively small, was consistently negative. The Know-Nothing vote in New York was only moderately anti-antislavery in 1854, but it was increasingly concentrated in nonantislavery areas. Comparing the votes for Know-Nothing candidates in New York between 1854 and 1856 and in Ohio between 1855 and 1857 (considering the 1855 Whig vote together with the two Know-Nothing votes), we see that almost every antislavery indicator has an increasingly negative correlation with the vote in successive years (Tables 5.2 and 5.3).

Does this close, negative relation between antislavery and the Know-Nothing vote prove that people voted for the party because they were opposed to antislavery rather than because they were nativists? It is not conclusive. An ideological affinity between nativism and opposition to antislavery might account for the relation without implying that these voters were insincere nativists. But there is little reason to suppose that any such affinity existed. If anything, the presumed common roots of antislavery and nativism in evangelical Protestantism should have produced the opposite relation: nativism should have been strongest among antislavery voters.

The most plausible conclusion, therefore, is that most Know-Nothing voters were not particularly nativist; that they were motivated not by the desire to restrict immigrants but by opposition to antislavery and a desire to preserve the union even at the cost of appeasing slaveholders. They apparently foresaw in a Know-Nothing victory the prospect of defusing the dispute which threatened to disrupt the union. Perhaps they hoped xenophobia would be a symbol strong enough to make the unity of the nation more important than the competing issue of slavery (Higham, 1958, p. 151). And voters who were attracted to the party because of its presumed nativism were used by the unionist majority for their own ends.

The Know-Nothing vote was as little related to revivalism as to

Republicanism. The relation of Know-Nothing support to revivalism and Liberty party support in Ohio, though weak, is negative (Table 5.3); in New York, it is negative and very strong (Table 5.2). The premise of the argument that nativism and antislavery went together and contributed jointly to the rise of the Republicans is that both were based in evangelical religion. But in New York and Ohio, nativism was not nurtured by the revivals, and was inconsistent with the beliefs those revivals taught. Although revivalists did not actively defend the rights of immigrants, they did not vote for the party which espoused nativism.

The transformation of American politics in the 1840s and 1850s is summarized in the graphs presented in Figures 5.1 and 5.2, which show the changing positions of the parties that contested office during that period. I have loosely referred to the factors in both states as representing "antislavery," and that name seems justified because the factor loadings of the time series follow the flow of events and correspond to the increasing salience of slavery as a political issue. But in what sense was the electoral realignment due to antislavery? The relationship was indirect, because voters' responses to the slavery issue were conditioned by party politics.

Figures 5.1 and 5.2 show that in both states the Whig/Republican vote fluctuated much more than the Democratic vote, indicating that the Whig party was much more affected by the political currents of these decades than was the Democratic (this is reflected as well, of course, in the fact that the Democratic party survived while the old opposition party was replaced by a new one). But the difference between the two parties is much greater in Ohio than in New York: in Ohio the loadings of the Democratic party vary very little.

The time series of Democratic loadings in Ohio does not approximate the step function which would suggest the occurrence of a critical election, but rather appears to represent a gradual trend slightly quickened between 1852 and 1856. And the narrow range of those loadings suggests that the change in the Democratic party's constituency was too small to be called a realignment. Indeed, the areas of Democratic strength remained nearly constant over the period (between the 1844 and 1864 presidential votes, $r = .85$).

Rather than a realignment of the two parties, the factor represents the transformation of the Whig into the Republican party, with very little permanent change in its composition, but with considerable intermediate movement during the realigning period. This transformation occurred in two steps, as the composition of the Whig vote was first affected by the antislavery parties, and then by the anti-antislavery party. From 1844 to 1853, the Whig curve declined irregularly but steeply. It then rose sharply between 1853 and 1857 as anti-slavery men joined the new Republican party and Unionist Whigs left it, and finally declined again to 1860 at which point the coalition became more or less stable.

The demographic sources of the realignment[18] are shown in Table 5.7. The most important is Yankee origins; revivalism and (negatively) southern origins also have an impact. But the realignment must be explained in political rather than demographic terms, for the several demographic variables presented in Table 5.7 together hardly predict the realignment factor better than any single Free Soil vote (for 1848, $r = .74$; for 1851, $r = .69$).

TABLE 5.7
Determinants of the Pre-Civil War Electoral
Realignment, Ohio[a]
(Multiple Regression)

Independent variable	0-order r	Beta weight
% Yankee, 1870	.660	.530
% Southern, 1870	−.484	−.072
% Catholic, 1850	.052	.070
Farms per capita, 1850	.254	.212
Revivalism	.432	.252
Multiple R	.743	

[a]First principal component of Whig and Republican presidential and gubernatorial votes, 1836–1884.

This close association of the factor with the Free Soil vote demonstrates that the movement of the electorate during the period was principally determined by voters' opposition to slavery. There is no independent indicator of sentiment on slavery comparable to the suf-

[18]The factor analysis which yields the dependent variable in Table 5.7 differs from the factor analysis whose loadings are presented in Figure 5.2: the Figure presents a factor analysis of the votes for all parties, while the factor used in the table is based only on the analysis of Whig and Republican votes. The reason for this discrepancy is that the factor based on all parties is not statistically independent of the party votes from which it is derived, so that a correlation between it and a minor-party vote would be misleadingly high. The table presents the factor based on Whig and Republican votes rather than that based on Democratic votes because, as noted, the realignment in Ohio had little effect on the Democratic party. The factor derived from Democratic party votes is related, though rather weakly, to the same variables that determine the Whig/Republican factor scores.

frage referendum in New York. But the legislators of the Ohio Free Soil party repealed the Black Code and passed personal liberty laws for fugitives; voters in the areas which supported the party protected fugitive slaves and elected some of the Congress's strongest opponents of slavery. Both legislators and voters demonstrated a singleness of purpose which makes clear that the Free Soil vote, and therefore the electoral movement during the period, were based on opposition to slavery. Insofar as that movement left the ultimate composition of the two parties similar to their composition at the beginning, however, one cannot say that opposition to slavery brought about a realignment of the Ohio electorate.

In New York a realignment occurred, but its relation to slavery attitudes was more complex. The demographic determinants of the realignment are shown in Table 5.8. The primary influence on the realignment was the urban–rural dimension; it was in rural areas that Republicans gained, and in urban areas that they lost, over previous Whig strength (indeed, farms per capita alone explains the realignment almost as well as the full set of variables). The influence of the size of the Catholic Church is also notable; relative Democratic strength increased in Catholic areas during this period.[19] The effect of revivalism (which will be discussed more fully below) is relatively small.

TABLE 5.8
Determinants of the Pre-Civil War Electoral Realignment,
New York[a]
(Multiple Regression)

Independent variable	0-order r		Beta weight
% Yankee, 1855	.466		.211
% Catholic, 1850	−.413		−.189
Farms per capita, 1850	.712		.505
Revivalism	.346		.108
Multiple R		.757	

[a]First principal component of Whig and Republican presidential and gubernatorial votes, 1836–1880.

[19]It might be asked whether one could equally well claim that this was an effect of Protestantism in the areas that realigned toward the Republican party, rather than of Catholicism where they did not. This is not the case. A rough measure of Protestant strength (subtracting the size of Catholic churches from the combined size of all churches) shows virtually no correlation with the realignment.

Politically the realignment reflects the complexity which antislavery politics assumed in New York. Just as in Ohio, antislavery politics affected the Whigs more consistently than it did the Democrats. This can be seen in Figure 5.1: neither the Liberty nor the Free Soil party offered candidates for governor in 1846 and 1850. The Democratic loadings between 1844 and 1854 form a nearly horizontal line, with the exception of 1848. The Whig loadings, on the other hand, fluctuate with the presence or absence of an antislavery candidate.

Antislavery was a symbol of factional struggles as well as a moral issue. The 1848 election was the only one seriously affected by the Democrats' factional struggle; for the Whigs, though the struggle was more continuous, the crucial years were 1854 and after, when the Know-Nothings opposed them. And these factional struggles, more than the moral question, were what determined the realignment.

Table 5.9 shows the relative importance of the political sources of the realignment,[20] measured by the 1848 Free Soil vote, the 1856 Know-Nothing vote, and the 1846 suffrage referendum. Of them, the first two are most important. The suffrage referendum has virtually no direct effect; in fact, its coefficient, though very small, is negative. This does not mean that areas which supported suffrage abandoned the Republican party in the realignment, as the zero-order relationship shows. It means, rather, that the realignment was much more closely determined by partisan shifts than by attitudes toward blacks.

The pre-Civil War realignment in New York thus depended on a combination of issues, all related to slavery but in complex ways. Most of those voters who left the Democratic party for the Republican were not supporters of black suffrage, and one can assume that moral opposition to slavery was not a major factor in their change of allegiance. While the Republicans did gain the votes of abolitionists, the crucial gains came from areas where voters were not abolitionists but left the Democratic party for other reasons. Gains from the Know-Nothings indicate that those Whigs who valued preservation of the union far more than they cared about slavery were also members, if reluctant ones, of the Republican coalition.

Abolitionism, then, was not the basis of Republican supremacy in New York. The Barnburners opposed southern dominance of national

[20]For reasons stated in footnote 18, the dependent variable in Tables 5.8 and 5.9 is derived from a factor analysis of Whig and Republican votes only. The factor derived from Democratic votes is quite similar to that derived from Whig and Republican votes ($r = .95$), and its demographic determinants are similar to those shown in Table 5.8. Its political determinants differ from those shown in Table 5.9 in that the Free Soil vote has a somewhat greater effect and the Know-Nothing vote a somewhat smaller effect, but both are more important than the suffrage referendum.

TABLE 5.9

Political Determinants of the New York
Electoral Realignment[11]
(Multiple Regression)

Independent variable	0-order r	Beta weight
Suffrage referendum, 1846	.437	−.062
Free Soil, President, 1848	.744	.499
Know-Nothing, President, 1856	−.770	−.555
Multiple R	.879	

"First principal component of Whig and Republican presidential and gubernatorial votes, 1836–1880.

politics and the extension of the southern economic system, and the Know-Nothings fought the Republican threat of disunion. Both positions were defined by attitudes to the relation between north and south, so slavery was an essential element of the two viewpoints. But it was a political, not a moral issue.

As antislavery politics grew, therefore, abolitionist politics declined, and with it the influence of the revivalist ethos. Throughout this chapter I have mentioned the statistically measured effects of revivalism, but only in passing, for they are generally small. Both the small size of those effects and the narrative of events demonstrate the decline of revivalism as an independent political force. Tables 5.10 and 5.11 summarize the change over time in the effects of revivalism, showing those effects on antislavery votes between 1840 and 1860 and on the electoral realignment.[21] The coefficients of revivalism decline almost steadily, especially in Ohio, with a breaking point upon the founding of the Republican party. Though the simple correlations of revivalism with antislavery votes decline little (especially in New York), the regression coefficients show that its direct effect became considerably less important.

[21]The tables show the correlation coefficients between revivalism and antislavery political indicators, the standardized partial regression coefficient of revivalism when several other variables are controlled, the factor loading on (or correlation with) the realignment as measured by the first principal component of votes for all political parties, and (in the case of votes) the percentage of the electorate voting for the party or measure.

Within each state, the regression coefficients are comparable because the same independent variables have been used in each regression (for the same reason, the coefficients are not necessarily equal to those presented in earlier tables). Between states, the coefficients are not comparable, both because the independent variables are different and because revivalism is measured differently.

The tables also show the factor loading of each electoral variable on the realignment factor and the percent of the vote won in each year. Both are inversely related to the effect of revivalism. The relationship is not perfect for either state, but in general, as the size of the vote and the relationship to the realignment increase, the effect of revivalism decreases. As the impending realignment became more and more evident in shifts in voters' allegiances, the particular effect of revivalism on those shifts steadily decreased.

Abolitionists continued to act independently through the Civil War. Though most voted Republican, they did not adopt the Republican version of antislavery but continued to oppose slavery on moral grounds and to insist on fair treatment of blacks. Gerrit Smith gave John Brown financial assistance. The list of stations on the underground railroad in Ohio reads like the roll of a report of revivals nearly three decades earlier; although the estimate that forty thousand fugitives passed through Ohio is surely exaggerated, Ohioans regu-

TABLE 5.10

Effects of Revivalism on Political Behavior,
Ohio, 1838–1860

Dependent variable	0-order r^a	Beta weight[b]	Factor loading[c]	% of total vote
Anti-Slavery Societies	.427	.371	.368[e]	
Liberty President, 1840	.317	.185	.006	0.3
Liberty President, 1844	.421	.321	.044	2.6
Liberty Governor, 1846	.371	.331	.072	4.4
Free Soil President, 1848	.452	.251	.269	10.8
Free Soil Governor, 1851	.447	.246	.206	6.0
Free Soil Governor, 1853	.397	.325	.266	17.6
Republican President, 1856	.277	.112	.228	48.5
Know-Nothing President, 1856	−.157	−.044	−.172	7.3
Republican President, 1860	.295	.154	.100	52.3
Realignment[d]	.432	.252	.988[e]	

[a]Zero-order correlation coefficient of revivalism with the dependent variable.

[b]Standardized partial regression coefficient of revivalism, in a regression equation with the following additional independent variables: percentage born in New York, 1870; percentage born in Virginia, West Virginia, and Kentucky, 1870; percentage Catholic, 1850; farms per capita, 1850.

[c]On the first principal component of the factor analysis of all parties, president and governor, 1836–1884. For variables not entered into the factor analysis (Anti-Slavery Societies and the realignment factor based on Whig/Republican votes alone), the entry is the correlation with the factor based on all parties.

[d]First principal component of Whig/Republican presidential votes, 1836–1884.

[e]These are correlation coefficients, not factor loadings, as explained in footnote c.

TABLE 5.11

Effects of Revivalism on Political Behavior,
New York, 1838–1860

Dependent variable	0-order r^a	Beta weight[b]	Factor loading[c]	% of total vote
Anti-Slavery Societies, 1838	.427	.264	.185[e]	
Liberty President, 1840	.443	.352	.007	0.6
Liberty Governor, 1842	.551	.414	.021	1.8
Liberty President, 1844	.456	.261	.050	3.3
Suffrage referendum, 1846	.512	.298	.431[e]	27.6
Free Soil President, 1848	.472	.325	.251	26.4
Free Soil President, 1852	.452	.243	.082	4.9
Republican President, 1856	.486	.236	.251	46.3
Know-Nothing President, 1856	−.505	−.315	−.167	20.9
Republican President, 1860	.516	.197	.102	53.7
Realignment[d]	.346	.108	.991[e]	

[a]Zero-order correlation coefficient of revivalism with the dependent variable.
[b]Standardized partial regression coefficient of revivalism, in a regression equation with the following additional independent variables: percentage born in New England, 1855; percentage Catholic, 1850; farms per capita, 1850.
[c]On the first principal component of the factor analysis of all parties, president and governor, 1836–1880. For variables not entered into the factor analysis (Anti-Slavery Societies, the referendum, and the realignment factor based on Whig/Republican votes alone), the entry is the correlation with the factor based on all parties.
[d]First principal component of Whig/Republican presidential votes, 1836–1880.
[e]These are correlation coefficients, not factor loadings, as explained in footnote c.

larly rescued fugitives or agitated to prevent their recapture. Revivalists continued to pressure the churches and the benevolent societies to embrace abolitionism. During the Civil War, finally, abolitionists insisted that the Union was fighting for abolition and that the southern states must not be allowed to rejoin the union until they had ended slavery (Bradford, 1947, p. 94; Gara, 1961, pp. 99–100; McPherson, 1964, pp. 6, 52–133; Wyatt-Brown, 1969, pp. 329–38).

But after the Liberty party was merged into the Free Soil party, abolitionism and the revivalist ethos no longer had a major effect on political developments. Revivalists had entered politics with two objectives: they wanted to make slavery an issue, and they wanted to make the country more nearly a sinless society. They succeeded in their first objective. Slavery did indeed become a major political issue, the defining issue, so that one's position on slavery determined his political loyalties and positions on many other issues. But its abolition came about in a manner which was not consistent with their desire to create a society without sin. Slavery was abolished, not through the repentance and conversion of slaveholders, but by force of arms. Neither the north nor the south admitted its guilt or conceded that blacks were fully human.

Revivalism, therefore, failed in its attempt to remake the nation's political life, just as it failed to remake the nation's social life. In order to become viable politically, abolitionism had to be transformed into antislavery so that it would accommodate motivations other than the piety of the revivalists. It had to be identified with intersectional hostility and in some instances with antipathy to blacks themselves; it was used to mobilize support by politicians who wanted to gain an advantage over their opponents either within their own party or in the opposing party.

The impact of ideology on politics is necessarily constrained by the social structure within which it emerges and attracts adherents. The existing structure of norms and opportunities for political influence affects any new political group. An ideology must compete with other ideologies, and must establish a relationship with groups whose interests are determined by material conditions and by existing organizations. The failure of the revivalist ethos illustrates the limitations on the autonomous force of ideas in politics. Abolitionists did not even succeed in maintaining an independent political party: as their "one idea" was transformed to attract a broader constituency, their own base was merged into the more broadly-based Republican party.

The Constitution prevents third parties from being important for long periods of time, so the demands of any group must ultimately be incorporated into the agenda of a major party if they are to be heard. When neither of the major parties presented a candidate distinctly appealing to the revivalist ethos, then, revivalists had no opportunity to express their beliefs through their vote. Though most of them voted for the Republican party whose positions came closer to the ethos, they lost their independent impact. The failure of revivalism may be due merely to the American political system's characteristic nonresponsiveness to ideological demands. The system generally deals with challenges through bargaining within a general consensus on the norms of its operation, including the norm that all political goals are negotiable. The parties and other organizations capable of flourishing in such a system are pragmatic and incremental; they do not make demands that might incite their opponents to withdraw from the system. But when the elimination of sin becomes a political objective, it is not negotiable, and movements with nonnegotiable goals are unwilling to defer to the norms of civility and restraint.

Movements making such unrestrained demands are often regarded as disruptions that disturb the smooth functioning of the system and hamper its ability to achieve workable solutions. But organizations dedicated to pragmatism and negotiation contribute as much to crises as to ideologically motivated movements. Precisely because they are incrementalist, they do not acknowledge that some problems are not amenable to solution by negotiation. The solutions they propose may suffice to delay crises, but not to avert them (Burnham, 1970b, pp. 135–36). The Civil War is a case in point. The pre-Civil War decade was the one period in American history when the norms of its political life broke down over a nonnegotiable goal (Burnham, 1967, pp. 293–95; McCormick, 1967, p. 116), proving that the compromises that had been attempted for decades were insufficient.

That crisis arose out of the normal functioning of the political system as much as it was instigated by any extremist political movement. It was Whigs, Republicans, and Democrats, not abolitionists or revivalists, who made the Civil War inevitable. The crisis also wrought a transformation of the political cleavages in the nation, but the new lines of division were not those drawn by revivalism, either geographically or ideologically. Its role in the actual process was a minor one, and it clearly did not determine the outcome.

Despite its relatively small effect on the reshaping of political alliances, however, revivalism nevertheless prepared the way by bringing into public consciousness a situation which the beliefs it inspired rendered intolerable. The spread of opposition to slavery must have been in part due to others coming to adopt those beliefs or at least some of their implications, even if it was also due to disputes which arose from the rivalry of sections and political factions.

From the viewpoint of politicians, revivalism created a problem, which they—the politicians—were left to solve. From their own viewpoint, however, revivalists only pointed to a problem that already existed. But neither group was able to solve the problem, and the interim resolution dealt only with what was for the revivalists its most superficial aspect.

It commonly occurs that the effect of ideologically motivated political activists with little experience in politics is limited to "creating" problems, not determining their outcome. Walker, discussing the lunch-counter desegregation sit-ins in Atlanta in 1961, says that it is the role of activists "to start fights they are unable to finish," leaving the resolution of the problem to the normal channels of political bargaining (Walker, 1963, p. 121). But if the failure of revivalism and the abolitionists it inspired to resolve the slavery controversy to their own satisfaction testifies to their lack of political effectiveness beyond the raising of issues, the Civil War and the subsequent history of blacks in America testify to the equal incapacity of the incremental, nonideological politicians who preempted them. The sit-ins in Atlanta in 1961 offered continuing proof that politicians were no more able than moralists to solve the problems created by slavery.

6
Persistence and Decline

The influence of revivalism on politics has persisted well past the Civil War. Before the war it was important in making antislavery political. It had very little effect on the resolution of the slavery controversy, as we have seen, but it had a more important impact on the area where the revivals had occurred and the antislavery crusade began. It became incorporated into the culture of that area, and in some places it has continued to influence politics into the present. Its influence is not constant; in a part of the original revival district it has vanished, and elsewhere it has only sporadic and irregular importance. And though aspects of post-Civil War voting behavior are explained by the revivalist past, the meaning of the symbols which revivalism makes salient is different from the meaning they had during the revival period itself: the influence of the revivalist ethos took a different form after the war than it had had before.

The later history of revivalist politics illustrates the transformation of an ethos from an ideology to a cultural pattern: from a newly created belief system with revolutionary consequences for its adherents to a set of beliefs identified with prevailing institutions and passed on through the normal processes of cultural transmission. That change in the character of the ethos was accompanied by a change in its meaning, from a justification of the demand for political change to an affirmation of the desire to preserve existing institutions. The process also illustrates the conditions which enable a cultural pattern arising out of critical events to become institutionalized; the ethos has been preserved in New York, where many revivalist communities have remained rural and experienced little immigration. It has vanished in Ohio, where much of the revival district has experienced industrialization and a high degree of population growth.

The first major political manifestation of revivalism was a movement which frontally challenged national institutions, creating a conflict which was ultimately unresolvable through normal political mechanisms. It produced a dynamic, innovative ideology appropriate to the dynamism and expansion of the communities in which the revivals had occurred. But it was possible for the revivalist ethos to become a part of the traditional culture of those communities precisely because they were rural, had stopped expanding after a few decades, and since then remained small and relatively untouched.

A counternormative belief system is different from an orthodoxy even if they have identical content. The functions of the two belief systems and the kinds of political activity they inspire will be different. Some of the differences between the effects of the ethos before the Civil War and its effects afterward can be explained as a result of this different relation to community belief systems. But the content of the beliefs whose expression is rooted in the revivalist ethos also changed, and changed differently in the two states.

The most salient issue for the revivalist ethos before the Civil War was, of course, slavery. It was the clearest example of a secular violation of the religious principles which underlie the revivalist ethos: namely the belief in freedom and man's ability to save himself, with which any form of bondage was inconsistent. But there were other forms of bondage to which revivalism addressed itself. The most important of these was bondage to alcohol. Revivalism promoted temperance societies which encouraged their members and others to take a pledge to abstain from alcoholic beverages. The rhetoric of these organizations insisted that drinking was a form of slavery (as well as proclaiming that great horrors would be visited upon those who drank, and great rewards upon those who abstained).

With the slavery issue resolved, the demand for temperance became the main expression of the ethos in New York's revivalist communities. When temperance and related matters (particularly the proscription of gambling) have been at issue the ethos has affected New Yorkers' votes. They vote distinctly in nonpartisan referenda, and their partisan votes are sometimes affected as well: when campaigns have been fought over issues which revivalism made salient, voters in revivalist counties have deviated from their usual party norm to support candidates whose positions have more clearly conformed to the tenets of revivalism.

But the ethos has had a different meaning for them than it had had for their ancestors. Instead of a protest calling for positive change in national institutions, it became a defensive reaction against the growth of urbanization and economic enterprise which they believed threatened their way of life. Their politics became an attempt to legitimize the definition of virtue which prevailed in their static rural communities. Though it arose as the political expression and realization of the belief in human freedom, the revivalist ethos was turned into a justification of a way of life which was under attack from outside. Though temperance, the main symbol of that justification, was derived from the preachings of the original revivalists, it acquired a new meaning which made a decisive change in the ethos's implications.

In Ohio, the influence of the ethos was transformed in a different direction. While the revivalists' embrace of the Republican party was less wholehearted than had been their support for antislavery parties, revivalism nevertheless created a strong tradition of Republican loyalty. With very minor exceptions, that loyalty was resistant to any influence of current issues, even when it appeared that the ethos would lead voters to abandon their favored party. Though Republican loyalty grew out of revivalism, it became detached from its revivalist roots and persisted autonomously. Party loyalty was therefore less affected by its revivalist origins than by the movement of the party system itself. Republicanism was held to fiercely for seven decades. But when the depression and the New Deal created the conditions for a realignment of party loyalties, revivalism had little impact: partisanship changed under the impact of socioeconomic changes and political forces, and revivalism ceased to be a measurable component of partisan sentiment.

The effect of revivalism after the Civil War, then, was very different from the effect it had had on the first generation. The differences are likely to be obscured by the data analysis, however, for the measurement of that effect is performed in the same way as in previous chapters. Multiple regression reveals many examples where the vote of revivalist counties is different from the vote of other counties and can only be explained as a result of past revivals. But the greater Republicanism of revivalist counties in Ohio may be independent of any obvious issue content, and prohibition may have had for voters in the late nineteenth and twentieth centuries a different meaning than abolitionism had for early nineteenth century voters. The analyses in this chapter must, therefore, be understood as revealing historical effects of revivalism rather than effects of the revivalist belief system described earlier. The similarities between the belief systems which motivated earlier and later voters are only partial.

There are several contrasts between New York and Ohio which

explain both the different kinds of voting behavior to which a revivalist history led after the Civil War and the longer survival of the
ethos in New York. These contrasts include demographic differences
between the revivalist and nonrevivalist sections of the states at the
time of the revivals themselves; the subsequent development of those
sections; and the different degrees of political competition in the late
nineteenth century. It is difficult to determine, however, which of
those differences were crucial.

Political developments in the 1840s and 1850s divided the two
states into sections which, respectively, supported and opposed antislavery politics. But the differences did not develop randomly; they
were dependent not only on the occurrence of revivals but also on the
demographic composition of the respective sections. The antislavery
sections were quite similar in composition, having been settled by
New Englanders. But the non-Yankee, nonrevivalist areas of the two
states were quite different. In New York the contrast was between
Yankees and Yorkers; in Ohio, it was between Yankees and southerners. The subsequent development of the respective political sections
was also very different in the two states. In New York, the areas that
were already urban in 1850 became even more so, and most of upstate remained rural (even though some of the state's largest cities
grew up there later). In Ohio, most of the later urban development
was concentrated in the Yankee-settled areas of the state.

Finally, politics was considerably more competitive in New York
than in Ohio between 1860 and 1896. Though the realignment of the
1850s created a party system in which voters' allegiances remained
remarkably stable for many years thereafter, the stability was considerably greater in Ohio: in New York, there were occasional deviations.
And in New York, the division corresponded to important contemporary demographic distinctions among the state's population groups;
in Ohio, partisan divisions persisted until the New Deal despite considerable changes in the composition of the state's population.

In New York the contrast between Yankee and Yorker had already partially given way to that between rural natives and urban
immigrants before 1860. In 1850, 21% of New York's residents were
foreign born. The cities in which they lived continued to be the principal destinations of foreign immigrants, and the upstate areas outside
of the major cities continued to be dominated by the descendants of
their first settlers. The revivalist areas continued to be rural. Indeed,
differences between them and nonrevivalist areas increased: the correlation of revivalism with farms per capita increased between 1890 and
1930 (from .22 to .33), as did its correlation with proportion foreign-
born (from −.11 to −.37).

In New York, continued stability permitted the revivalist ethos to become firmly established in the areas where it had taken root. Its persistence, however, did not take the form of a stable division between parties along the geographical lines of revivalism, but rather of occasional outcroppings of voting behavior which deviated from normal party allegiance in ways consistent with the ethos. Traditional voting patterns were closely related to revivalism, but this relation was due almost entirely to the association between revivalism and other, more important variables. Table 6.1 shows that the vote in 1880, a typical election of the period, is primarily explained by the fact that Yankee counties voted Republican and immigrant counties Democratic, and much less by the past occurrence of revivals. The number of farms was no more important than revivalism. Non-Yankee rural counties were not noticeably more Republican than urban counties.

But there were many deviations from traditional partisanship on which revivalism had a more marked effect. The first of these occurred as early as 1872 when, as Figure 5.1 shows, the election deviated from the pattern established by the pre-Civil War alignment. The year marked the revolt by the Liberal Republicans, who opposed the hardline reconstruction policy being maintained in Congress by the Radicals. The movement attracted many who had been among the strongest antislavery men in the Republican party before the war, including Schurz, Sumner, and Charles Francis Adams, the latter two considered as presidential candidates (Haynes, 1916, pp. 9–13).

The movement's principal goal was the liberalization of recon-

TABLE 6.1

Determinants of 1880 Republican Vote
and 1872 Democratic Z-Score, New York
(Multiple Regression)

| | Dependent variable | | | |
| | Republican President, 1880 | | Z-score, 1872 | |
Independent variable	0-order r	Beta weight	0-order r	Beta weight
% Yankee, 1855	.625	.484	.482	.276
% Foreign, 1870	−.274	−.215	−.548	−.341
% Catholic, 1890	−.099	.142	−.408	−.081
Farms per capita, 1870	.496	.129	.642	.112
Revivalism	.369	.114	.426	.257
Multiple R		.674		.731

struction, but it also organized support for civil service reform and a reduced tariff. When it met in convention, it nominated Horace Greeley for the presidency. Greeley, the former antislavery Whig and radical Republican, was a well-known protectionist, but many in the movement felt they needed the support of his New York *Tribune* if they were to have any hope of success. Consequently, the convention adopted no tariff plank (Alexander, 1969, vol. 3, pp. 281–85). In addition, Greeley was a teetotaler, and the Republicans responded to his nomination with a platform plank against "sumptuary legislation" (Odegard, 1966, p. 246).

The Democrats, seeing no hope of victory with a candidate of their own, accepted a coalition with the Liberals and accepted Greeley. The nomination of Greeley was hard for New York's wet Democrats to take, and it was particularly hard for the leaders of the party who had so often been the victims of his barbs in *Tribune* editorials (Alexander, 1969, vol. 3, p. 287). His presence on the Democratic ticket caused a deviation from the pattern that had already become traditional: he won the votes of many Republicans and induced even more Democrats to vote for Grant. The deviation of the 1872 vote is seen from the lower than usual correlations of the 1872 Republican vote with demographic variables (with proportion Yankee, $r = .61$ compared to .69 for 1868; with proportion foreign-born, $r = -.25$ compared to $-.45$ for 1868). The 1872 deviation was similar to the much greater one that would occur in 1896.

A deviant voting pattern can be accounted for by comparing its correlations with relevant variables to the correlations of previous elections with those same variables, but the differences will be masked by the fact that even when an election is deviant each party will normally have the same electoral base, so that only slight changes in the correlations will be evident. The direction and degree of an election's deviation from the traditional division between the parties can be measured directly, however, with Burnham's "pseudo Z-score," which measures the extent to which the vote in a given election in each county differs from the four elections immediately preceding.[1]

[1]The formula is
$$\frac{X_j - X.}{\sqrt{\sum_{i=1}^{4} (X_{j-i} - X.)^2}},$$
where X_j is the proportion in each county for a party in the deviating election, X_{j-i} are the proportions for the party in the four preceding elections, and $X.$ is the mean of the four preceding elections. The use of the pseudo-variance in the denominator gives more weight to a county that has been stable in the four preceding elections than to one in which the vote has fluctuated. See Burnham (1968, p. 10).

The 1872 Democratic Z-score, then, will be high where the Greeley vote was unexpectedly high. Its analysis shows that Republicans were most likely to vote for Greeley and Democrats least likely to abandon him in Yankee-settled, revivalist areas that had been strongly abolitionist (Table 6.1; the correlation of the Z-score with the 1852 Free Soil vote is .55). Although Greeley's platform was not closely related to the issues he had endorsed in previous decades, his following apparently remained similar. Moreover, although temperance was not a widely discussed issue in the campaign, his opinions probably influenced some voters.

The temperance question was the issue which most aroused the sentiments of the revivalist ethos in New York. The origin of the temperance movement and its relation to revivalism and the benevolent enterprise have already been discussed, as has the flurry of political activity over temperance in the 1850s. The temperance movement, like the crusade against slavery, grew out of revivalism. At the beginning, the movement's goal was to reform individuals, to persuade men to give up drinking of their own free will. Temperance revivals invited men to take a public pledge of abstinence. Consistent with revivalist principles, the preachers told those who drank that they were sinners, but that they could confess their sin, renounce it, and live a sinless existence. By 1850, however, the movement had taken a different direction, trying to control alcoholic consumption by legislation. Although temperance advocates had disagreed among themselves about whether legal coercion was appropriate, the Maine law inspired most of them to demand similar legislation in other states. New York was among the several states which, for brief periods, placed some restrictions on the sale of alcohol. The legislature adopted a local-option statute in 1845, but repealed it two years later. Then in 1853 the legislature passed a Maine law, but it was vetoed by Governor Horatio Seymour. The new legislature elected in 1854 at the height of the Know-Nothing campaign passed the law again in 1855. This time it was signed by Myron Clark, but it was later found unconstitutional (Griffin, 1960, pp. 129, 133–34, 229; Gusfield, 1963, p. 61; Krout, 1967, pp. 277–83).

But as the campaign against slavery increasingly absorbed the evangelicals' political energies, temperance proved to be a transient issue. In New York the movement for prohibition was quite literally overtaken by the Civil War: In 1861 the Legislature passed a prohibition amendment to the state constitution (it was approved by the Assembly a week before Fort Sumter was fired on), but it never got the second reading the following year which was necessary prior to its submission in a referendum (Colvin, 1926, p. 137).

After the war, agitation for control of the liquor trade was renewed. The movement identified itself with the antislavery movement and took much of its inspiration from the latter's success; many of its leaders were former abolitionists and were inspired by the same religious doctrine. The politicized prohibition movement took a very different course, but two aspects of the abolitionists' political experience had important effects on it. The first of these was at least implicit in the abolitionists' behavior, but the second was quite contrary to their intentions.

The first was the decision to make the movement political. Abolitionists hesitated to make that decision, for they believed that their campaign should succeed—indeed, could only succeed—by individual repentance and conversion. To begin to use political means implied the abandonment of that assumption. However, many abolitionists did not recognize this, for they were unrealistic in their expectations and believed that they could persuade slaveholders through politics, as they had attempted to persuade them through other means, to free their slaves peacefully.

Abolitionism probably had to become political to succeed: slavery was a sin whose principal victims were not its perpetrators, and the exploiters of slave labor would not willingly give it up. It became evident that the only way to free the slaves was to exert coercion over those who coerced them.

The case with alcohol was different, however. Its principal victims voluntarily accepted their condition. Although temperance rhetoric identified innocent wives and children as victims of the drunkard's sin, the movement's preachers primarily argued that those who drank were harming themselves. To deny the drunkard his drink by force of law, then, meant explicitly to deny him his freedom in the interest of what temperance advocates chose to define as his own good. Having practiced politics to achieve abolition, they adopted the assumption that coercion might be necessary to achieve freedom for others. But they failed to question the impropriety or recognize the distinction between slavery and drunkenness. Their activity was inconsistent with the tenets of revivalism which made them regard drinking as sinful, but they did not concern themselves with the contradiction inherent in the idea of compelling others to be free.

The second way in which the antislavery crusade prepared the way for prohibition's different course was in the outcome of the earlier campaign: legal reform turned out to be its only accomplishment. Even though slaves were freed, neither were they given the legal rights abolitionists demanded for them nor were their former masters converted. The crusade had been undertaken because abolitionists believed slavery to be an example of a more general evil—the denial of freedom, which was inconsistent with the will of God—and had accordingly advocated goals that went beyond change in the legal condition of the slave. But as the struggle continued, its goal came to be identified more narrowly and objectified in the fact of slavery and the demand for emancipation. Once emancipation was accomplished, many abolitionists (including even Garrison) believed that their work was ended. The campaign died with abolition, even though many of the evils which grew out of slavery remained.

This limitation of abolitionism to the goal of legal change had a heavy impact on the temperance movement after the war. The campaign against alcohol was pursued exclusively through politics (indeed, it had been moving in this direction during the flurry of activity after 1850), and became a campaign for legal prohibition. Though temperance advocates continued to preach and attempted to reform individuals, their principal effort was to make it legally impossible to sin by consuming alcohol. They identified the success of their crusade with the achievement of prohibition. Moreover, it was easier than it had been for abolitionists to maintain this narrow goal, because alcohol was consumed throughout the nation, and prohibitionists could achieve partial victories by legal change within their own states and localities.

The National Prohibition party was founded in Chicago in 1869, and its first convention reunited many abolitionists. Gerrit Smith wrote the convention's address, which began, "Slavery is gone, but drunkenness stays." Hoping to evoke the support of those who had opposed slavery because it violated God's law by depriving men of freedom, Smith went so far as to say that "the lot of the literal slave, of him whom others have enslaved, is indeed a hard one; nevertheless it is a paradise compared with the lot of him who has enslaved himself—especially of him who has enslaved himself to alcohol" (Colvin, 1926, pp. 69–75).

The Prohibition party regularly sought office in New York beginning in 1874 when its candidate for governor was Myron Clark. Only rarely did it get as much as 3% of the vote, but it achieved a steady, small percentage for over forty years. This vote was concentrated in rural, Protestant areas (the correlations of the 1884 presidential vote with farms per capita and proportion Catholic, 1890, are .46 and −.49). Support for Prohibition candidates was also related to support for abolition: the 1888 vote correlates .46 with the 1852 Free Soil vote. Not surprisingly, then, the Prohibition party vote was higher in revival counties (with the 1888 vote, $r = .20$); however, the direct effect of revivalism on the vote was generally small.

Prohibition continued to be agitated for in the legislature, and became important in some political campaigns. The Republican party attempted to maintain a delicate ambiguity on the issue, hoping not to alienate either supporters or opponents of prohibition: its 1883 state platform called for the submission of a state constitutional amendment "in regard to" the sale and manufacture of liquor. The Republican legislature passed high-license bills in 1887 and 1888, only to see them vetoed by Democratic Governor David B. Hill (Colvin, 1926, pp. 134–35; McSeveney, 1972, pp. 24, 142–47).

Unlike slavery, prohibition by itself was not a sufficiently important issue to secure revivalists' votes for independent candidates in any great degree. In the 1896 presidential election, however, prohibition combined with other symbols to bring a resurgence of revivalist voting. In that election the traditional partisan cleavage was even more sharply disrupted than it had been in 1872. The election brought disaster to the Democrats in New York. Responding to the depression which had begun during Cleveland's administration, large numbers of Democrats voted Republican: the vote for Bryan was almost ten percentage points smaller than for any Democratic presidential candidate since 1872.[2]

Republican gains were almost constant statewide: they do not correspond closely to any demographic differentiation among the state's counties (the correlation of the Republican Z-score with proportion foreign, 1890, is −.09; with farms per capita, 1890, −.13). However, Democratic losses do not correspond exactly to Republican gains. Those losses were partially compensated in some areas by the votes of those who had supported Populist or Prohibitionist candidates in the past (there was of course no independent Populist candidate in 1896, and the Prohibition vote fell by nearly two-thirds between 1892 and 1896; the correlations of the 1896 Democratic Z-score with the 1892 Prohibitionist and Populist votes are .40 and .39, respectively). Bryan's particular appeal, enabling him to hold on to Democrats and pick up third-party adherents, was localized in specific areas of the state. As Table 6.2 shows, they were the rural and revivalist areas.

Since the vote for Bryan was such a considerable deviation from the normal political loyalties of the time, it demands an explanation. Many attributes have been suggested as defining characteristics of populism in its many international manifestations, and most of these have been attributed to Populism in its late nineteenth-century

TABLE 6.2

Determinants of 1896 Democratic
Z-Score, New York
(Multiple Regression)

Independent variable	0-order r	Beta weight
% Yankee, 1855	.214	−.161
% Foreign, 1890	−.399	−.001
% Catholic, 1890	−.225	.082
Farms per capita, 1890	.510	.556
Revivalism	.383	.322
Multiple R	.595	

American version.[3] Of these, three are particularly important.

Populism has been viewed, first, as a revolt of the economically dispossessed against dominant economic institutions and local business elites (Gusfield, 1963, pp. 94–97; S. Parsons, 1973; Rogin, 1967, pp. 168–71, 180; Woodward, 1959, p. 63). In this interpretation, Populism was a radical movement representing the class demands of those who were hurt by the agricultural depression and an attempt to initiate fundamental changes in the structure of American society.

A second interpretation represents Populism as a revolt of the periphery against the center, a vehicle of protest for the attacks of the nation's "colonial" areas against its metropole (Burnham, 1970b, pp. 44–46, 52–53). Populism is interpreted as a protest against a status revolution in which urban areas and their immigrant inhabitants were overtaking the nation. The protest was thus a nostalgic evocation of a disappearing rural society (Hays, 1967, p. 174; Hofstadter, 1955, pp. 60–65).

Finally, Populism has been interpreted as a Protestant revival, in which William Jennings Bryan epitomized the belief that social problems were essentially religious, and that the traditional Protestant virtues were sufficient evidence of a man's worthiness to govern

[3]Populism, like revivalism and abolition, is an ambiguous term (see the essays in Ionescu and Gellner, 1969, especially those of Wiles, pp. 166–79, and Worsley, pp. 212–50).

As used here it is a proper noun, referring to the movement and party which grew up in the western United States in the 1890s and captured the Democratic party in 1896. Its significance in New York does not appear to have been the same as its significance in the west, however, as will be shown below.

(Hofstadter, 1948, p. 191; Jensen, 1971, pp. 275–79; Rogin, 1967, pp. 179–80). None of these interpretations necessarily excludes any of the others; in particular, the third has been seen by advocates of both the first two as an essential part of the very different Populisms they describe.

Whatever may explain Populism in the west, it is highly unlikely that the same explanation serves for New York. In New York, Populism was not a mass movement; if Populism itself (rather than the general orientations it symbolized) had any influence on the behavior of New Yorkers, that influence in most cases probably did not extend beyond a single day in November of 1896.

Bryan's appeal in New York was apparently not based on agrarian radicalism. The vote for the Populist party in preceding years had been concentrated not only in rural areas but also in areas where the Greenback party had won votes two decades earlier (the correlation of the 1892 Populist vote and the 1876 Greenback vote is .64). But despite Bryan's strength among those who had voted Populist, his support was much less closely related to the Greenback vote (with the Z-score, $r = .25$). The relation between the distributions of the votes in the 1896 and 1964 elections offers confirmation of the different explanations of Bryan's support in New York and in the west and south. As I will show below, the Populist states' preference for Goldwater in 1964 confirms the center-periphery explanation, but the revivalist areas of New York rejected Goldwater. The revolt against the metropole and the revivalist ethos seem to have been identified in the same candidate in 1896; they led in opposite directions in 1964.

It appears, instead, that it was Bryan's evangelicalism that appealed to New Yorkers of the revivalist orientation. It is true that the Tribune attacked his "Cross of Gold" speech as blasphemous and that many Protestant clergymen condemned him (McSeveney, 1972, pp. 181–82). But even though he did not support national prohibition until 1910, he epitomized the spirit of the temperance movement and he used a religious rhetoric in which he compared himself to Biblical figures and showed no hesitation about identifying righteousness and sin (Gusfield, 1963, p. 125; Jensen, 1971, pp. 277–79). The image he projected enabled him to attract voters in revivalist counties. In fact, the independent effect of revivalism on the Democratic Z-score is larger than its effect on most other variables representing events influenced by the ethos. As Table 6.2 shows, this effect is not explained either by ruralism or earlier New England settlement. The effect of New England settlement, moreover, is actually negative when controls are introduced. The results in Table 6.2 compare interestingly to those in Table 4.3 for the Liberty party votes and the 1846 suffrage referendum. Abolitionism was in some cases more closely related to Yankee settlement than to revivalism. Events in the later nineteenth century, however, show that revivalism was more responsible than Yankee settlement for the institutionalization of the ethos.

Moreover, a Yankee culture was a more important determinant of the ethos than the presence of New England natives. The proportion Yankee of the 1855 population is a much better predictor of every manifestation of the revivalist ethos than the proportion Yankee of the 1870 population[4] (for example, the correlation of proportion Yankee, 1870, with the 1872 Democratic Z-score is .34; with the 1896 Democratic Z-score, .14). The influence of New England origins on voting during the last half of the nineteenth century depended not on the backgrounds of individuals but on the ethos of the community.

The vote for Bryan is important, because most of the evidence that revivalism created an enduring political ethos is from voting behavior normally associated with Republicanism. Since the Democrats lost heavily in almost every county in 1896—there were only five counties in which Bryan received a higher proportion of the votes than Cleveland had in 1892—it is likely that few if any Republicans supported him, even in revivalist areas. If this is so, the Bryan vote offers some of the strongest evidence that the phenomenon is a common cultural condition that affected whole areas, for it apparently restrained Democrats from abandoning the party when it presented them with a new kind of candidate, whereas their copartisans in other parts of the state were not so restrained.[5]

The Democrats sustained losses in 1896 from which they only partially recovered during the next several years. Before 1896 the party was competitive; it won five of the nine presidential elections between 1860 and 1892, and six of the fifteen gubernatorial elections. But after the 1896 election it became a permanent minority: the only presidential election carried by a Democrat from then until 1928 was that of 1912, in which Taft and Roosevelt divided the usual Republican majority, and Wilson won the state's electoral votes with only 41% of the popular vote. Until the rise of Al Smith, the Democrats did almost as badly in gubernatorial elections. The 1896

[4]The 1870 census reports, for New York, the number in each county born in Connecticut, Massachusetts, and Vermont, and these form the basis of what is referred to here as the 1870 proportion Yankee. The three adjacent states supplied 85% of the New England-born population of 1870, so this measure is almost certainly very close to the actual proportion.

[5]Burnham (1970b, pp. 46–50) shows that similar areas of Pennsylvania also remained Democratic in 1896 to a much greater degree than the rest of the state.

election was not a realigning one, however. The two parties' areas of relative strength in the state were not permanently changed. The geographical distribution of the 1896 vote itself was quite different from the previous pattern (with the 1892 election, Democratic, $r = .66$). But though for many years the Democratic total remained lower than it had been, the party's presidential vote even in the years in which Bryan ran again was more closely associated with the 1892 vote than with that of 1896.

Prohibition as an issue grew in importance over these years, however, and continued to provide an outlet through which the revivalist ethos expressed itself. The Prohibition party did not benefit from this increased importance; its fortunes declined as other organizations, notably the Anti-Saloon League, took up the fight for prohibition. Between 1900 and the ratification of the prohibition amendment in 1919, the Anti-Saloon League pursued a different strategy: it endorsed sympathetic candidates in the major parties. A definitive test of the League's effectiveness in New York is not possible, but it is likely that the League was an important factor in some elections; for example, in 1906 thirty-six assemblymen who were opposed for reelection because they had supported local option received League support, and all were elected (Odegard, 1966, pp. 97–98). There were apparently no statewide elections in which prohibition was clearly a deciding issue, however, until after the eighteenth amendment was enacted.

The vote for Prohibition party candidates during this period fell to extremely low levels, seldom more than 1.5%. Its strength continued to be located in the same areas of the state, the rural, revivalist areas (the 1908 and 1912 votes for Prohibition candidates for president correlate .28 and .35 with revivalism). But it was so small that, by itself, it cannot be considered very strong evidence that the revivalist ethos significantly influenced the voting behavior of these areas.

But later evidence shows that the revivalist ethos continued to have an effect. After the ratification of the eighteenth amendment to the Constitution, referenda on the amendment were presented to New York voters in 1926 and 1933.[6] In both, New Yorkers overwhelmingly called for its repeal. But even though far more people

---

[6]The 1926 referendum called on the state to request that Congress modify the Volstead Act so that each state could decide what beverages were alcoholic. The 1933 referendum (like the Ohio 1933 referendum referred to below) was actually a vote for delegates to a convention to consider ratification of the twenty-first amendment. Both were overwhelmingly approved in New York, the first with 75% in favor and the second with 88% in favor.

supported prohibition in the referenda than had voted for any Prohibition candidate, support came from much the same areas. Both referenda correlate very closely with the Prohibition vote in the 1912 presidential election (in each case, $r = -.74$). In fact, the areas of support for prohibition remained similar for forty years: the vote for the Prohibitionist in the 1888 election correlates $-.65$ with the 1926 referendum and $-.64$ with the one in 1933.[7]

During this time support for prohibition became much more restricted to rural areas than it had previously been. As Table 6.3 shows, the rural nature of counties was by far the most important determinant of support for prohibition in 1933. Nevertheless, revivalism still contributed to dry sentiment.

TABLE 6.3

Determinants of Support for
Repeal of Prohibition, New York, 1933
(Multiple Regression)

Independent variable	0-order r	Beta weight
% Yankee, 1855	−.414	−.104
% Foreign, 1930	.757	.196
% Catholic, 1936	.511	.238
Farms per capita, 1930	−.883	−.531
Revivalism	−.455	−.173
Multiple R	.928	

In the absence of statewide campaigns fought over prohibition, the ethos seems to have been dormant from 1896 until the 1920s. During this period, especially after about 1912, the lines of cleavage that would dominate the state's politics for several decades were beginning to be established. The salient conflicts in the state became organized on urban–rural lines; the polarization that had decreased following the election of 1896 reappeared and became more intense than it had been.

This realignment did not depend on the revivalist ethos, but it provides the background to the occasional resurgences of the ethos. It occurred from about 1918 to 1936, but it was not really the gradual change that the long time period appears to indicate. Rather, it

[7]The correlations are negative because a "yes" vote on the referenda was a vote against prohibition.

occurred in two discrete but fairly abrupt stages, the first affecting voting for state offices and the second affecting voting for the presidency.

The Democratic party in New York anticipated the reorientation of the national party by several years with its nomination of Al Smith for governor in 1918 (and in every successive biennial election through 1926; he won all these contests except in 1920). Smith's gubernatorial canvasses are much more closely related to the post-New Deal presidential votes than to those before 1928 (the 1920 gubernatorial vote correlates .54 with the 1920 presidential vote, and .91 with that in 1932).

Figure 6.1 reveals the temporal sequence of the realignment, represented by the first principal component of a factor analysis of presidential and gubernatorial votes between 1904 and 1968. The figure shows a sharp, steady increase in Democratic gubernatorial election loadings from 1918 to 1926, followed by a parallel increase in presidential election loadings from 1924 to 1936, with a slight interruption in 1932 (and with corresponding decreases in the Republican loadings).[8] With a few exceptions, this realignment has remained the basis of division of the electorate since 1936. Most of the fluctuations, moreover, have been within a fairly narrow range compared to the differences between elections before 1920 and those after 1936.

Table 6.4 shows the demographic determinants of the realignment. Voters in urban, foreign-settled, and Catholic areas turned to the Democrats much more strongly than they had in the past.[9] The negligible direct effect of depression unemployment demonstrates that the "New Deal" realignment was not to any great degree a response to the New Deal (just as the time series in Figure 6.1 shows that old party affiliations had been disrupted long before the depression began), and can probably more appropriately be called the "Al Smith realignment."

Table 6.4 also shows some political correlates of the realignment. Dissatisfaction with the earlier structure of the two national parties was evident before voting patterns changed, as is shown by the

[8]The lack of symmetry between Republican and Democratic loadings in several years is explained by unusually large votes for third-party candidates who attracted more voters from one party than from the other. Of these, only that in 1930 is relevant to the present discussion, and it receives further attention below.

[9]MacRae and Meldrum (1960, p. 675) find that Catholicism was not an important determinant of the New Deal realignment in Illinois; but in New York, where the realignment was due in great degree to the person of Al Smith, religion evidently played a more important part.

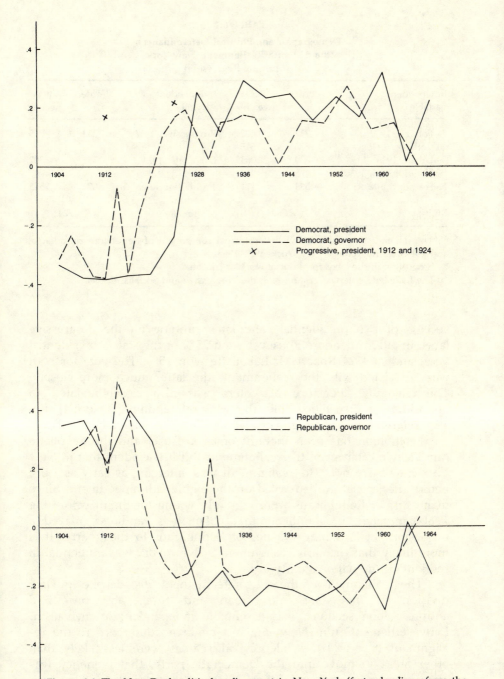

Figure 6.1 The New Deal political realignment in New York (factor loadings from the first principal component of election returns, 1904–1968).

TABLE 6.4
Demographic and Political Determinants of
the Al Smith Realignment, New York[a]
(Multiple Regression)

Independent variable	0-order r	Beta weight	Independent variable	0-order r	Beta weight
% Foreign, 1930	.717	.602	Progressive, 1912	.259	−.005
% Catholic, 1936	.675	.515			
% Urban, 1930	.630	.063	LaFollette, 1924[c]	.581	.302
% Unemployed, 1930[b]	.475	−.017			
Farms per capita, 1930	−.599	.111	Prohibition refer-endum, 1933	.679	.515
Multiple R		.862	Mutiple R		.724

[a]The dependent variable is the first principal component of Republican presidential and gubernatorial returns, New York, 1904–1968.
[b]Proportion of the labor force out of work or laid off.
[c]The LaFollette vote was cast on both the Progressive and Socialist tickets.

success of two presidential candidates running on the Progressive label: in 1912, Theodore Roosevelt won 25% of the state's presidential vote, and in 1924 Robert M. LaFollette won 15%. The vote for both was associated with the realignment, the latter much more closely. The changing allegiance of voters was also closely related to opposition to prohibition (like the 1933 referendum [Table 6.4], the 1926 referendum has a high correlation, .76, with the realignment).

Prohibition has been thought of as a cause, and the LaFollette candidacy a catalyst, of the realignment. But it is evident that in New York they were not. The realignment was emerging as early as 1918, before the legislature had voted on the eighteenth amendment. Since many former Republicans were regularly voting for Smith before the 1924 campaign, it is unlikely that LaFollette's candidacy played a major part in loosening the ties of Republicans to their party. It is more likely that the early realignment in New York was influential in reorienting the national party.

The realignment of the electorate in the 1920s, despite its clear division of the state into urban and rural, and pro- and antiprohibition sections, was essentially independent of revivalism. Early settlement from New England made no difference to the realignment ($r = -.01$). While revivalist areas were less likely than other areas to move into the Democratic party, that tendency was almost entirely due to other factors (the correlation between revivalism and the realignment is −.20, but when revivalism is added to the variables in the left panel of Table 6.4 in a multiple regression equation, its coefficient is only −.04).

That the ethos remained important in the mid-twentieth century is evident, however, from the second principal component of the same factor analysis. Factor analysis yields several components, but in the analysis of election returns over a period of time spanning a realignment, there is usually a single dominant component and several others of considerably smaller magnitude. For the 1904–1968 period in New York, the second principal component is more than half as large as the first, and is also worth investigating. The temporal sequence of this second component is shown in Figure 6.2 (for convenience of presentation, only Republican loadings are shown, although the factor analysis includes all the parties and elections presented in Figure 6.1). The elections which stand out are those of the period 1922–1936 and 1964; most in the first set have high positive loadings, and 1930 and 1964 have high negative loadings.

The high positive values for the presidential elections between 1928 and 1936 indicate a greater than expected Republican vote in the counties that load positively on the component and a lower than

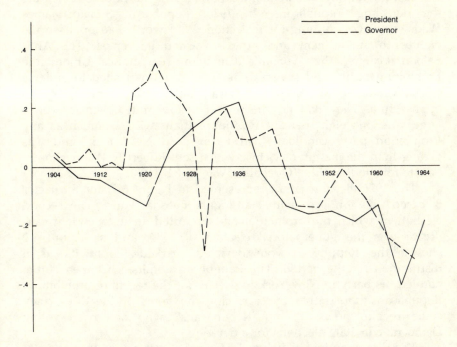

Figure 6.2 Factor loadings from the second principal component of election returns, New York, 1904–1968 (loadings for Republican vote only).

expected Republican vote in the counties that load negatively. The factor is closely related to the two referenda on prohibition ($r = -.59$ and $-.60$); it thus represents a fear of and then a repudiation of the Democrats' wet policy. Even though the issue had been settled by 1936, there remained resistance to the man whose election in 1932 had settled it.

It must be remembered that this factor is orthogonal to the first, so that the effects of the New Deal realignment have been controlled for. Despite the close relationship between the New Deal realignment and prohibition sentiment, there remains in the voting of the period a large residual also explained by prohibition.

In two campaigns an independent candidate running exclusively to defend prohibition won many usually Republican votes. The Anti-Saloon League had been opposed in principle to supporting independent one-issue candidates before the passage of the prohibition amendment; instead it endorsed major-party (usually Republican) candidates who supported its cause. After the amendment was in effect and began to come under attack, however, the Republican party moved toward repeal, and the prohibition forces considered running independent candidates in the hope of defeating the defecting Republicans. In 1926, Republican Senator James Wadsworth was running for reelection. Wadsworth had opposed the eighteenth amendment and now advocated its repeal. The Anti-Saloon League, the Women's Christian Temperance Union, the Prohibition party, and several other organizations united to endorse F. W. Cristman, a former Republican state senator and a dry, to oppose him. They had no illusions of victory, but Cristman won a large vote; his eight percent was more than twice as much as any Prohibition party candidate had received in New York, and was greater than the margin of victory which sent Robert F. Wagner to the Senate for the first time (Odegard, 1966, pp. 101–03).

The 1926 election is not represented in Figure 6.2, for the factor is based only on presidential and gubernatorial votes. The second election in which the prohibitionists supported an independent candidate was the gubernatorial election of 1930, and as Figure 6.2 shows, the Republican vote deviated markedly from its usual distribution for the period. The Republican nominee, Charles Tuttle, had led his party in New York to declare for the repeal of prohibition. Republicans hoped that by sacrificing the votes of the dries, they could regain the "Al Smith Republicans" who had been voting Democratic in state elections for a decade.

The dries nominated Robert P. Carroll. Once again, they did not expect to win, but they hoped that the Carroll vote would defeat

Tuttle and show the national Republican party that it could not abandon prohibition (*The New York Times*, November 2, 1930, p. 19; November 5, 1930, pp. 1–2). This time, however, the dries could not even claim responsibility for a Republican defeat: Roosevelt, running for reelection, won by a record margin with 56% of the vote, so Carroll's 6% had no effect on the outcome.

The vote for the dry candidates in these two elections came from much the same places (the correlation between them is .76), the counties that had customarily supported prohibition. As Table 6.5 shows, their vote was rural and (especially in 1926) concentrated in revivalist counties. The defection of dries deprived the Republican party of much of the support it received in other state elections during this period. Its vote in the 1930 election, for example, has a very low correlation with all other Republican gubernatorial votes between 1920 and 1942 (with 1928, $r = .45$), even though each of those votes has a correlation of at least .90 with almost all of the others. The Republican vote was much more urban than usual. The party failed, however, to recapture the Democratic defectors, then or later, and as Figure 6.1 shows, the Al Smith realignment became permanent.

The election of 1964 also deviated from the pattern established by the Al Smith and New Deal elections. Johnson won 69% of New York's popular vote (Roosevelt in his best year, 1936, had won 59%). Democratic gains were not uniform throughout the state, however (with 1960, $r = .79$), but were greatest in traditionally Republican areas where on earlier occasions revivalism had influenced political

TABLE 6.5

Determinants of Support for Prohibition Candadates,
New York, 1926 and 1930
(Multiple Regression)

| | Dependent variable | | | |
| | Senate, 1926 | | Governor, 1930 | |
Independent variable	0-order r	Beta weight	0-order r	Beta weight
% Yankee, 1855	.466	.247	.394	.127
% Foreign, 1930	−.685	−.267	−.618	−.118
% Catholic, 1936	−.395	−.290	−.393	−.184
Farms per capita, 1930	.715	.188	.740	.455
Revivalism	.537	.287	.423	.185
Multiple R	.837		.781	

preferences. The defection of these areas represented a reaction against Goldwater apparently based on his opposition to the protection of the civil rights of blacks. Burnham has shown the remarkably close relationship between the 1964 Z-score and the 1860 referendum on black suffrage (Burnham, 1968, pp. 21–23). The Z-score is also related to revivalism ($r = .31$). Goldwater's nomination and the Republican convention's rejection of the proposed civil rights plank evidently evoked the revivalist ethos's condemnation of unequal treatment of blacks, the issue which had first made the ethos politically salient.

The relation between support for Bryan and support for Goldwater in different parts of the country confirms that the interpretation of Populism was different in the northeast than in the rest of the country. Support for Goldwater (measured as a deviation from traditional Republicanism) was *positively* related to support for Bryan in 1896 in the nation at large. Burnham discusses the functional similarities between the Republican convention in 1964 and the Democratic convention in 1896: in both conventions, the nation's periphery revolted against its center (the northeast) which traditionally controlled the nomination; in each case, the strategy for constructing a coalition excluded the northeast; and in each case, massive dislocations from traditional voting behavior in the northeast prevented the victory of those seeking to build a new coalition. "The Gold standard and a civil-rights plank may have little enough in common on the overt level, but they may share a partial common identity as stalking horses for a major confrontation between regional power interests and political subcultures" (Burnham, 1968, p. 8).

This common identity is indeed only partial, however. Though civil rights may have represented an imposition by the northeastern metropole to the formerly Populist states of the periphery, it represented to some New Yorkers an affirmation of the revivalist ethos. Those parts of the northeast which had identified with Bryan rejected Goldwater, for his stand on civil rights violated the ethos which had created a favorable response to Bryan.

Burnham regards the 1964 election as representing a "curious timelessness," in which sentiments not prominent in national politics since the previous century were drawn upon (Burnham, 1968, p. 40).[10] Examination of New York voting, however, shows that the same cultural tradition which affected the 1964 election was important

[10]Although I believe Burnham underestimates the influence of the phenomenon he discusses, this article has been extremely useful to my understanding of New York voting behavior.

in determining the results of elections at the beginning of the New Deal, and during the time of Bryan, as well. Anti-Democratic deviations in the 1928–1936 presidential elections and anti-Republican deviations in 1964 constitute a single dimension, as the second component of the factor analysis reveals. The areas that were particularly strong in the rejection of Goldwater were equally strong in rejection of Smith and of Roosevelt in his first two presidential elections.

The component demonstrates the persistence of the revivalist ethos into the twentieth century. Based on voting between 1904 and 1968, it shows a remarkably close correlation to the 1860 suffrage referendum (.80!). It is also related to early New England settlement ($r = .65$) and to revivalism ($r = .47$). As Table 6.6 shows, the component is not determined by contemporary ethnic or religious differentiation; it is related to rural–urban differences, but these are to some extent explained by nineteenth century settlement and revivalism. The component is more closely related to proportion foreign-born than to proportion urban (1930, $r = -.23$); it is also negatively related to population growth (with increase between 1910 and 1930, $r = -.35$). The persistence of the ethos depends on the joint effects of the conditions which brought it into existence and the stability of the areas in which it has survived.

TABLE 6.6

Determinants of the Persistence of Revivalism and of Support for Parimutuel Betting, 1939, New York (Multiple Regression)

	Dependent variable			
	Revivalism, twentieth century[a]		Parimutuel betting, 1939	
Independent variable	0-order r	Beta weight	0-order r	Beta weight
% Yankee, 1855	.654	.436	−.523	−.220
% Foreign, 1930	−.405	.023	.700	.169
% Catholic, 1936	.035	.063	.360	.189
Farms per capita, 1930	.516	.307	−.793	−.388
Revivalism	.466	.202	−.580	−.309
Multiple R	.728		.888	

[a]The dependent variable is the second principal component of a factor analysis of Republican presidential and gubernatorial votes, 1904–1968.

As a political phenomenon, moreover, the factor represents what is *common* to support for prohibition around 1930 and the racial issue in 1964: their relation to revivalism. The factor (an unanticipated statistical construct derived directly from party voting statistics and thus not determined either by revivalism or by prohibition) is more closely related to revivalism than is either the vote on the prohibition amendment and for dry candidates or the partisan deviation of 1964. While revivalism only partly explains each of these latter phenomena, it explains their common elements more completely.

Since the 1930s, New Yorkers have voted on several referenda liberalizing the constitution's provisions on gambling, and these offer additional evidence for the persistence of the ethos. The amendments have allowed parimutuel betting (1939), bingo by local option (1957), and the establishment of a state lottery (1966). All were opposed in revivalist areas. They demonstrate the joint importance of the conditions which brought the ethos into existence and the conditions which enable it to survive. The analysis of the 1939 referendum in Table 6.6 shows this in particularly clear relief. It was opposed in areas of Yankee heritage and revivalist tradition which had remained rural and free of immigration in the intervening century. The ethos has survived where the group maintaining it has been insulated against the cultural change that would result from changing economic conditions or the assimilation of culturally distinct groups.

All the gambling referenda are also closely related to normal partisanship: Republicans voted against them much more than Democrats, and party vote is in general a much better predictor than any demographic characteristics, either contemporary or from the nineteenth century. However, even when party vote is controlled, there is still a strong independent effect of revivalism (controlling for Democratic vote in 1936, the regression coefficient of revivalism on the 1939 referendum is $-.35$). Gambling, while never the object of an active crusade as drinking had been, was frequently associated with it in temperance propaganda for over a century (Griffin, 1960, p. 105). The revivalist ethos led voters to oppose the state's attempts to legalize it.

There is thus a clear continuity in New York's political behavior from the 1840s until at least 1964. The continuity is not perfect: it is interrupted, and the tradition that has been maintained is not relevant to the political issues of every election. The tradition becomes important on those occasions when issues defined as personal and spiritual issues in the revivals of the early nineteenth century assume political importance. Those revivals imposed upon converts the duty to convert others to their way of life, by legislation, if not by persuasion.

But these issues have a different meaning than they had when the revivalist ethos originated. The ethos has survived in communities where ruralness and stability permit traditions to be preserved; because of those same characteristics, however, the impulses those communities express through politics are not the same impulses that they expressed in the early nineteenth century when they were still dynamic and expanding. If revivalists respond to some of the same symbols that their ancestors responded to, they give those symbols different meanings and have done so since soon after the Civil War.

In preserving a culture which values voluntarism and independence, rural communities have long found themselves threatened by the rise of industrialism. Their values and their security have been threatened by the country's economic growth and the changed social circumstances it has brought in its wake. When they feared a decline in status, they took temperance as the symbol of their thrift and abstinence in contrast to what they regarded as the laziness and profligacy of urbanites, particularly the immigrants who formed the bulk of the industrial labor force. By imposing prohibition on the rest of the country, they could achieve public recognition that their values and practices were preferable to those of the groups that threatened them (Gusfield, 1963, pp. 3–11 and passim; Hofstadter, 1955, pp. 288–93).

As prohibition came to represent the values and status of rural Protestants, it ceased to represent what temperance had meant to the earlier revivalists: one among many expressions of the belief that man, being free, must choose to exercise his faculties for the glory of God. Slavery could only have been abolished by coercing slaveholders, but in coercing them abolitionists could achieve freedom for the enslaved. In contrast, it was in principle possible to win drinkers by persuasion, and to win them by persuasion would have been more in keeping with the revivalist understanding of the nature of man. The fact that prohibitionists opted exclusively for a coercive solution demonstrates that temperance no longer symbolized the liberation of men from sin so that they might freely will their salvation. Instead, it symbolized the control of social values by one group in society.

So the dynamism of the revivalist ethos in dynamic post-frontier communities gave way to preservatism and reactiveness. The use of such a symbol as a means of social control over another group does not imply that it was used hypocritically. On the contrary, prohibition was an effective symbol only because it was believed in. Those who accepted the revivalist ethos perceived their activity in the same way their ancestors had: they thought that they were doing good, and that coercion was in the best interests of the coerced. But the stability which enabled revivalist communities to preserve the ethos also led them to use it in a different way.

It may seem paradoxical that I find in these later manifestations of revivalism an expression of status politics, when I have explicitly denied that status politics explains the relation of the revivals to abolitionism. But neither the social conditions of revivalist communities in the early nineteenth century nor the symbol they used fit the status-politics explanation. Revival communities were still expanding before the Civil War, and did not feel threatened by industrialism and urbanization. Even if they had, opposition to slavery would not have been an appropriate symbol to assert their status, because it did not exemplify the contrast. With the end of the nineteenth century social conditions had changed, rural Protestantism was in retreat, and the politics of prohibition which revivalists chose to support did represent their culture in contrast to the culture which seemed to be superseding it. To the extent that prohibition implied nativism, they, unlike their ancestors, were nativist. The new, coercive politics, then, grew out of revivalism but departed markedly from the principle that had inspired its politicization in the first place.

The revivalist ethos outlasted the Civil War in Ohio as well. But if the past occurrence of revivals had a stronger and more consistent effect on voting behavior in Ohio than in New York, it produced political patterns even farther removed from those which the revivalist belief system had initially inspired. Revivalism became Republicanism: for seven decades Republican support was distinctively high in counties with a revivalist history. This distinctiveness persisted despite the considerable growth in many of those counties and the change in their economy and population composition. But with the depression and the New Deal, many revivalist counties moved to the Democratic party, and past revivalism was no longer an important determinant of political differences.

As the previous chapter shows, the Republican party of Ohio was more successful than that of New York at incorporating abolitionists or, more accurately, the abolitionists were more effective in dominating the emerging Republican organization, of which they were the principal organizers. However, in the process the Ohio Republicans were also more ready to compromise the principles they had espoused as abolitionists. Ohio's abolitionist voters also became faithful supporters of the Republican party.

After the war ended, the political loyalties that had been established dominated the partisan cleavage so effectively that current politics was rarely able to alter that cleavage. Whitlock (1914) amusingly describes the political sentiments apprehended by a boy growing up in Ohio in the decades after the war:

> In such an atmosphere as that in the Ohio of those days it was natural to be a Republican; it was more than that, it was inevitable that one should be a Republican; it was not a matter of intellectual choice, it was a process of biological selection. The Republican party was not a faction, not a group, not a wing, it was an institution. . . . It was a fundamental and self-evident thing, like life, and liberty, and the pursuit of happiness, or like the flag, or the federal judiciary. It was elemental, like gravity, the sun, the stars, and the ocean. It was merely a synonym for patriotism, another name for the nation. One became, in Urbana and in Ohio for many years, a Republican just as the Eskimo dons fur clothes. It was inconceivable that any self-respecting person should be a Democrat. There were, perhaps, Democrats in Lighttown; but then, there were rebels in Alabama, and in the Ku-Klux Klan. (p. 27)

He goes on to describe the reunions of the 66th regiment, when townspeople were reminded that "the Republican Party had saved the Union, won liberty for all men, and there was nothing left for the patriotic to do but to extol that party, and to see to it that its members held office under the government" (p. 28).

Though Whitlock is presenting a child's perception, the stability—not to say stagnation—of electoral politics in Ohio for seventy years suggests that party loyalty was equally a matter of convention for voters. From the time the Republican party first contested offices in 1855 until 1910, both the size and the geographical distribution of the two parties' votes were virtually unchanged: Republicans won every presidential election, and twenty-one of the twenty-eight gubernatorial elections, but only rarely received more than 55% of the popular vote. The areas supporting each party also remained the same: the correlation is .79 between the Republican presidential votes in 1860 and 1908, a typical pair. With a few exceptions (notably the three-way contests of 1912 and 1924 and the religion- and prohibition-dominated election of 1928), elections up to 1932 displayed the same geographical distribution (between 1860 and 1932, $r = .69$). Elections such as those of 1872 and 1896 which brought large-scale shifts in the voting patterns of New York and other states brought virtually no change in Ohio. Such tremendous regularity implies that current political concerns rarely if ever affected the vote. What Fenton describes as the "issueless politics" (Fenton, 1966, p. 117) of Ohio in the 1950s appears to have prevailed since the last third of the nineteenth century.

Nor was this stability affected by the industrialization and urbanization of some parts of the state, accompanied as it was by considerable changes in population composition. The Western Reserve had been Ohio's hotbed of both revivalism and abolitionism, and it was in the part of the Reserve that bordered Lake Erie and its neighboring counties that most of this development was concentrated. Revivalist counties grew faster than other counties (revivalism correlates .34 with population growth between 1890 and 1910, and .46 with population growth between 1910 and 1930; proportion Yankee correlates .27 with both these variables). Since internal migration in the eastern United States had dwindled by this time, most of the new inhabitants were foreign immigrants, and the population did not create newly settled farming areas, but cities. The influx of new residents changed the composition of revivalist counties: by 1910, they were more urban ($r = .25$) and contained more foreign-born ($r = .46$ than the state as a whole. The revivalist counties did not remain homogeneous and rural as they did in New York. But they nevertheless remained Republican.

Throughout the last part of the nineteenth century, the effect of revivalism on the Republican vote was large and stable. Republican strength was concentrated not only in revivalist areas, but also in nonfarm areas with large foreign-born populations but few Catholics. Table 6.7 shows those relations for several election years; relations in the omitted years (except, as noted, 1912, 1924, and 1928) show only slight differences. It is striking that the Republican vote is concentrated in counties with foreign-born populations but not in those with Catholic populations, since the two are highly correlated (for 1890, $r = .73$). Evidently the Democrats monopolized the Catholic vote while the Republicans won the votes of other foreigners and of the native voters in the (largely urban) foreign-settled counties.

TABLE 6.7

Determinants of Republican Presidential Vote, Ohio
(Multiple Regression)

Independent variable	\multicolumn{2}{c}{Dependent variable}				

	1868		1888		1932	
Independent variable	0-order r	Beta weight	0-order r	Beta weight	0-order r	Beta weight
% Foreign[a]	−.022	.006	−.070	.077	.167	.210
% Catholic[b]	−.174	−.289	−.281	−.468	−.319	−.535
Farms per capita[a]	−.118	−.247	−.007	−.214	−.193	−.204
Revivalism	.315	.348	.219	.217	.351	.237
Multiple R	.435		.419		.573	

[a]The independent variables are for 1870, 1890, and 1930, respectively.
[b]For 1868 and 1888, the variable is % Catholic, 1890; for 1932, % Catholic, 1936.

The effect of revivalism remained fairly constant up until 1932, despite the urbanization and increasing concentration of foreign, non-Catholic voters in revival counties. The persistence of the effect of revivalism is particularly striking in light of the changing effects of other variables. For example, the coefficient of proportion foreign-born increased from .077 in 1888 to .210 in 1932 (although these two electoral variables correlate .82). The tradition of Republicanism created by revivalism was resistant to demographic changes in the counties that had experienced it. The near invariance in the effect of revivalism demonstrates that the ethos had been transmuted into loyalty to a particular party. The effect of revivalism in Ohio after the Civil War was to create party loyalties which were immutable even when issues related to the original belief system became politically salient.

The issue which most often evoked revivalist voting in New York was prohibition. In Ohio the fight over prohibition was even more intense. Like New York, Ohio had briefly experimented with statutory control of the liquor trade before the Civil War. The Democratic legislature elected in 1853 hoped to pacify rural temperance sentiment by passing a law forbidding the consumption of alcohol on the premises where it was purchased. But both the law and its enforcement were very weak. Despite continued agitation, the move for prohibition waned in Ohio until after the Civil War as it did in New York (Roseboom, 1944, pp. 224–25).

When it revived, Ohio was one of the centers of the nationwide campaign. It was one of the first three states where the Prohibition party was organized and the first where an independent prohibition ticket ran for office (in an 1869 municipal election in Cleveland). It was the home of two of the campaign's leading organizations: the Women's Christian Temperance Union founded in Hillsboro in 1873, and the Anti-Saloon League in Oberlin in 1893. The Anti-Saloon League maintained its national headquarters at Westerville. These two organizations, together with the Prohibition party, were the leaders of the struggle for prohibition. They were often at odds, however: the Anti-Saloon League and the Prohibition party had opposite strategies. The Women's Christian Temperance Union occupied an intermediate position, closer to the Prohibition party for a period but later working more closely with the Anti-Saloon League (Colvin, 1926, pp. 65–67; Dohn, 1959, pp. 132–33; Gusfield, 1963, pp. 85–86; Odegard, 1966, pp. 3–5).

Throughout the more than fifty years that prohibition was an issue, Ohio's voters had numerous opportunities to vote on it. From 1874 to the repeal of the twenty-first amendment in 1933, referenda relating to the liquor traffic were submitted to voters with great frequency. The wording of the question varied: some called for the regulation of the liquor trade through taxation; some called for home rule; others for outright prohibition. After statewide prohibition was accepted in 1918, measures to strengthen or weaken it (and, ultimately, in 1933, to repeal it) were also submitted.

Through that half century, prohibition was supported by rural, Protestant voters, as in New York. But the relation between revivalism and support for prohibition was inconsistent. Though at some points prohibition was a vehicle through which revivalists endorsed symbols related to their ethos, there were many other elections in which prohibition was clearly an issue, but in which revivalist areas were not disproportionately influenced. On the whole, the persistence of revivalism through prohibition was less consistent—and therefore less important—than its persistence through traditional party loyalties.

There were two important differences between New York and Ohio which altered the relation of revivalism to prohibition: first, the contrast between revivalist and nonrevivalist areas in Ohio was not as extreme as in New York: though Yankees and southerners had had polar positions on slavery, both groups were native and Protestant. The culture of an area and its response to mobilizing events interact in the formation of an ethos. Since in Ohio a cultural base existed for support of prohibition in both revivalist and nonrevivalist areas, the occurrence of revivals did not make as much of a difference to prohibition sentiment as it did in New York.

Second, as the state's demographic composition changed, so did the location of support for prohibition. While the areas of revivalism were the most rapidly growing and urbanizing parts of the state, the southern-settled areas remained relatively stable. The size of the southern-born 1870 population is negatively correlated with later population growth ($r = -.25$ both for growth between 1890 and 1910 and between 1910 and 1930) and urbanization (with percentage urban, 1910, $r = -.14$). The urbanizing areas became less favorable to prohibition, so the 1883 referendum correlated only .33 with the vote to retain the Eighteenth Amendment fifty years later. This represented a much lower degree of continuity over that time span than was found in New York.

In its early years as a political issue, prohibition did not polarize the state as it would later. Table 6.8 shows the determinants of the vote for prohibition in 1883. While support was concentrated in rural areas, among Protestants and Republicans, the relationships later became stronger, as they did in New York.[11] As the table shows, re-

TABLE 6.8

Determinants of Support for Prohibition and
for Prohibition Presidential Candidates, Ohio
(Multiple Regression)

| | Dependent variable | | | | | |
| | Prohibition referendum, 1883 | | Prohibition President, 1884 | | Prohibition President, 1908 | |
Independent variable	0-order r	Beta weight	0-order r	Beta weight	0-order r	Beta weight
% Foreign[a]	−.210	.243	−.058	.192	−.076	−.126
% Catholic, 1890	−.410	−.482	−.241	−.203	−.346	−.374
Farms per capita[a]	.311	.193	.343	.359	.075	−.140
Revivalism	.086	.049	.440	.407	.299	.352
Multiple R	.459		.583		.483	

[a]For 1883 and 1884 the independent variables are for 1890; for 1908 the independent variables are farms per capita, 1910 and percentage foreign white, 1910.

vivalism had a negligible effect on the vote.

The Prohibition party ran candidates for president and governor in nearly every election from 1869 to 1916 and again in 1928 and 1932. As Table 6.8 shows, revivalism had a large and consistent effect on the vote for the Prohibition party. However, the vote for that party is not an adequate indicator of support for prohibition in Ohio, because it remained extremely small. The best showing made in Ohio by a Prohibition candidate was that of John B. Helwig who, running for governor in 1889, received 3.4% of the popular vote. The outcome of the 1883 referendum shows that support for prohibition was much more widespread: it was approved by 59% of those voting on the question (although it failed because it did not receive a majority of those voting in the election; it cannot be known, of course, how many blank ballots were intended as votes against, but that was their effect).

The much lower vote for Prohibition candidates than for prohibition amendments (which were supported by a majority again in 1918

[11]It can be noted in passing that the relationship between foreign settlement and opposition to prohibition is entirely explained by the former's association with Catholicism. The relation is similar for referenda in later years (Table 6.10). In those later years, though the sign of the coefficient of percentage foreign is not reversed, the coefficient is still very much smaller than the correlation coefficient.

and 1920) does not necessarily imply that support for the party was unrelated to support for prohibition, but the association between the two is only moderate (the correlations between the vote in the 1883 referendum and the votes for Prohibition presidential candidates in 1884 and 1888 are .34 and .37, respectively). Because prohibition forces in Ohio were concentrated in the Anti-Saloon League, neither the size nor the distribution of the party's vote fully reflected prohibition sentiment.

Prohibition was only rarely an issue in contests between the major parties. On most of the few occasions when it was, revivalism did not contribute uniquely to the outcome; rather, revivalist counties maintained their usual levels of Republican support. One such occasion was the gubernatorial campaign of 1889, when Republican Governor Joseph Foraker embraced the cause and was defeated for reelection.[12] However, Democratic gains in 1889, though related to opposition to prohibition in 1883 (with the Z-score, $r = -.23$), were unrelated to revivalism ($r = .09$).

Populism and the election of 1896 confirm the inability of the revivalist ethos to influence voters to deviate from their traditional party. As an electoral force, Populism had no major significance, either as a third party or incorporated into the Democratic party in 1896. In the four elections which the Populists entered as a third party (the presidential contest of 1892 and the gubernatorial elections of 1891, 1893 and 1895), Populist strength was very small: the largest total was 6%, won by Jacob Coxey running for governor in 1895, the year after he had led "Coxey's army" to Washington.

Populism in Ohio was not related to prior episodes of agrarian radicalism: it was virtually uncorrelated with the Greenback voting strength of the late 1870s. It was not even particularly rural: the correlation of the four Populist candidates with the number of farms per capita, 1890, ranges from $-.04$ to $.15$. In contrast to New York, third-party Populism was not associated with support for prohibition (the correlation of the 1883 referendum with the four Populist candidates ranges from $-.17$ to $.01$). Nor was it related to revivalism (the correlations range from $-.10$ to $.03$).

---

[12]Kleppner (1970, p. 125) claims that the gubernatorial elections of 1873 and 1883 were also determined by prohibition sentiment (with 1889, these were the only Republican defeats in gubernatorial elections before 1905), because Republican voters, especially German Lutherans, objected to the Republicans' support of temperance measures in those years. But in only one of those years, 1883, were Democratic gains at all associated with the size of the 1890 German population (with the Z-score, $r = .64$; for the other two years, $r = .05$ and $.08$), and Democratic gains in 1883 were unrelated to prohibition (the correlation of the 1883 Z-score with the 1883 referendum is .04).

Bryan had as little impact on Ohio's voting patterns as third-party Populism. The Republicans received 52% of the vote, compared to 48% in 1892, and the Democratic total decreased by less than one percentage point (as Bryan apparently received the votes of Populists and Prohibitionists). Bryan's strength came from areas that were rural and in favor of prohibition: accessions to the Democrats in 1896 (measured by the Z-score) correlate .56 with farms per capita, 1890; .34 with the vote in favor of prohibition, 1883, and .45 with the vote for the Prohibition candidate for president, 1892. They were not closely related to the previous Populist votes, except for that in 1895 (the correlations of the Z-score with the 1891, 1892, 1893, and 1895 votes are .11, .17, .14, and .33). Nor were they related to revivalism ($r = .07$). These correlations in any case are based on extremely small differences between the vote in 1896 and earlier years. The Bryan election did not mark a realignment, or even a major deviation: the correlations of the 1892 and 1896 votes ($r = .94$ for the Democrats, .97 for the Republicans) are almost as high as any pair of elections of the immediately preceding period, and the correlations for the subsequent elections before 1912 are similarly high.[13]

The election of 1905 was the only campaign in which revivalist voters gave unusual support to a candidate favoring prohibition. The Republican governor, Myron T. Herrick, who was running for reelection, had forced an amendment weakening the 1905 local option bill, and the Anti-Saloon League supported John M. Pattison, the Democratic candidate. The election was fought on the local option issue, and an observer remarked that it was a new kind of campaign for the Democrats—the first in which one could hear "amens" from the audience at rallies (Dohn, 1959, pp. 115–21).

Pattison won, becoming the first Democratic governor to be elected since 1889. Republican losses were closely related to support for prohibition measures: the Republican Z-score correlates $-.35$ with the 1883 referendum, and $-.52$ and $-.53$ with referenda submitted in 1912 and 1914 on prohibition-related issues. It was also closely related

---

[13]Kleppner's assertion (1970, pp. 329–32) that Bryan won the vote of pietists in the 1896 election and initiated a party realignment are simply not borne out by the data. Kleppner's method of data analysis is unreliable, because it draws conclusions from the voting behavior of homogeneous units, which can provide estimates of voting behavior quite contrary to those derived from the analysis of all units, as the present example and the one referred to in the preceding note show (see Kousser, 1976). Moreover, Kleppner's understanding of the election in 1896 is apparently hampered by a misreading of his own Table 32 (p. 282). Finally, his claim of a realignment in Ohio in 1896 fails even to consider whether the voting shifts he erroneously detects persisted in later elections.

TABLE 6.9

Determinants of Republican Z-Score, Ohio, 1905
(Multiple Regression)

Independent variable	0-order r	Beta weight
% Foreign white, 1910	.120	−.133
% Catholic, 1890	.456	.381
Farms per capita, 1910	−.370	−.302
Revivalism	−.283	−.299
Multiple R	.595	

to revivalism: Table 6.9 shows that when other variables are controlled, revivalism exerts a sizable independent effect.

As the national campaign for prohibition became more intense,
Ohioans were frequently presented with prohibition-related referenda. In 1912 a referendum on a constitutional amendment to regulate the liquor traffic was submitted to voters; it had a very slight relation to revivalism. Amendments for statewide prohibition submitted
in 1914, 1918, and 1920,[14] however, had a much stronger relationship
(Table 6.10; the relationship for 1918, omitted, is similar to those for
1914 and 1920). There is no obvious reason why this relationship
should have been inconsistent. When revivalism affected the vote,
however, it did so despite the considerable changes revivalist counties
had undergone. By 1910 counties that had experienced revivalism
were predominantly foreign-settled and nonfarm (the correlations of
these two variables with revivalism are .46 and −.18). Foreign-settled
counties opposed and farm counties supported prohibition, as Table
6.10 shows. Nevertheless, revivalism exerted an independent effect in
favor of prohibition. Revivalist counties were more likely to support
prohibition than other counties with similar proportions of foreign-
born and of farmers. This effect was also independent of the revivalist
counties' traditional Republicanism: if the 1908 presidential vote is
added as an independent variable to the regressions of the 1914 and
1920 referenda results, the coefficient of revivalism decreases only
slightly.

The vote on the repeal of the eighteenth amendment in 1933 also
showed an effect of revivalism: As Table 6.10 shows, its effect was
still large, even though nonfarm and foreign-settled counties were

[14]Prohibition was approved in 1918; the 1920 referendum offered the opportunity to
repeal it, but a majority favored its retention.

TABLE 6.10

Determinants of Votes in Prohibition Referenda, Ohio
(Multiple Regression)

Independent variable	1912[a] 0-order r	1912[a] Beta weight	1914 0-order r	1914 Beta weight	1920 0-order r	1920 Beta weight	1933[a] 0-order r	1933[a] Beta weight
% Foreign[b]	.572	.198	−.403	−.154	−.510	−.174	.589	.251
% Catholic[b]	.736	.513	−.664	−.497	−.808	−.645	.639	.354
Farms per capita[b]	−.611	−.228	.500	.190	.569	.155	−.673	−.460
Revivalism	.075	−.086	.157	.289	.080	.224	.085	−.226
Multiple R	.790		.730		.846		.815	

[a]The 1912 referendum was on regulation of the liquor trade, which was opposed by prohibitionists, and the 1933 referendum was on the 21st Amendment. Positive coefficients, therefore, represent votes against prohibition.
[b]For the first three dependent variables the independent variables are percentage foreign white, 1910; percentage Catholic, 1890; and farms per capita, 1910. For the last, they are percentage foreign, 1930; percentage Catholic, 1936; and farms per capita, 1930.

even more strongly opposed to prohibition than they had been in the earlier years. The 1933 referendum, however, presents the last measurable trace of the influence of revivalism: prohibition was not debated or voted on again when the amendment was repealed, and the partisan realignment of the New Deal era eliminated the influence of revivalism on the traditional Republican vote.

In summary, the relationship of revivalism to prohibition was inconsistent. It had a strong effect on the vote for Prohibitionist candidates, but that vote was always extremely small. In the 1883 and 1912 referenda it exercised little effect; in referenda held in later years its effect was larger. Of three elections where prohibition sentiment influenced voters to deviate from their usual party loyalties (1889, 1896, and 1905), those deviations were related to revivalism in only one. Revivalism shaped party loyalties much more strongly and consistently than it created support for prohibition in Ohio; it formed them so strongly that even when prohibition became an issue affecting the vote in partisan campaigns, revivalists usually remained with their party in the normal degree rather than deviating in its favor when it supported or against it when it opposed prohibition.

The impact of revivalism on Ohio's post-Civil War politics, then, was principally in the formation of stable party allegiance. But if revivalism continued to affect Ohioans' votes for a century after the revivals occurred, it appears that the revivalist belief system did not. In New York revivalist counties remained attached to some of the original symbols of the ethos but the ethos became detached from its original content. In Ohio even the symbol of temperance was abandoned, or at least adhered to with considerably less regularity. The ethos acquired a new content. The Republican allegiance that it formed became self-sustaining, and the historically revivalist roots of Republicanism ceased to be important.

As the population composition of revivalist counties changed, moreover, the base for the perpetuation of the ethos vanished. The depression brought a partisan realignment, but revivalism had no particular impact on it. Its issues were not the issues of revivalism, and there was no occasion for revivalism to continue to affect voting behavior. Many of the revivalist counties, now urbanized and industrialized, were the areas where Roosevelt could be expected to have had a broad appeal. As occurred elsewhere in the country, the Democratic party gained new, permanent supporters in these areas, except that in Ohio they happened also to be the areas where the influence of revivalism had continued to be felt, in however attenuated a form. With the realignment the relationship between revivalism and party vote vanished. Since the 1932 election was much like previous ones in

TABLE 6.11

Determinants of Republican Presidential Votes, Ohio
(Multiple Regression)

Independent variable	1936		1940	
	0-order r	Beta weight	0-order r	Beta weight
% Foreign, 1930	−.489	−.060	−.455	−.276
% Catholic, 1936	−.568	−.404	−.080	.278
Farms per capita, 1930	.535	.335	.602	.540
Revivalism	−.210	−.032	−.303	−.023
Multiple R		.667		.660

the distribution of Ohio's votes, this change was not felt until 1936.[15] But as Table 6.11 shows, the partisan division in 1936 and later (persisting for the elections for which the data are not shown) was no longer influenced by revivalism.

[15]The Ohio realignment is analyzed in detail in Hammond (1976, pp. 66–72).

To say that the political impact of revivalism ended with the New Deal in Ohio while it persisted, though sporadically, in New York, requires an explicit comparison between those two states: in New York, the revivalist ethos made a difference on several later occasions (the referenda on questions related to gambling) which have no parallel in Ohio. One might, therefore, argue that there is no proper test for the comparison. However, the principal manifestation of revivalism in Ohio was not in referenda related to moralistic politics but in partisan votes. The analysis of subsequent partisan votes reveals that it had no further impact.

Moreover, there is one occasion on which the revivalist ethos manifested itself in New York and for which there is a precise parallel in Ohio: the 1964 election. The Goldwater election cost the Republicans a large share of their votes in Ohio (Johnson won 63% of the vote, whereas Democratic candidates between 1952 and 1960 had all won less than 47%), and the 1960 and 1964 elections were more dissimilar in their distributions than most pairs of successive elections ($r = .80$). Johnson's gains in 1964 came from areas similar to those where he gained in New York: they were rural, native counties. But the deviations, measured by the Z-score, were not associated with revivalism ($r = .01$). Since revivalism had created a system of party loyalties rather than a set of responses to political issues in Ohio, it vanished when party loyalties were changed by exogenous forces. It no longer existed to influence the vote in 1964.

So revivalism has ceased to be a determining force in the outcome of elections in Ohio, even irregularly as in New York. Most of the revivalist counties of the state have lost the distinctive character which encouraged revivals in the early nineteenth century. Accordingly, their residents no longer maintain the traditions which revivalism created. The distinctiveness was less to begin with than in New York, since native Protestants dominated the state as a whole. It finally vanished in the twentieth century, as urbanization and industrialization changed the character of revivalist areas.

In New York, on the other hand, revivalist areas have remained stable. They are still predominantly rural, have experienced relatively little foreign immigration, and have grown much more slowly than the rest of the state. Their populations have remained essentially unchanged in more than a century, and differences between them and the rest of the state have remained as identifying marks of solidarity. In these areas, the ethos created by the revivals of the early nineteenth century continues to influence the voting decisions of residents.

New York and Ohio thus offer an instructive contrast for understanding the perpetuation of an ethos. The situations in which it re-mains effective in New York, in addition, illustrate the conditions which make the ethos salient. Not since the 1840s does revivalism ap-pear to have been responsible for the initiation of important political developments; it has, rather, remained in the background and functioned only reactively.

To what, then, does it react? I have referred earlier to suggestions that symbolic politics of the kind manifested in the revivalist ethos is most likely to emerge in times of prosperity, when immediate economic interest is relatively unimportant to voters. But the revivalist ethos has been most salient in 1896, the New Deal period, and 1964. At two of these times the country was shaken by a major depression, yet in both cases the effect of the revivalist ethos was apparently in-dependent of the response to economic difficulties. In both years the depression led most voters to reject the party in power: in 1896 the northeast voted Republican, and in the 1930s many turned to the Democratic party. Yet in both cases much of the variation in voting behavior cannot be explained by the typical response to economic dif-ficulty, and in both cases the revivalist tradition drove voters against the prevailing tide.

What all three episodes have in common is that one of the major parties presented a new image and a new kind of candidate. The or-dinary standards of party choice did not serve, and voters sought other standards to enable them to make a choice. It was in just such a time that the revivalist ethos first became political. When slavery was regarded by revivalists as the principal issue to be decided, the exist-ing parties did not differ sufficiently, and neither of them offered a sufficiently antislavery position. At that time, however, revivalism it-self contributed to the reorientation of the party system by making slavery a major issue.

In these later periods, the changes in the parties' images and plat-forms emerged from outside. Revivalism was not a source of political change. Even in the 1850s its influence had been limited when its issue was adopted and diluted by other political forces. Now its influ-ence was even more limited because the major parties only rarely underwent changes which made the ethos a relevant standard for political choices. But on these occasions the ethos gave its adherents a unique interpretation of images and issues: in 1896 prohibition was important, but it is likely that it was only a part of the image Bryan presented. Between 1928 and 1936 it is more clear that prohibition was the defining issue for those who reacted to electoral choice in terms of the revivalist ethos. In 1964 it is likely that race was the major issue, and that the revivalist heritage demanded support for a candidate whose platform promised a greater hope of equal treatment for blacks.

So the response to issues which symbolize religious traditions of the past does not depend on the absence of other "more real" issues, as Berelson et al. (1954, p. 185) suggest. Instead, the ethos provides guides to behavior when the more customary guides do not apply. Revivalism perhaps remains dormant most of the time, but it is available in the relatively unpredictable situations in which voters can base decisions on it.

7

The Meaning of the Revivalist Ethos

The Protestant ethic "prowls about in our lives like the ghost of dead religious beliefs" (Weber, 1958b, p. 182). So, too, the revivalist political ethos prowls about, if not in the lives of many of us, then in our politics. Though I have called it the "revivalist" ethos, it grew out of a perhaps unique interaction among several conditions. The revivals gave the ethos its content, but a pervasive Yankee culture, which made the categories of thought presented by the revivals congenial to those who heard them, was a necessary foundation. The revivals were dramatic events which altered the consciousness of their converts. The conflict which developed into the Civil War reinforced the new consciousness by calling upon it intensively, so that the orientations dependent on the ethos became second nature.

Although the ethos became embedded through conflict, it was able to survive only in the absence of conflict. But the paradox is apparent rather than real. In Ohio the ethos was destroyed by a conflict of attrition which gradually obliterated the group identity of those who had held it; in contrast, the Civil War period during which the ethos solidified was one in which the solidarity of the group holding it was heightened, because the enemy was distant. When groups are clearly distinguished from each other, conflict between them is likely to promote solidarity within each of them; when they are in stable interaction, assimilation is likely to weaken their distinct traits (Simmel, 1955, pp. 91–93).

Will assimilation make the revivalist ethos vanish? Its influence has been merely sporadic at least in the twentieth century, and the likelihood of its complete extinction is suggested by discussions of two long-term tendencies in American politics: secularization and the national homogenization of political behavior.

It has been argued that secularization, the generalized weakening of ultimate belief, has modified conflict over ultimate values in Western societies, including the United States (Alford, 1963, p. 50). With the growth of instrumental orientations, in this view, men's concern with problems of ultimate meaning will not be satisfied by answers which are not intellectually acceptable (Wilson, 1969, pp. 17–18).[1] If ultimate values cease to be matters of importance to individuals, they will not generate conflicts that are fought in the political sphere.

The Ohio case appears to exemplify the loss of influence of ultimate values on political behavior. But I have suggested that the failure of the revivalist ethos to persist there was due not to any decline of religion (whether or not that occurred) but rather to the loss of a homogeneous cultural environment. Without such an environment, group identity did not remain strong and without it the group's distinctive orientations were lost.

A number of overlapping explanations for secularization have been offered, of which the growth of instrumental orientations is but one. Another explanation suggests that heterogeneity of religious membership in a community, apart from heterogeneity of belief, weakens the power of the church as an agency of social control, for religious values cease to be community values (Wilson, 1969, pp. 51–52).

In this sense, secularization may explain the Ohio case. But heterogeneity is not developing in the New York communities where the revivalist ethos continues to exist. While these communities have a diversity of denominations, they remain predominantly Protestant. According to Herberg, the several Protestant denominations in the United States have adopted a homogeneous faith in which one denomination is roughly substitutable for another (Herberg, 1960, pp. 35–41). Though the conditions he describes are not conducive to the preservation of a locally distinct tradition like the revivalist ethos, it may be that the adaptation of churches in communities with such a tradition is to the norms provided by that tradition rather than to the norms prevailing in the larger society.

In any case, I have suggested that the preservation of the ethos has not depended on the continuing influence of religion after it was institutionalized. If secularization suggests the weakening of religious influence over politics, however, the widely noted nationalization of political forces suggests that any local tradition is in danger of disap-

---

[1]By this interpretation, there is evidence of secularization in Finney's revival preaching itself, as he struggled to make religious belief and practice harmonious with the "laws of mind."

pearing in the face of the increasing influence of more centralized forces.

Political behavior seems to be more and more similar throughout the nation, and therefore less subject to unique local conditions. Examination of voter participation and partisan division in Congressional elections from 1870 to 1960 shows that in the nineteenth century the differences among congressional districts were great, presumably in response to differing local conditions. But variations in turnout have steadily become more constant throughout the nation, and correspondingly less unique to Congressional districts; the tendency in partisan division, though less distinct, has been in the same direction (Stokes, 1967, pp. 193–96).

This change has been attributed to the development of mass communications (Stokes, 1967, p. 196) and to the increasing importance in politics of economic interests extending beyond particular localities (Hays, 1967, pp. 166–67). If such conditions prevail, it is evident that the influence of local traditions on voting behavior must inevitably decrease.

That these two trends are occurring there can be little doubt. The question, however, is whether they are affecting the whole nation equally, and in particular, whether they are sufficient to destroy the locally unique influence of the ethos in the region where it still leaves its traces. The previous chapter suggests that the revivalist ethos is resilient. Though its influence in the twentieth century has been quite sporadic, neither secularization nor the nationalization of politics appears to have destroyed it yet. Its recent resurgence in 1964 suggests that any reports of its death would be premature.

The last chapters have described the limits which the political system places on politics inspired by the revivalist ethos. In conclusion, however, I will return to the ethos itself. The intention of those who adopted it has been to moralize politics—not necessarily to make it more moral, but to make people bring moral criteria to bear on their political decisions. Often their behavior has been merely reactive. Even in the case of the movement they most clearly initiated (the abolition movement, through which revivalism also had its greatest effect), their moralism did not determine the outcome without the intervention of political, economic, and military factors. The ability of moralists to achieve their political goals has always been limited by the constraints of social and economic structure. But despite the difficulties imposed by these constraints, moralists do act. They are convinced that they are under obligation: in the case of the revivalists, obligation to God to make the world express his will.

The implications of this study contradict the prevailing interpretation of the revival movement. That interpretation views the movement as a source and an expression of national consensus. It has taken three forms: the revivals have been identified as the bearer of pietist political dispositions; as the religious expression of Jacksonian democracy; and as the source of a common national culture. Each of these identifications I believe to be wrong. All of them, in attempting to integrate the revivals into the mainstream of American cultural history, ignore the strength of conviction which motivated the revivalists to political opposition. They emphasize formal aspects of the revival, neglecting the content of revival preaching and the content of the political action it inspired. They disregard empirical evidence about the political behavior of revivalist areas. In all these respects, these three interpretations are bound up with assumptions stemming from a consensus interpretation which homogenizes American history and disregards its repeated political conflicts.

The dichotomy between pietist and liturgical religion has recently been proposed by many scholars (who collectively identify themselves as the "new political historians") as the principal determinant of nineteenth-century American voting behavior. That dichotomy might, at first glance, be taken to subsume my discussion of the revivalist political ethos. Examined more closely, however, their explanation of voting behavior is quite different from the one I have proposed.

The "new political historians" present an ethnocultural model of voting behavior which argues (usually in opposition to a class model) that "at least since the 1820s, . . . ethnic and religious differences have tended to be *relatively* the most important sources of political differences" in the American electorate (Benson, 1964, p. 165). Though some place a greater weight on ethnicity, my attention will be confined to their discussion of religious influences on voting.

They argue that the major cleavage in the electorate has been between people accepting two general religious orientations. Various terminologies identify the first as evangelical, puritan, or pietist, and the second as nonevangelical, ritualist, or liturgical.[2] Kleppner (1970) summarizes the distinction by saying that pietists emphasized "right behavior" while liturgicals emphasized "right belief" (p. 73). Hays (1960) elaborates: pietism

> stressed strict standards of behavior derived from Puritan sources, especially Sunday observance, and prohibition of gambling, dancing, and, above all, drinking alcoholic beverages. It was evangelistic: it exhorted individuals to undergo a

---

[2]Despite the terminological discrepancy, the descriptions of the two poles in the discussions referred to are quite similar. Moreover, these historians' treatments of the nineteenth century are regarded as similar both by themselves and by several recent review essays (Foner, 1974; McCormick, 1974; Wright, 1973). For consistency I will use the terms pietist and liturgical, rather than the separate terminology of each author.

> dramatic transformation in their personal lives, to be converted, and it sought to impose these standards of personal character on the entire community by public, legal action. But there were others, whose . . . religion consisted more of a sequence of rituals and observances through which one passed from birth to death, with the primary focus of religion being the observance of those practices. For many of them Puritan morals meant little; Germans, for example, were accustomed to the continental Sunday of relaxation in beer gardens or to using wine for communion services. (p. 196)

Moreover, Formisano and Benson implicitly regard belief in the positive, active state as an attribute of pietism (in that they identify the Whigs with both): "The Whig political philosophy postulated an activist, positive state, responsible for improving the material and moral well-being of society" (Benson, 1964, p. 212). Evangelical religion, in their interpretation, was activist, and its activism applied equally to moral regulation and economic development. Finally, pietism was nativist: pietists were hostile to foreigners simply because they were foreigners or because they practiced different customs, and in politics nativism implied measures restricting naturalization and banning the use of foreign languages in schools (Benson, 1964, pp. 114–22, 214; Formisano, 1971, pp. 85, 99–100, 142).

Some of these scholars have argued that a pietist orientation motivated the behavior which I attribute to the revivalist ethos. Hays considers it the principal source of the electoral realignment and the Republican advantage in the north in the 1850s (Hays, 1967, pp. 158–59). Formisano claims that it was at the basis of the benevolent societies' activities and of abolitionism in Michigan (Formisano, 1971, pp. 111, 120). Benson claims most Liberty voters in New York were members of "evangelical sects" and held "radical religious beliefs" (Benson, 1964, pp. 210–11).

It might appear that these explanations overlap so much with my own that they are identical except for terminology. There are certainly similarities between these writers' pietism and what I call the revivalist ethos. The revivalist ethos, too, demanded personal conversion and a consequent transformation of personal life. It was in the end not reluctant to call on the state to enforce its morality on others. Moreover, some ethnoculturalists attribute pietism's strength to revivals (Formisano, 1971, p. 116; Jensen, 1971, p. 62). But there are several differences of emphasis between pietism as they conceive it and what I have described as the revivalist ethos, and there is a fundamental difference between the respective explanations of religion's influence on politics. There are also inadequacies in some of these authors' conceptualizations and investigations, but I will discuss only those that are related to the contrast between pietism as they define it and revivalism as I define it.

They claim that pietism inspired voters to endorse government intervention on an extremely broad platform of issues—in the economy, against slavery, in favor of temperance and Sabbath observance, and against foreigners. The implicit claim is, then, that all these positions formed a syndrome, and that the same people supported all of them. But the connections among these ideas are not obvious; that such a broad range of issues formed a coherent package can only be established empirically, by seeing whether the same population groups supported them all when presented with the opportunity in elections.

I have shown that antislavery and temperance did form such an ideological package for revivalist voters. However, most of them opposed nativism at the polls; also, by deserting the Whigs and the Democrats to vote for antislavery parties, they opted out of the choice between a party representing active government and a party representing laissez-faire (abolitionist leaders, moreover, differed considerably among themselves on economic policy and fought over the economic platform of the Liberty party).

If the pietism the ethnoculturalists discuss is too diffuse in content, it is also too diffused in the population. They attribute almost complete explanatory weight to differences between pietists and liturgicals, so much that one gets the impression that everyone was one or the other (and, incidentally, in about equal proportions). But the only one who presents data shows that about half of his samples were unchurched (Jensen, 1971, p. 311).[3] The conflict between pietism and liturgicism could not have had too great an effect on those with no religious connection, so it cannot explain how they voted.

Related to these scholars' assumption that pietism was widely diffused is their explanation of how individuals adopted a pietist orientation. They present the process as a static one of cultural transmission rather than active consciousness-formation. Some explicitly attribute pietistic politics to revivals, as noted above. But they treat revivals as a culturally sanctioned experience which reinforced dispositions the church had already created rather than a transforming experience affecting converts' beliefs.

They do not discuss the process which might have created the set of beliefs, either for the individual or for the group which passed them on. They appear to regard the denomination as the preserver and transmitter of pietist (or liturgical) culture. While all the writers emphasize that several denominations contained both pietist and liturgical factions, they nevertheless offer no other determinant of the

[3]To be fair, reliable data on the extent of church membership before the Civil War are not available.

distinction between pietists and liturgicals, and denomination is the only operational variable they use in assessing the impact of orientations on political behavior.

I do not believe that pietism, as these writers use the term, is adequate to explain what I have identified as the consequences of the revivalist political ethos. Converts were a select group even within revivalist denominations. Moreover, the political projects, such as abolitionism and temperance, which they adopted in the 1830s simply cannot be explained by denominationally-created doctrinal dispositions. New political activities must be explained by new political circumstances; if the activities are a result of religious motivations, either those motivations or the environment in which they act must change to create the activities.

The new political historians therefore provide a static interpretation of religious influences. They believe, for example, that pietism took for granted that the state should interfere in private lives to regulate morality. But this claim on state authority was not a natural assumption of pietist culture; in fact, a variant of it had been defeated in the eighteenth and early nineteenth centuries in the battle for disestablishment, which most pietists endorsed. The idea that the state should enforce their morality had to be developed and, in the case of the abolitionists, it developed only gradually and over heated opposition, not only from opponents of abolitionism, but even from within their own ranks.

If the new political historians' conception of religion is too static, so is their conception of politics. Though the new political history provides ample scope for conflict within the political system, that conflict is not over the major manifest issues of public debate, but over symbolic issues establishing boundaries between groups. These historians share with the consensus interpretation of American history the assumption that basic issues of distribution and power were solved or for some other reason were of little concern to citizens.

They reduce politics, therefore, to cultural conflict between ascriptive groups. Even when concrete issues like slavery become manifest, the position of particular groups on these issues is only to be interpreted as a reaction to the position of their opponents.[4] The ethnoculturalists leave unresolved a logical problem: where does an initial position come from? One side has to act first before the other can react. But even granting that an initial position may proceed directly from

<hr/>

[4]One of the new political historians even takes to task another for being "conceptually old-fashioned" because his voters "are still the old issue-oriented types." See Kleppner (1972, p. 23) commenting on Jensen (1971).

religious doctrine, they imply that the only purpose in advocating such a political position and enforcing on others the morality prescribed by the doctrine is to display the group's moral superiority over others who do not share its beliefs or practices.[5] As Formisano (1971) puts it, evangelicals believed

> their values . . . to be the true American heritage. Elected officials were men designated by the community to represent it before man and God. That "representation" should not be sinful. With symbolic issues it does not matter if the law is violated by parts of the community, particularly by the subterranean, unseen, or unlived-with. Form counts more than substance for those who are looking for recognition, either for themselves or their values. It matters that the letter and spirit of the law exist, bestow sanction, and indicate the approved direction of society. (p. 126)

So, in this view, issues are merely symbolic—"merely," because winning concrete political struggles is of no importance compared to asserting the group's superiority.[6] My earlier discussion of symbolic issues pointed to a problem with the concept, that of establishing what it is that is symbolized by a particular issue. I have pointed out there that the empirical evidence on abolitionism does not support the status-conflict hypothesis, and that abolitionism was not an appropriate issue to symbolize that conflict because it opposed a custom practiced by neither group.

Similarly, I believe that abolitionism served no better as a symbolic bearer of the hypothesized conflict between pietists and liturgicals. Though the use of religious doctrine to establish group superiority has a certain plausibility as an explanation of temperance, Sabbath observance, and the attempt to impose American ways on foreigners, it fails as an explanation of abolitionism. The group being attacked, slaveholders, was geographically removed (and shared many of the abolitionists' religious and cultural orientations); the fight against slavery was hardly the most appropriate means of attributing inferiority to neighboring groups of a different culture.

---

[5]I differ with McCormick, who argues that the ethnoculturalists espouse three distinct theories of ethnocultural voting: that the vote represents a reaction to a negative reference group, a means of extending or protecting cultural practices of one's own group, and an expression of religious beliefs and world views (McCormick, 1974, pp. 358–59). I believe that for the ethnocultural historians discussed here, affirmation of group identity and protection of cultural practices are expressions of the same impulse, and that they are far more important than the expression of religious values. Even Kleppner, who identifies the pietist–liturgical distinction with religious doctrine (in the opposition between "right belief" and "right behavior"), believes that group antagonisms outweigh religious inspiration in determining voters' orientations (Kleppner, 1970, pp. 35–91).

[6]Burnham (1971, p. 63), criticizing the new political historians for their disregard of manifest political issues, has suggested that their methodology is biased against discovering that issues made a difference to the vote.

The empirical evidence equally refutes the claim that revivalists' politics were a symbolic expression of their group membership. Statistically, revivalism has a much greater effect on abolitionist voting than does denominational composition, and revivalist communities which supported abolitionist candidates cast very low votes for nativists. Something other than intergroup hostility must explain the relation between revivalism and abolitionism. The explanation is the one I have presented in this book, that revivalism's doctrine and practices created a distinctive political ethos which in itself motivated political behavior; this explanation is quite different from the one posited by the ethnoculturalists.

The pietism-ritualism hypothesis more nearly fits the institutionalization of the revivalist ethos in the post-Civil War period, with which most of the hypothesis's exponents deal.[7] Republican loyalty and especially temperance provided an opportunity to express group solidarity in the midst of cultural conflict at the same time that they were an expression of political positions derived from religious values. But the hypothesis implies that the influence of pietist or ritualist orientations is constant and pervasive, whereas the last two chapters have shown that the influence of revivalism is irregular and somewhat dependent on the actions not of revivalists themselves but of party leaders. The hypothesis, moreover, explains with equal facility phenomena that are inconsistent with each other—party identification and deviation from party identification in support of specific positions—and does not explain the conditions under which party identification or positions will influence voting behavior when they conflict with each other.

A second way in which American cultural historians have attempted to incorporate revivalism into the mainstream of American political and cultural development has been to identify the revivals, and Finney in particular, as the natural religious expression of Jacksonian democracy. In Miller's (1965) words,

> the kind of revival stimulated by Finney in upstate New York, though it refrained from politics and was not necessarily confined to Democrats, was a mass uprising, a release of energy, a sweep of the people which made it an expression of that energy we call Jacksonian America. (p. 30)

Further, according to McLoughlin (1960),

> in its underlying assumptions about nature, man and society, [Finney's *Lectures*] was in its way as ebullient an embodiment of the spirit of Jacksonian democracy as the speeches of Andrew Jackson, the editorials of John L. O'Sullivan and William Leggett, or the essays of Ralph Waldo Emerson. . . . [The] deep emotional

[7]Although I have, in passing, indicated some inadequacies in their general formulation; moreover, in Chapter 6 I pointed out some specific errors in Kleppner's discussion of Ohio politics.

reliance upon the leadings of God's spirit. . . . indicates a common bond between Finney's antiecclesiasticism and the Jacksonian's anticlericalism. Egalitarian
reliance upon the innate common sense of the common man is, after all, only a
secular form of the doctrine of the priesthood of all believers. (pp. vii, xxxii)

The problem with this identification is that it is contradicted by
the concrete behavior of the adherents of the two movements. The
revivalist ethos gave people an interpretation of their own political
role and a set of positions on concrete issue diametrically opposed to
those held by Jacksonians. Comparison is difficult, because the political meaning of revivalism is only implicit in its doctrine. Moreover,
"Jacksonian democracy" can describe the politics of a particular party,
but it has also been used to characterize the new form of politics
which all parties practiced as the second American party system developed. By either definition, however, the political practices now regarded as having typified the age of Jackson were not the political
practices of the revivalists.

There are certain similarities between the two, to be sure. As
Jacksonianism was the politics of the common man,[8] so revivalism
was the religion of the common man (even though Finney, while
conscientiously directing his preaching at ordinary and poorly educated people, was nevertheless proud when he could claim that
"the highest classes of society" were being converted by a revival;
Finney, 1876, p. 289). Each established equality and the universal
right to participate; Jacksonian democracy flourished during the
period when what was regarded as universal suffrage was established
and national political parties were created in their modern form, giving all (white male) citizens the right and the opportunity for political
participation. The revivals emphasized the individual responsibility of
each believer to act positively to secure his own salvation. Both thus
created not only a participatory opportunity but a participatory burden on individuals, whether their participation was expected in party
politics or in the achievement of salvation.

Both had aspects of mass mobilization campaigns. The rebirth of
party competition in the 1820s and 1830s gave rise to the first mass
political rallies and stimulated a style of oratory intended to move
people, just as the revival movement used mass meetings and exhor-
tatory preaching to convince those in attendance.

Both established institutions which facilitated the participation
they demanded: universal suffrage was a hallmark of the Jacksonian
period, but perhaps more important was the opportunity created

[8]I am deliberately accepting a conventional description of Jacksonian democracy,
since McLoughlin and Miller do so in identifying Finney with it. For a review of literature challenging that conventional view, see Pessen (1960, pp. 384–93).

through the erection of a national party structure, the political convention, and the proliferation of elected offices, all of which provided occasion and incentive for mass participation. Similarly, revivalism, through both revival meetings and benevolent societies, gave individuals numerous occasions and avenues to express their convictions in concrete behavior.

Both, though creating institutions to facilitate participation, had important anti-institutional aspects. Both arose, to some degree, as insurgent movements opposed to a traditional order. The revivals were an effort to overcome the stodginess and rigidity of Calvinist church life, and Jacksonianism challenged banks, state-incorporated monopolies, and other structures which threatened to consolidate the privileges of the few (Hofstadter, 1948, pp. 57–63). Anti-institutionalism in both cases not only led to attacks on specific institutions, but generated principles opposed to institutional rigidification and hierarchy. The revival, though typically located in denominational churches, deemphasized church structure, hierarchy and dogma, believing that no establishment was worthy to question an individual's religious certainty. Jacksonian democracy opposed centers of power which it saw as dangerous because they defended vested interests and threatened popular democracy.

Similarities between revivalist and Jacksonian practices can be traced to the similar social conditions which gave rise to them. The settlement of the American west (even when the west was in New York or Tennessee) precluded the perpetuation of established classes through inheritance and necessitated reliance on individual responsibility. American conditions did support democracy both in politics and in religion, for no human authority had the legitimacy to claim deference from the common man. In that sense, both Jacksonian democracy and revival religion appropriately, perhaps even inevitably, recognized the existence of equality and the absence of constricting institutions on the frontier.

But these similarities were overshadowed by greater differences. Revivalism was egalitarian in inviting all to be saved, and its practices made salvation accessible to those with little education and few intellectual attainments. But revivalists did not assume that all were equal. Those who believed were saved, and those who did not were damned. The equality was an equality of opportunity.

Moreover, revivalism and Jacksonianism were opposed both on concrete political issues and on general orientations to the political system and to public morality. Once suffrage ceased to be an issue and structures for universal political participation were established, their differences came to the fore.

The differences arose in the realm, broadly speaking, of morality.

Jacksonian democracy had little room for an explicit morality. Its attitude was one of laissez-faire, and its folklore glorified the frontier rowdiness which would have horrified the revivalists. Jackson himself caused consternation among them: a Mason, a dueler, and a drinker (though a church-going Presbyterian), his rowdy inaugural reception shocked the evangelicals, and addresses to the American Education Society in 1824 and the American Home Missionary Society in 1829 made specific reference to the dangers of government by irreligious men (Griffin, 1960, pp. 55–56).

For the Jacksonians, politics was not constrained by morality. Politicians were not expected to be governed by moral codes but to be responsive to the demands of political alliance. The creation of national parties required an accommodation of diverse interests in terms which made impossible the quest for absolute values through politics; in particular, the major accomplishment of the second party system was to achieve a truce between the opposed interests of north and south (a truce which, to be sure, was only temporary, and whose collapse ultimately destroyed the second system) (McCormick, 1967, pp. 115–16). The spoils system was a vivid expression of Jacksonianism's preference for accommodation over morality, and came to be its most hated symbol to its opponents. In a word, Jacksonian politics were pragmatic and anti-ideological.

The disregard for morality both in private life and in official conduct naturally precluded any assumption that the state might regulate the moral life of its citizens. The Jacksonian state was largely negative, removing obstacles rather than imposing them. The main thrust of Jacksonian policy was to enforce conditions for the free exercise of individual capitalist initiative. Any notion that the state might impose restrictions on private behavior was out of the question.

In all these respects, the revivalist political ethos differed diametrically. It clearly established an individual morality. If proclivities to individual thrift and success in worldly calling created by that morality may have contributed indirectly to the capitalism which Jacksonianism also sustained, that was not its explicit intention. The intention, rather, was to govern individual life by a renunciation of worldly pleasures and by benevolence toward others. Neither of these intentions could find Jacksonian democracy particularly congenial.

The personal morality of the revivalist ethos was of course projected into politics. Even those who did not believe that revivalism's moral code should be enforced on all through politics believed that the same morality which they enjoined for private life could guide and inspire appropriate political conduct and demanded that public figures be governed by it.

Finally, revivalism inspired some adherents to enter political life, but their conception of the appropriate use of state power entirely opposed that of the Jacksonians. They believed that the state could appropriately be employed to enforce their morality, and regarded politics as an appropriate arena in which to bring about such state enforcement, because the revivals led them to accept as compellingly binding the obligations which revival doctrine imposed on them. The struggle for absolute ends did not permit a politics of pragmatism and accommodation.

I have earlier claimed that the pragmatism of revival measures led to a pragmatic view of politics. Revival doctrine did not specifically envision political activity; rather, politics was simply one among many means for spreading their views and for enforcing the behavior they believed to be right, and since it was available it should be used. The pragmatism of revivalist politics, however, differed from the pragmatism of Jacksonian democracy. Jacksonian pragmatism excluded political struggle over absolute ends in favor of struggle for limited advantages through compromise. The revivalist ethos was pragmatic as to means, but the means it accepted were aimed at the achievement of an absolute end. Revivalists, in fact, entered politics refusing to admit that the nature of political activity might place limits on the achievement of the end which motivated their pragmatism.

True, they were accused by the antipolitical Garrisonians of engaging in impermissible compromise simply by entering politics at all. True, also, the political resolution of the slavery controversy involved a considerable compromise of their goals, and was only achieved when their political influence was considerably diminished. Nevertheless, the revivalist ethos brooked no restriction of its objectives in response to the need to accommodate the objectives of others.

Beyond these differences of general orientation, Jacksonian and revivalist politics diverged both in style and in positions on concrete issues. The issues dividing them were, most notably, antislavery and temperance. But there were a host of others: revivalists demanded the suspension of Sunday mails and the declaration of national fast days. (Miller [1965] claims that "it is a mistake to suppose that all revivalists, or even a majority of them, were opposed to Jackson" for his rejection of a petition to declare a day of national humiliation [p. 39], but offers no examples of supporters.)

In arguing the relation between the two phenomena, both Miller and McLoughlin acknowledge that Finney was not politically identified with the Democrats:

> Finney never took the stump for Andrew Jackson. . . . His pietistic evangelicalism made him see politics through moralistic eyes, and he cast his vote

in terms of particular moral issues rather than in terms of party politics.
(McLoughlin, 1960, p. ix)

But that is just the point. He saw politics in light of moral issues, and
instead of distinguishing those issues from politics he determined his
partisan choices according to them. His followers, of course, went further: they created a party which would advocate for abolition, the
most important of their moral causes.

Both Miller and McLoughlin refuse to take seriously the revivalists' political preferences. They attempt to place religion in a
metaphorical relationship with politics rather than in a relation of
cause and effect. But the concrete political behavior of revivalists was
removed from and opposed to the concrete political behavior of Jacksonians. Their respective assumptions about the general role of the
state and the practice of politics were equally opposed. To attempt to
assimilate them as parts of a common movement is to ignore the intentions of their respective practitioners and to ignore the substance
of the lively political conflicts between them.

The final of these three related interpretations of the political consequences of the revivals is that they created a common national experience which in turn formed a universally shared identification with
the nation and made a major contribution to its cultural unity. Like
the ethnocultural interpretation, this view claims that revivalism was
very widespread, affecting broad segments of the population (but it
differs from the ethnocultural interpretation in claiming that the effects of revivalism were not limited to those groups that shared the
evangelical religious heritage, but came to dominate American culture
generally), and that revivalism also created an extremely diffuse political orientation which did not specify positions on particular issues
but which formed a general political mentality.

The idea that the revivals forged a cultural unity is related to the
identification between revivalism and Jacksonianism not only in that
Miller and McLoughlin are proponents of both, but also in the claim
that the religion of the common man created a common political mind
which (both in principle and in practice) overcame divisions of ideology, class and section. The Jacksonian interpretation also reinforces
the claim that the revivals produced cultural unity in a more concrete
way: it could be argued that Jacksonianism and revivalism were the
principal contestants for the political allegiance of early nineteenth
century Americans. If they can be amalgamated or shown to have
basic principles in common, it is entirely natural that the subsequent
formation of political orientations should be one of unity derived from
those common principles.

Like the two interpretations just discussed, this one attempts to deny the existence of fundamental political conflicts in American society, and sees the revivals both as a source and an expression of harmony. Even more than the first two, it is a declaration that within religion and culture a fundamental consensus has pervaded American life since the country was founded. Also like the first two, it reaches its conclusions only by discounting the revivalists' fervor and their conviction that the defense of their belief obligated them to concrete political activity. It ignores both the content of revivalism and the empirical evidence about the kind of politics that characterized individuals and areas affected by the revivals.

How, according to this argument, did the revivals contribute to the cultural unity of the nation? The revivals were a response to disestablishment, the religious liberty established by the Constitution, and the accompanying denominational pluralism. In the absence of an establishment, some procedure was necessary to guarantee the church's survival without state support. Since each denomination was free to exist, each was implicitly competing with the others for adherents, and thus each had to find means to produce converts. So the revivals were a natural organizational response to denominational fragmentation.

In this view, however, their major effect was not to strengthen the individual denominations. Because the revivals emphasized individual experience and because the practitioners in the several denominations used similar techniques, those who underwent them shared a common experience. Because the revivals were widespread—almost universal, in this view—that experience was common to the whole nation. Because the revivals had little concern for fine points of doctrine, denominational differences were minimized. Despite the denominations' natural tendencies to compete, "the voluntary principle [became] a mechanism not of fragmentation but of national cohesion" (Miller, 1965, p. 44). "Revivalism replaced the establishment as the American method of maintaining moral order. . . . The evangelical Protestant denominations became a kind of national church" (McLoughlin, 1965, p. 168).

Revivalists' millennialism is cited as evidence that they optimistically identified the nation with the kingdom of God. Finney believed "that the United States was to be the first nation in which the whole population would be completely converted" (McLoughlin, 1960, p. xli). The spread of the revivals to the cities in the 1850s led to "the expectation of an immediate attainment through a national religion of the millennium, so long and so ardently sought in America" (Miller, 1965, p. 93). McLoughlin (1960) identifies Finney with the Jacksonian

John L. O'Sullivan who believed that "Americans were 'a chosen people' with a 'glorious destiny,' which would be guided by the unseen hand of Providence" (p. xlviii). The inherent democracy of the revivals led revivalists to view America's development of democratic institutions as a sign that God had singled the country out (McLoughlin, 1960, p. xli).

Therefore, according to Matthews (who is commenting on the whole period of the Second Great Awakening in the half century after the revolution), the revival, because it was so widespread, and despite its diversity and localism, "was a nationalizing force that created a 'common world of experience.' . . . American nationalism in part, therefore, rested . . . on . . . the relevance, power, and similarity of thousands of local organizations" (Mathews, 1969, pp. 42–43). Ahlstrom (1972) summarizes: the denominations which grew in the early nineteenth century

> were forging a mainstream tradition of American Evangelical Protestantism. Theologically it was Reformed in its foundations, Puritan in its outlook, fervently experiential in its faith, and tending, despite strong countervailing pressures, toward Arminianism, perfectionism, and activism. Equally basic, and almost equally religious, was its belief in the millennial potential of the United States as the bearer and protector of these values. This mainstream would play a vast sustaining and defining role in the life of the nation during the entire nineteenth century. . . . Despite the legal separation of church and state this American Protestant mainstream would enjoy the influence and self-confidence of a formal establishment. (p. 470)

Revivalistic Protestantism, according to these historians, was the forerunner and nineteenth century equivalent of what Bellah has more recently called America's "civil religion," which finds God's design in American history and ensures civil harmony by enforcing an appropriate moral code (Bellah, 1968).

This analysis of the revivals makes assumptions similar to those often made in the functional analysis of religion generally (although none of the writers explicitly draws on functionalism). Functionalism analyzes social institutions from the standpoint of their contribution to (i.e., their "function for") the maintenance of social order. The functional analysis of religion derives from Durkheim (1965), who assumes that religion is an expression of the solidarity of society, and society the real object of worship. Accepting that assumption, functional analysts assume further that religion reinforces the commitment of individuals to their society: religious rites "regulate, maintain and transmit from one generation to another sentiments on which the constitution of the society depends" (Radcliffe-Brown, 1965, p. 157; see also Parsons, 1960, p. 302). They therefore regarded religion as an indispensable institution assuring social integration. "The reason why religion is necessary is apparently to be found in the fact that human society achieves its unity primarily through the possession by its members of certain ultimate values and ends in common" (Davis & Moore, 1945, p. 244).

That religion *can* contribute to social integration is not in doubt. But functional analysts often take as a postulate that societies are integrated, and that whatever religions exist must contribute positively to integration. Though it has been suggested that the contribution of religion to the integration of religiously pluralistic societies is problematical (Merton, 1957, p. 29; Yinger, 1970, pp. 110–14), some functionalists reject that suggestion for the United States: Talcott Parsons (1973, pp. 164–65) explicitly invokes Bellah's concept of civil religion to explain the integrative function of American religion.

But the analysis which attributes inevitably integrative functions to religion—like much of functional analysis—errs in adopting three interrelated and erroneous assumptions. Merton calls these the postulates of functional unity: that "all parts of the social system work together with a sufficient degree of harmony or internal consistency, i.e., without producing persistent conflicts which can neither be resolved nor regulated" (Radcliffe-Brown, quoted in Merton, 1957, p. 26); of universal functionalism: "that all standardized social or cultural forms have positive functions" (Merton, 1957, p. 30); and of functional indispensability: that "every custom, material object, idea and belief . . . represents an indispensable part within a working whole" (Malinowski, quoted in Merton, 1957, p. 32). These assumptions, as Merton points out, blind the investigator to the possible dysfunctions of social institutions, including those of religion. That the revivals did not contribute uniformly to social order is evident from the discussion of their political consequences in the previous chapters.

The cultural unity interpretation, which imputes order-preserving or order-establishing functions to the revivals, can be removed from the realm of assumptions and subjected to empirical test, because it implies that the political behavior of those influenced by revivalism should follow certain patterns. Revivalists should have believed that God's purposes were already realized in existing political institutions. Their politics should have demonstrated a commitment to preserving civil order rather than to producing social and political change.

This pattern of behavior did not characterize the revivalists. Rather, they practiced what Walzer (1969, pp. 317–19) calls a politics of sainthood, confronting the world as if at war with it, struggling to make it free of sin. They fought those institutions which, in their view, permitted sin to flourish. Their attitude toward society was opposition—not, to be sure, the opposition either of revolution or of total withdrawal, but rather a pragmatic opposition motivated by their desire to reform it.

The revivals hardly contributed unequivocally to national unity. Their immediate effects were often divisive. The very first revivals sowed divisions in the communities of western Massachusetts, and similar incidents occurred as revivals spread west over the next century. Divisions arose within nearly all the denominations affected by them, leading often to internal conflict and sometimes to schism. Miller (1965) recognizes this divisiveness, but dismisses it:

> These divisions—though frequently argued with dismaying ferocity—are of little importance before the terrific universality of the Revival. . . . Organizational conflicts . . . were not of great importance in the area of what I term the religious mentality. There, the simple fact of the Revival . . . was central. Whether it produced formal unity or created new churches was of less import than the omnipresence of the Revival. (pp. 7, 23)

The fact of disunity, though acknowledged, is ignored.

The moral crusades the revival inspired were also highly divisive. Individuals were publicly accused of being sinners, and new issues injected into politics created conflicts which persisted for many years. One of the moral crusades, of course, aroused opposition to slavery, and played no small part in the genesis of the most traumatic conflict the United States has experienced. The circumlocutions with which these historians refer to the Civil War are symptomatic: "The slavery question proved so disruptive [that it produced] secession and all its woes" (Miller, 1961, p. 367). "The movement [the second Great Awakening] achieved unity just in time for the abolitionists to tear it apart" (Mathews, 1969, p. 42).[9] The war is mentioned directly only when its importance is denied: "the revival movement . . . could not prevent the Civil War. . .; but . . . could . . . formulate a religious nationalism which even the war could not destroy" (Miller, 1961, p. 360).

It appears that to call the war by name is to utter a profanity. But what is profaned by its mention is not the nation's unity but the belief that there was any. Like the secular consensus historians, those who see Protestant revivalism as a unifying force are unable to account for the major event in American history.

It is true that evangelical Protestantism became a civil religion after the war. It inculcated the moral standards which became those

[9]In a separate article (Mathews, 1968, p. 13) in which Mathews confronts the abolitionist movement directly, he is less sanguine about the revivals. There he acknowledges that the "common world of experience" allegedly created by the revivals was a "fiction."

of the nation, found the American form of government congenial, and minimized denominational differences (Mead, 1963, p. 141). Especially after the Civil War, Protestantism celebrated the virtues with which the nation was identified and the social and economic relations emerging from them.

But the individuals and communities affected by the revivals, in their community conflict, in their benevolent activities, and in their voting, even after the Civil War, rejected some of the implications of that civil religion and still, at least occasionally, marched to a different drummer. They recognized that the war had not brought the freed slave into full fellowship and equality, they advocated prohibition, and in 1896 they supported a man who represented their values in opposition to exultation in the industrial development and imperial expansion of their country. They did not share the contentment felt by so many Protestants at being part of a growing, industrious society. Because revivalism emphasized personal experience and rejected dogmatism, and because the religious rhetoric that inspired and accompanied the Civil War permitted some to see the north's victory as God's vindication of the national cause,[10] Protestantism did help to promulgate the civil religion. But it was not the revivalist areas that embraced it.

Nor was the civil religion consistent with the intentions of the revivalists. The revivalists were optimistic, but not because they thought American institutions were the full realization of God's will. Their millennial expectancy was based on what they thought was clear evidence: the results of the revivals. As long as the revivals continued to win believers they could believe that the kingdom would soon come. (Many of the millennially optimistic statements Miller quotes were written at the height of the revival or of the later revival of 1857–1858.) This expectancy did not last long after the revivals died down.

Similarly, their sense that America's institutions marked a realization of God's purposes was highly contingent. Most revivalists were not subtle thinkers, and they failed to realize that their effort to reform American society might have its ultimately unhappy consequences. But they often feared that America was going to hell: at Jackson's election, during the panic of 1837, and when the Civil War loomed, they revived the "Jeremiad" of eighteenth-century New England. Finney believed that if the whole nation were converted, slavery would be abolished automatically, but he correctly feared that without the conversion of the nation a civil war over slavery would erupt.

---

[10]Among those who did so was "that magnificent weathervane of respectable opinion," Henry Ward Beecher (Mead, 1963, p. 143).

And even when revivalists did express great hope for their country's future, the hope was usually accompanied by a warning. They believed that their expectations would be fulfilled only if the evangelization of America were completed, and prophesied dire outcomes if it failed. James Batchelder's statement that "we absolutely must . . . evangelize our beloved country, that she may serve as 'the hope of the world in a political and religious sense' " is quoted by Miller (1965, p. 55) to represent the revivalists' identification with American institutions. But if Batchelder was optimistic that his country would inspire the world, he still believed that it would do so only if he and his colleagues fulfilled their duty. In two separate essays, Miller extensively discusses a document entitled "The Necessity of Revivals of Religion to the Perpetuity of our Civil and Religious Institutions," arguing that this 1831 article identifies evangelical Christianity with the nation and even subordinates religion to national ideals (Miller, 1961, pp. 362–63; Miller, 1965, pp. 68–70). But his own discussion reveals that the document is as emphatic about the great moral dangers the nation faces. In particular, it alerts the faithful to the "corrupting influence of a preeminent national prosperity" (Miller, 1961, p. 363). Such a warning is completely inconsistent with celebrations of America at the end of the century by Protestants for whom prosperity confirmed that God had blessed the country.

The cultural unity interpretation of revivalism, like most functional analysis which accepts the postulates of functional unity, universality, and indispensability, has conservative political implications.[11] To favor order over disorder is necessarily to favor an existing set of social institutions over all possible alternatives. The consensus historians, glorifying American culture and political institutions, find in the revivals both an anticipation of their views and an explanation for the phenomena they discern. But they do so only by ignoring both the extensive history of conflict in America and the inequalities in the social institutions which produced it, and in so doing they commit an injustice against the revivalists, whose understanding of those social institutions was far more perceptive and far more critical.

Many church historians recognize that the political culture of consensus contradicted the revivalist ethos, and that the revivalist impulse was destroyed in the later nineteenth century. Specifically, revivalism came to concentrate on individual conversion rather than social reform (Mead, 1963, p. 137). As revivalism became more indi-

---

[11]Cf. Merton (1957, pp. 37–45) although, as Merton points out, these implications are not inherent in the logic of functional analysis. Geertz (1957) provides an attempt to apply functional analysis to religious change.

vidualistic, the mainstream of American religion, culture, and society left it behind. More generally, the revivalist impulse was destroyed when revivalism's prophetic, oppositional stance was abandoned in favor of what Mead calls the complacency of a culturally dominant Protestantism in the late nineteenth century (Mead, 1963, pp. 142, 154). "Protestants shared the general cultural conviction of the time that they were living in the best of all possible worlds" (Hudson, 1961, p. 124). Religion was institutionalized and nationalized: "Henceforth the kingdom of the Lord was a human possession, not a permanent revolution. It is in particular the kingdom of the Anglo-Saxon race, which is destined to bring light to the gentiles by means of lamps manufactured in America" (Niebuhr, 1937, p. 179). To the extent that revivals forged a unified national culture, they abandoned the very distinctiveness which had made them an important national political force.

The consensus historians misinterpret revivalism. It inspired political movements which responded to moral convictions, not to group antagonisms; it did not fortify the prevailing Jacksonian political culture of the early nineteenth century; and it did not contribute unequivocally to a complacent, culturally united society after the Civil War. These historians err by ignoring fundamental aspects of revivalists' (preachers' and converts') acts. To demonstrate that ideas have consequences, one cannot get by simply with an analysis of the ideas themselves. Empirical evidence about the political behavior of the revivalist communities forces us to conclude that the meaning of the revivals was vastly different from that presented by historians who wish to incorporate the revivals comfortably into American cultural history. To understand the role of revivalism before the Civil War, and even to understand its political manifestations in revivalist communities afterward, one must recognize that it created not complacent patriots but people committed to the realization of their ideals within their nation, however much they might violate social order and national harmony.

Consensus was part of the revivalists' goal, but they did not want to establish consensus for its own sake. They did want to create a homogeneous America, but of a particular kind. They hoped to create agreement on a specific set of beliefs, among them that all men are created equal and that enslavement is contrary to the will of God. Nor was their goal to disrupt, at least not for the sake of disruption. They began their work without recognizing the cost of achieving their goals; they were optimistic that a voluntary process of conversion would suffice. But they did not hold back when stronger means were required. Their pragmatism as to "the right use of means" was in the

service of the goals they held absolutely—it permitted them to accept
or to challenge national harmony, as occasion demanded. They did
not realize all their goals, but they did create a political ethos which
stood outside of and had profound effects on the national consensus.
The world for which they strove remains beyond reach, but the ideal
inspired them and their descendants.

Appendix A

Data: Sources and Transformations

The data used in this study, with the exceptions noted below, were provided by the Inter-University Consortium for Political and Social Research. The data were supplied in partially-proofed form and the Consortium bears no responsibility for either the analyses or interpretations presented here. The Consortium provided all data referred to from the United States Census (that is, all demographic data for years whose last digit is zero), and county vote totals from all presidential, senatorial, and gubernatorial elections from 1824 to 1968. All these election returns were examined, although not all have been used.

Data not available from the Consortium were found in the following sources:

1. *Both States*

Anti-Slavery Society Membership: American Anti-Slavery Society. *Fifth Annual Report of the Executive Committee* . . . New York: William S. Dorr, 1838. Pp. 138–51.

2. *New York*

Percentage of population born in New England, 1855. In *Census of the State of New York, for 1855*. Albany: C. Van Benthuysen, 1857.

Referenda, 1846, 1860, and 1869. In *The Tribune Almanac for 1870*.

1855 election. In *The Tribune Almanac for 1856*.

Twentieth century referenda. In *Manual for the Use of the Legislature of the State of New York*, 1928–1968. Published by the New York Secretary of State at Albany, New York.

3. *Ohio*

1867 referendum results were kindly provided by William P. Lewis, Director, State of Ohio Legislative Reference Bureau.

1883 referendum. In *Annual Report 1883*. Columbus, Ohio: 1884.

1912 referendum. In *The Constitution of the State of Ohio and the Several Amendments Submitted at the Election Held September 3, 1912*. Columbus, Ohio: F. J. Heer, 1912.

Referenda, 1914–1927. In *Vote for State Officers*, 1914–1928.

1933 referendum. In *Ohio election statistics*, 1934. Published by the Ohio Secretary of State at Columbus, Ohio.

The sources of the data on revivalism are described in Appendix B.

The county is the unit of analysis for this study. The necessity of using counties is in some respects unfortunate: it has the consequence that the more than 900,000 voters in Kings County in 1964 are given the same importance as the fewer than 3,000 in Hamilton County. The need to use units whose boundaries do not change over time precludes the use of any smaller units, such as wards, in the larger counties. The resulting distortion appears to be slight, however: Pomper (1971) has shown in at least one analysis at the state level that results were similar whether states were weighted equally or according to their population (pp. 206–07).

Counties themselves do not form units with consistent boundaries through the whole period under study. In the nineteenth century new counties were frequently formed by dividing old ones, and a rather complicated procedure was devised to take account of this: composite counties were created out of those counties which were divided or newly organized after 1836. In some cases this required combining into a composite county two or more which had been organized before 1836, when a new county had been formed from parts of each of the old counties.

Counties were combined as shown in Tables A.1 and A.2.[1] This

TABLE A.1
Composite Cases, New York

1. Bronx New York	3. Nassau Queens
2. Fulton Hamilton Montgomery	4. Genesee Wyoming
	5. Chemung Schuyler Steuben Tioga Tompkins

[1]County organization data for Ohio are taken from Downes (1927); for New York, from New York Secretary of State (1916, pp. 220–21).

TABLE A.2
Composite Cases, Ohio

1. Ashland	6. Carroll
Delaware	Columbiana
Erie	Harrison
Huron	Jefferson
Knox	Mahoning
Lorain	Medina
Marion	Portage
Morrow	Stark
Richland	Summit
Wayne	Trumbull
	Tuscarawas
2. Allen	
Auglaize	7. Guernsey
Mercer	Monroe
Van Wert	Morgan
	Noble
3. Defiance	
Paulding	8. Ottawa
Williams	Sandusky
4. Fulton	9. Athens
Henry	Hocking
Lucas	Jackson
Wood	Vinton
5. Cuyahoga	10. Crawford
Geauga	Wyandot
Lake	

procedure provided a set of units for each state which was consistent from 1836 on. The five composite counties shown in Table A.1, together with the forty-eight counties whose boundaries were not changed after 1836, form a set of fifty-three cases for New York; the ten composite counties shown in Table A.2, together with forty-one unaffected counties, form a set of fifty-one cases for Ohio.

All the findings presented through Chapter 5 refer to these reduced sets of cases. Ohio's county organization was completed by 1851, and all findings in Chapter 6 are based on the full set of cases. In New York, findings presented for the period up to 1914 refer to the reduced set of cases, and findings for the later period refer to the full set.

The factor analyses of New York election returns between 1904 and 1968 are based on the full set of counties, except that New York and Bronx Counties have been combined. Where these factors have been correlated with other variables, the factor scores for the composite county have been assigned to the two separate counties.

All correlations of revivalism with other variables based on the full set of cases use the revivalism scores of the composite counties. Because some counties did not exist when the revivals were occurring, it was impossible to assign a unique revivalism score to each modern county. The score for each composite county was therefore assigned to each of its component counties.

All voting data are computed as percentages of the total vote cast for the office. When a candidate was endorsed by more than one party, his total vote was attributed to the major party (for example, Johnson ran on the Democratic and Liberal lines in New York in 1964; his combined total is referred to as the percentage Democratic).

Certain variables are used in unconventional ways and require special comment. Church-size data in the 1850 census are not membership figures but seating capacities of church buildings. The size of a denomination in a county has been estimated by the number of seats in that denomination's churches divided by the 1850 population.

Internal migration data for Ohio are taken from the 1870 census even though they are used to estimate population origins for earlier years. Ohio, unlike New York, had no special state censuses in the nineteenth century (U.S. Dept. of Commerce, 1948, p. 52) and 1870 measurements of southern and Yankee settlement are used as the best available indicators of the population composition of counties before the Civil War. These data are evidently subject to unreliability, especially in the counties (mainly in southern Ohio) that were settled in the eighteenth century and the earliest decades of the nineteenth, where by 1870 most of the population was native to the state. One must assume that later migration followed a similar pattern to earlier migration, and that the 1870 measures are reasonably reliable indicators.[2]

The proportion of the 1870 population born in New York is used to estimate Yankee origins in Ohio. It is probably a valid measure of Yankee origins for the Western Reserve in which New Yorkers were concentrated, because most of the New Yorkers who migrated to Ohio were Yankees, and most of the Yankees who migrated to the Reserve came from western New York rather than directly from New England. However, New York origins has two known sources of invalidity as an indicator of Yankee settlement. The Ohio Company's

---

[2]At least some validity for the 1870 migration data as indicative of the pre-Civil War population composition is demonstrated by the correlation of .79 between the percentage born in New England, 1855, and the percentage born in Connecticut, Massachusetts, and Vermont, 1870, for the counties of New York.

Purchase, the area around Marietta, was settled in 1788 by families migrating directly from New England; further settlement was largely from New England. The northwestern corner of the state, which was Indian territory and unsettled by whites until the 1830s, received much of its population from the New York-settled Western Reserve, but most of these settlers were probably Ohio-born sons of migrants. In both of these areas the indicator fails to count a substantial Yankee population. Unfortunately, better data do not exist.

The number of farms per capita is used as the best consistently available measure of rural population. For the earlier censuses, the number living in rural areas and the number employed in agriculture are not reported.

Standardized rather than raw regression coefficients have been presented throughout. The reason for this is that many of the measures are indirect and therefore provide relative rather than absolute levels of variables. Among these are variables estimated by measures of the same variables at different points in time; variables only indirectly related to the variables they are intended to measure (such as the 1850 church statistics); and variables in which measurement error must be assumed (such as the number of revivals). Since the absolute levels and variances of the indicators differ from those of the true variables, the scales are arbitrary and standardized coefficients are more appropriate than raw coefficients.[3]

[3]For a discussion of the uses of raw and standardized regression coefficients in relating census and electoral data, see Hammond (in press).

Appendix B
Measuring Revivalism

A social scientist who attempts to quantify a religious experience like revivalism must feel somewhat presumptuous. But this study is based on the assumption that religious belief and religious emotion have effects on overt behavior and that that overt behavior is observable. Not only were revivals observable, but their occurrence was recorded in enthusiastic detail by those who approved of them. As early as 1740 Jonathan Edwards had suggested that accounts of revivals be published regularly to inspire congregations which had not yet been visited by the Spirit. In the nineteenth century religious journalism was flourishing, and both denominational and nonsectarian periodicals— like the one Huck Finn read at the Grangerfords—had wide circulation. Revivals were major news items for these publications, and their accounts make it possible to determine where revivals occurred.

To determine the incidence of revivals all extant issues of several religious periodicals were examined for the decade 1825–1835. Many of these were not used, either because too few issues were available or because the low frequency of reports of revivals suggested that no effort was made to cover them regularly. The following ten periodicals, which were relatively complete and reported revivals regularly, were examined in detail:

Home Missionary and American Pastor's Journal (New York), 1828–31.
Methodist Magazine (New York), 1825–28.
New York Observer, 1825–35.
New York Evangelist, 1832–34.
Rochester Observer, 1827–32.

Western Recorder (Utica), 1825–26.
Utica Christian Repository, 1833.
The Christian Advocate (New York), 1826–35.
The Evangelical Magazine and Gospel Advocate (Utica), 1830–31.
The Visitant (Utica), 1825–27.

Some of the reports were relatively detailed, telling how long the revival lasted and how many people were converted. Other accounts merely named the town in which a revival had occurred; when the movement was at its peak, a single issue might carry a long list of such towns. The editors of the day carried on an active exchange and often reprinted accounts from other papers.[1]

The first seven periodicals listed contained reports for both New York and Ohio, and the last three for New York only. Every revival reported in each of these periodicals was noted, together with whatever indication was given of the number of people converted.[2]

The reports had to be aggregated to the county level so that they could be correlated with the political and demographic data. Identifying the counties in which the towns were located was often a problem. In many cases, no town of the name could be located; more often, there were two or more towns with the same name in the same state, and the report contained no evidence about the town's location within the state. This was particularly a problem for Ohio, where approximately forty percent of the reports could not be identified as to county. In such cases the report had to be ignored.

Because the periodicals overlapped in their coverage it was necessary to determine whether two independent reports referred to the same event. A rather conservative procedure was used to avoid duplication: if two periodicals referred to a revival in the same town in the same year, they were regarded as a single event. If any one periodical carried more than one report from a town in a single year, it was assumed that the reports referred to the same event unless each report contained a reference to the number of people who had been converted and the second number was smaller than the first. By this procedure 1,951 reports for which the town could be located were deter-

[1] The report quoted in Chapter 3 from the *New York Observer* was reprinted from the *Cincinnati Christian Journal*.

[2] In locating these reports I received valuable assistance, greatly appreciated, from Professor Gaylord P. Albaugh, who provided me with the relevant sections of his unpublished bibliography of religious journals published in the American colonies and nation in the eighteenth and early nineteenth centuries (a small portion of which has been published in Albaugh, 1963 and 1964), and guided me in its use.

mined to identify 1,343 revivals in New York and 431 reports for which the town could be located were determined to identify 351 revivals in Ohio between 1825 and 1835.

From these reports, two measures of the incidence of revivalism in each county were derived. The first was simply the number of revivals occurring in the county during the decade. The second, more complicated measure was an estimate of the proportion of the population affected by revivals, derived from the reports of the number of people converted in each revival. According to these reports, about eighty new converts resulted from the average revival.

Some two-thirds of the reports (64% for New York, 68% for Ohio) contained some indication of the number of conversions. Where no such indication was given, it was assumed that other revivals in the same county were of similar proportions. The number of conversions was therefore estimated as being equal to the average number converted in other revivals (for which the information was available) in the same county in the same year. If no such information was available for that year, the estimate was equal to the average number for that county during the entire decade.[3] These numbers were summed for all the revivals in the county and the total was divided by the 1830 population to estimate the proportion of the population converted in revivals.

It is of course not assumed that this number is precise. Even apart from the necessity to estimate numbers for one-third of the revivals, the numbers which appeared were very likely exaggerated. But there is no reason to suspect that the exaggeration was systematically greater in some counties than in others, so the estimates should be reasonably accurate measures of the relative effect of revivalism in each county. Because this measure is speculative, however, I have limited its use to the discussion of the relation between population density and the impact of revivalism in Chapter 3. Elsewhere, the simple number of revivals in each county is used.

While these reports undoubtedly fail to provide an exhaustive count of revivals, the practice of editorial exchange probably guarantees that the count is not geographically selective—the more so because a congregation experiencing a revival felt impelled to broadcast the news, so that other congregations might profit by the example. Though the measures may not be subject to systematic error, however, they are certainly subject to random error—it is unlikely that all

[3]There were only two counties, both in Ohio, in which revivals were reported but no reports gave numbers of conversions. For them the number of conversions in each revival was estimated as being equal to the average number for all revivals in Ohio during the decade.

revivals were reported, and the county locations of many of the reports that were found could not be identified.

It is well known that random measurement error produces lower correlations between a variable of interest and other variables (Blalock, 1969; Costner, 1969). In particular, when two correlated variables, one well- and one poorly-measured, are jointly used as independent variables in multivariate analysis, effects that are in fact due to the poorly-measured variable may be attributed to the one that is well-measured (Gordon, 1968, pp. 599–601). One must therefore be cautious in interpreting results when an indicator is known to contain measurement error. The possibility of measurement error was particularly a problem in this study, where the most important variable could be measured with only moderate precision. Since I have been concerned to estimate the effects of revivalism relative to the effects of other independent variables, it was important to make its measurement as accurate as possible so that its effects were not spuriously minimized in the multivariate analyses.

The remedy for random measurement error is to derive several independent measurements of the same phenomenon. Accordingly, I examined and tabulated statistics of revivalism and of the membership of churches where revivals occurred from denominational sources. Of the various measures collected, one proved useful: the membership of the New School Presbyterian Church.

The New School Church arose from the Presbyterian schism of 1837, when the national General Assembly expelled three synods in western New York and the Presbytery of the Western Reserve in Ohio. The alleged basis for their expulsion was the legalistic claim that many of their churches had irregular forms of governance stemming from the Plan of Union. The real issues in the split, however, were the New School theology and the New Measures of Finney and his followers. Many other synods, presbyteries, and individual churches chose to leave the church and join the expelled synods in a new denomination commonly called the New School Presbyterian Church. Some churches within the expelled synods likewise chose to affiliate with the expelling group, which was called the Old School; each body, denying the legitimacy of the other, laid claim to the name "Presbyterian Church in the U.S.A." (Staiger, 1949, pp. 405–10).

Membership in the New School denomination can thus be taken as an indicator of revivalism since congregations affiliating with it demonstrated their acceptance of the principles and practices for which the synods were expelled from the Old School body. However, New School membership may not be an uncontaminated measure of revivalism. Contemporaries and historians have identified slavery as a latent issue in the split of 1837. Staiger (1949) claims that northern conservatives in the church feared the possibility of an impending geographical split over slavery, and attempted to head it off by using a pretext to rid the church of those congregations and synods that wanted to force the church into a strong antislavery stand. It is true that all the expelled synods had adopted resolutions declaring slavery sinful and slaveholding inconsistent with church membership (pp. 394–97).

At the same time, many southern churches went with the New School, and many New School congregations, upon deciding that even the New School Presbyterian Church was not sufficiently antislavery, later withdrew from it and became Congregational (Nichols, 1963, p. 156). If the schism was in part due to disagreements over slavery, it certainly did not resolve anything. Both wings split into northern and southern branches before the Civil War (Smith, 1957, p. 27).

But the possibility that the New School schism was due even in part to abolitionism must be considered with caution before its use as an indicator of revivalism. While random measurement error will lower the correlations between variables, systematic measurement error may well increase them. If New School membership has higher correlations with indicators of abolitionism than do other measures of revivalism, they may be due to the confounding effects of abolition in the schism rather than to the better measurement of revivalism. To use it as an indicator of revivalism would therefore exaggerate the effect of revivalism on abolitionism. New School membership is, in fact, more highly correlated with indicators of abolitionism than is the number of revivals reported in newspaper accounts.[4] These higher correlations appear to result from systematic measurement error in Ohio, but not in New York.

The evidence that the higher correlations between New School membership and abolitionism in New York do not result from systematic error is that correlations between New School membership and variables which demonstrate the effect of revivalism in later years are also higher than the correlations of those variables with the other measure of revivalism. I have argued that revivalism not only stimulated opposition to slavery but also created a political ethos which influenced the way people voted for many years. If the difference be-

---

[4]New School congregation membership in each county was tabulated from Presbyterian Church in the United States of America [New School], General Assembly (1841, pp. 31–62; 1843, pp. 5–69). Total membership was computed as a proportion of the 1840 county population.

tween the measured effects of New School membership and those of the number of revivals on abolitionism is due to the fact that the former measures abolitionism as much as revivalism, it should not be more highly correlated with the later variables.

TABLE B.1
Revivalism and Political Indicators, New York
(Correlation coefficients)

	Anti-Slavery Societies	Liberty, 1844	Suffrage referendum, 1846	Democratic Z-score, 1872	Prohibition referendum, 1933	Parimutuel betting referendum, 1939
Number of revivals	.204	.282	.279	.166	−.296	−.397
New School membership	.467	.433	.523	.501	−.461	−.566

Table B.1 shows the correlations of New School membership and number of revivals with several political variables for the years before and after the Civil War in New York. The correlations of New School membership with abolitionism indicators are indeed about twice as high as the correlations of number of revivals; but the magnitude of the difference between their respective correlations with post-Civil War variables is about the same. While there are historical grounds for arguing that the New School half of the schism represented abolitionism as much as it did revivalism, there are no such grounds for suggesting that it also represented Populism and prohibition. The pattern of differential correlations is more likely to be derived from differential random measurement error: New School membership appears to represent revivalism, measured with less error than the other indicator.

The argument could be accused of being circular: one must assume that revivalism had an effect on these several political issues in order to gain confidence in an indicator that will be used to prove that it had that effect. If one assumes, however, that New School membership represents revivalism-*cum*-abolitionism, its association with later political phenomena must then be explained by one of two arguments: either that it is due to the association of these later phenomena with abolitionism or that it is due to some set of demographic factors which determines both. The former explanation appears inferior to the widely accepted interpretation that the connection between abolitionism and other reform movements is their common source in revivalism. The effect of demographic factors as an explanation is ruled out by the multivariate analyses presented in the text. In all, it seems most persuasive to interpret New School membership as a valid indicator of revivalism in New York.

New School membership and newspaper reports of revivals can therefore be regarded as independent measures of revivalism. To minimize the effects of measurement error in each, they were combined into a single index. The index consisted of the sum of their standard scores, giving equal weight to each. This index is the measure of revivalism used for New York in all tables except in those few which explicitly indicate that the measure is either number of revivals or proportion of the population affected by revivals.

There is no such assurance that New School membership is an uncontaminated measure of revivalism in Ohio. Table B.2 shows its

TABLE B.2
Revivalism and Political Indicators, Ohio
(Correlation coefficients)

	Liberty, 1844	Free Soil, 1851	Republican, 1868	Republican, 1888	Democratic Z-score, 1905
Number of revivals	.421	.447	.315	.219	.234
New School membership	.648	.735	.334	.175	−.009

correlations with several political variables. Its correlations with abolitionist votes are so high that their level in itself must arouse suspicion. When they are compared to the correlations of the number of revivals with abolitionist votes, and the correlations of both indicators with later political variables, moreover, the pattern suggests systematic rather than random error. New School membership correlates with abolition much more highly than does number of revivals; correlations with later variables are approximately equal. It is likely, therefore, that New School membership in Ohio was due to abolitionism as much as to revivalism. Accordingly, New School membership has not been used as an indicator of revivalism in Ohio. The variable measuring revivalism is simply the number of revivals reported in each county in newspaper accounts.

All the data on which the measures of revivalism are based have been deposited with the Inter-University Consortium for Political and Social Research, Ann Arbor, Michigan, and are available for further analysis by others.

References

Ahlstrom, S. E. *A religious history of the American people*. New Haven and London: Yale University Press, 1972.

Albaugh, G. P. American Presbyterian periodicals and newspapers, 1752–1830, with library locations. *Journal of Presbyterian History*, September 1963, **41**, 165–87; December 1963, **41**, 243–62; March 1964, **42**, 54–67; June 1964, **42**, 124–44.

Alexander D. S. *A political history of the state of New York*, 3 vols. Port Washington, N.Y.: Friedman, 1969.

Alford, R. A. *Party and society: The Anglo-American democracies*. Chicago: Rand McNally, 1963.

Allinsmith, W., & Allinsmith, B. Religious affiliation and politico-economic attitude: A study of eight major U.S. religious groups. *Public Opinion Quarterly*, 1948, **12**, 377–89.

Almond, G., & Powell, G. B. *Comparative politics: A developmental approach*. Boston: Little, Brown, 1966.

Almond, G., & Verba, S. *The civic culture*. Boston: Little, Brown, 1963.

Banfield, E. C., & Wilson, J. Q. *City politics*. New York: Vintage Books, 1963.

Barnes, G. H. *The anti-slavery impulse 1830–1844*. New York: Harcourt, Brace, & World, 1964.

Barnes, G. H., & Dumond, D. L., Eds. *Letters of Theodore Dwight Weld, Angelina Grimké Weld, and Sarah Grimké*, 2 vols. New York: Da Capo, 1970.

Bass, H. J. The politics of ballot reform in New York state, 1888–1890. *New York History*, 1961, **42**, 253–72.

Beecher, L. *The autobiography of Lyman Beecher*, 3 vols. (B. M. Cross, Ed.). Cambridge, Mass.: Belknap, 1961.

Bellah, R. N. Civil religion in America. In W. G. McLoughlin & R. N. Bellah (Eds.), *Religion in American life*. Boston: Beacon, 1968.

Bendix, R., & Berger, B. Images of society and problems of concept formation in sociology. In L. Gross (Ed.), *Symposium on sociological theory*. New York: Harper & Row, 1959.

Benson, L. *The concept of Jacksonian democracy: New York as a test case*. New York: Atheneum, 1964.

Benson, L. An approach to the scientific study of past public opinion. In D. K. Rowney & J. O. Graham, Jr. (Eds.), *Quantitative history: Selected readings in quantitative analysis of historical data*. Homewood, Ill.: Dorsey, 1969.

Berelson, B. R., Lazarsfeld, P. F., & McPhee, W. N. *Voting: A study of opinion formation in a presidential campaign*. Chicago, Ill.: Univ. of Chicago Press, 1954.

Berger, M. L. *The revolution in the New York party systems 1840–1860*. Port Washington, N.Y.: Kennikat, 1973.

Berwanger, E. H. *The frontier against slavery: Western anti-Negro prejudice and the slavery extension controversy*. Urbana, Ill.: Univ. of Illinois Press, 1967.

Blalock, H. M., Jr. Multiple indicators and the causal approach to measurement error. *American Journal of Sociology*, 1969, **75**, 264–72.

Blau, J. L. The Christian party in politics. *The Review of Religion*, 1946, **11**, 18–35.

Bower, R. T. Opinion research and historical interpretation of elections. *Public Opinion Quarterly*, 1948, **12**, 455–64.

Bradford, D. H. The background and formation of the Republican party in Ohio 1844–1861. Unpublished Ph.D. dissertation, University of Chicago, 1947.

Burnham, W. D. Party systems and the political process. In W. N. Chambers & W. D. Burnham (Eds.), *The American party systems: Stages of political development*. New York: Oxford Univ. Press, 1967.

Burnham, W. D. American voting behavior and the 1964 election. *Midwest Journal of Political Science*, 1968, **12**, 1–40.

Burnham, W. D. The changing shape of the American political universe. In R. P. Swierengs (Ed.), *Quantification in American history: Theory and research*. New York: Atheneum, 1970. (a)

Burnham, W. D. *Critical elections and the mainsprings of American politics*. New York: Norton, 1970. (b)

Burnham, W. D. Quantitative history: Beyond the correlation coefficient: A review essay. *Historical Methods Newsletter*, 1971, **4**, 62–66.

Campbell, A., Converse, P. E., Miller, W. E., & Stokes, D. E. *The American voter*. New York: Wiley, 1960.

Carman, H. J., & Luthin, R. H. The Seward–Fillmore feud and the crisis of 1850. *New York History* 1943, **41**, 335–357.

Chaddock, R. E. Ohio before 1850: A study of the early influence of Pennsylvania and southern populations in Ohio. Unpublished Ph.D. dissertation, Columbia University, 1908.

Chalmers, L. Tammany Hall and New York City politics, 1853–1861. Unpublished Ph.D. dissertation, New York University, 1967.

Cole, C. C., Jr. *The social ideas of the northern evangelists 1826–1860.* New York: Columbia Univ. Press, 1954.

Converse, P. E. The nature of belief systems in mass publics. In D. E. Apter (Ed.), *Ideology and discontent.* New York: Free Press, 1964.

Colvin, D. L. *Prohibition in the United States: A history of the Prohibition party and of the prohibition movement.* New York: Doran, 1926.

Costner, H. L. Theory, deduction, and rules of correspondence. *American Journal of Sociology,* 1969, **75**, 245–63.

Crandall, A. W. *The early history of the Republican party 1854–1856.* Gloucester, Mass.: Peter Smith, 1960.

Cross, W. R. *The Burned-Over District: The social and intellectual history of enthusiastic religion in western New York, 1800–1850.* Ithaca, N.Y.: Cornell Univ. Press, 1950.

Curran, T. J. Know-Nothings of New York state. Unpublished Ph.D. dissertation, Columbia University, 1963.

Curry, R. O. (Ed.) *The abolitionists: Reformers or fanatics?* New York: Holt, Rinehart & Wilson, 1965.

Davis, D. B. *The problem of slavery in western culture.* Ithaca: Cornell Univ. Press, 1966.

Davis, H. E. Religion in the Western Reserve 1800–1825. *Ohio Archaeological and Historical Quarterly,* 1929, **38**, 475–501.

Davis, K., & Moore, W. E. Some principles of stratification, *American Sociological Review,* 1945, **10**, 242–49.

Dohn, N. H. The history of the Anti-Saloon League. Unpublished Ph.D. dissertation, Ohio State University, 1959.

Donald, A. D. Prelude to Civil War: The decline of the Whig party in New York, 1848–1852. Unpublished Ph.D. dissertation, University of Rochester, 1961.

Donald, D. Toward a reconsideration of abolitionists. In *Lincoln reconsidered: Essays on the Civil War era,* 2nd ed. New York: Knopf, 1966. Pp. 19–36.

Donovan, H. D. A. *The Barnburners.* New York: New York Univ. Press, 1925.

Downes, R. C. Evolution of Ohio county boundaries. *Ohio Archaeological and Historical publications,* 1927, **26**, 340–477.

Duncan, O. D., & Davis, B. An alternative to ecological correlation. *American Sociological Review,* 1953, **18**, 665–66.

Durkheim, E. *The elementary forms of the religious life*. New York: Free Press, 1965.

Edwards, J. Thoughts on the revival of religion in New England, 1740. In *The works of President Edwards in four volumes*, Vol. 3. New York: Carter, 1868. Pp. 333–425.

Ellis, D. M., Frost, J. A., Syrett, H. C., & Carman, H. J. *A history of New York State*. Ithaca, N.Y.: Cornell Univ. Press, 1967.

Fehrenbacher, D. E. Disunion and reunion. In J. Higham (Ed.), *The reconstruction of American history*. London: Hutchinson, 1962.

Fenton, J. H. *Midwest politics*. New York: Holt, Rinehart & Winston, 1966.

Filler, L. *The crusade against slavery 1830–1860*. New York: Harper & Row, 1960.

Finney, C. G. *Sermons on important subjects*, 3rd ed. New York: Taylor, 1836.

Finney, C. G. *Memoirs of Rev. Charles G. Finney*. New York: Barnes, 1876.

Finney, C. G. *Lectures on revivals of religion*. Cambridge, Mass.: Belknap Press, 1960.

Fladeland, B. *James Gillespie Birney: Slaveholder to abolitionist*. Ithaca, N.Y.: Cornell Univ. Press, 1955.

Fletcher, R. S. *A history of Oberlin College from its foundation through the Civil War*. Oberlin: Oberlin College, 1943.

Flinn, T. A. Continuity and change in Ohio politics. *Journal of Politics*, 1962, **24**, 521–44.

Foner, E. Politics and prejudice: The Free Soil party and the Negro, 1849–1852. *Journal of Negro History*, 1965, **50**, 239–56. (a)

Foner, E. Racial attitudes of New York Free Soilers. *New York History* 1965, **46**, 311–29. (b)

Foner, E. *Free soil, free labor, free men: The ideology of the Republican party before the Civil War*. New York: Oxford Univ. Press, 1970.

Foner, E. The causes of the American Civil War: Recent interpretations and new directions. *Civil War History*, 1974, **20**, 197–214.

Foner, P. S. *Business and slavery: The New York merchants and the irrepressible conflict*. Chapel Hill, N.C.: Univ. of North Carolina Press, 1941.

Formisano, R. *The birth of mass political parties: Michigan, 1827–1861*. Princeton, N.J.: Princeton Univ. Press, 1971.

Fox, D. R. The Negro vote in old New York. *Political Science Quarterly* 1917, **32**, 252–72.

Fox, D. R. *Yankees and Yorkers*. Port Washington, N.Y.: Friedman, 1963.

Fox, D. R. *The decline of aristocracy in the politics of New York 1801–1840*

(R.V. Remini, Ed.). New York: Harper Torchbooks, 1965.

Galbreath, C. B. *History of Ohio*. Chicago: American Historical Society, 1928.

Gara, L. *The liberty line: The legend of the underground railroad.* Lexington: Univ. of Kentucky Press, 1961.

Geertz, C. Ritual and social change: A Javanese example. *American Anthropologist*, 1957, **59**, 32–53.

Geertz, C. Ideology as a cultural system. In D. E. Apter (Ed.), *Ideology and discontent*. New York: Free Press, 1964.

Geertz, C. Religion as a cultural system. In M. Banton (Ed.), *Anthropological approaches to the study of religion*. A.S.A. Monographs, No. 3. London: Tavistock, 1966.

Goldrich, D. J., Pratt, R. B., & Schuller, C. R. The political integration of lower-class urban settlements in Chile and Peru. *Studies in Comparative International Development*, 1967, **3**, 1–22.

Goodman, L. A. Some alternatives to ecological correlation. *American Journal of Sociology*, 1959, **64**, 610–25.

Gordon, R. A. Issues in multiple regression. *American Journal of Sociology*, 1968, **73**, 592–616.

Griffin, C. S. *Their brothers' keepers: Moral stewardship in the United States, 1800–1865*. New Brunswick, N.J.: Rutgers Univ. Press, 1960.

Gusfield, J. R. *Symbolic crusade: Status politics and the American temperance movement*. Urbana, Ill.: Univ. of Illinois Press, 1963.

Guttman, L. The basis for scalogram analysis. In *Measurement and prediction*. Vol. IV of *Studies in social psychology in World War II*. Princeton, N.J.: Princeton Univ. Press, 1949. Pp. 60–90.

Hamilton, M. W. *The country printer: New York State, 1785–1830*. Port Washington, N.Y.: Friedman, 1964.

Hammond, J. D. *Political history of the State of New York*. Syracuse, N.Y.: Hall & Dixon, 1848.

Hammond, J. L. *The revivalist political ethos*. Unpublished Ph.D. dissertation, University of Chicago, 1972.

Hammond, J. L. Two sources of error in ecological correlations. *American Sociological Review*, 1973, **38**, 764–77.

Hammond, J. L. Minor parties and electoral realignments. *American Politics Quarterly*, 1976, **4**, 63–85.

Hammond, J. L. New approaches to aggregate electoral data. *Journal of Interdisciplinary History*, 1979, in press.

Harlow, R. *Gerritt Smith: Philanthropist and reformer*. New York: Holt, 1939.

Haynes, F. E. *Third party movements since the Civil War with special reference to Iowa: A study in social politics*. Iowa City: The State Historical Society of Iowa, 1916.

Hays, S. P. History as human behavior. *Iowa Journal of History*, 1960, **58**, 193–206.

Hays, S. P. Political parties and the community-society continuum. In W. N. Chambers & W. D. Burnham (Eds.), *The American Party system: Stages of political development*. New York: Oxford Univ. Press, 1967.

Hennessy, T. M. Problems in concept formation: The ethos 'theory' and the comparative study of urban politics. *Midwest Journal of Political Science*, 1970, **14**, 537–64.

Herberg, W. *Protestant—Catholic—Jew: An essay in American religious sociology*. Garden City, N.Y.: Doubleday Anchor, 1960.

Higham, J. Another look at nativism. *Catholic Historical Review*, 1958, **44**, 147–58.

Hill, C. *Society and Puritanism in pre-revolutionary England*. New York: Schocken, 1967.

Hofstadter, R. *The American political tradition*. New York: Vintage, 1948.

Hofstadter, R. *The age of reform*. New York: Vintage, 1955.

Hofstadter, R. Pseudo-conservatism revisited: A postscript. In D. Bell (Ed.), *The radical right*. Garden City, N.Y.: Doubleday Anchor, 1964. Pp. 97–103.   (a)

Hofstadter, R. The pseudo-conservative revolt. In D. Bell (Ed.), *The radical right*. Garden City, N.Y.: Doubleday Anchor, 1964. Pp. 75–96.   (b)

Holt, E. A. *Party politics in Ohio, 1840–1850*. Columbus, Ohio: Heer, 1931.

Holt, M. F. *Forging a majority: The formation of the Republican party in Pittsburgh 1848–1860*. New Haven, Conn.: Yale Univ. Press, 1969.

Hudson, W. S. *American Protestantism*. Chicago: Univ. of Chicago Press, 1961.

Ionescu, G., & Gellner, E. (Eds.), *Populism: Its meaning and national characteristics*. London: Weidenfeld & Nicolson, 1969.

Jensen, R. *The winning of the midwest: Social and political conflict 1888–1896*. Chicago: Univ. of Chicago Press, 1971.

Johnson, B. A critical appraisal of the church-sect typology. *American Sociological Review*, 1957, **22**, 88–91.

Kanter, R. M. *Commitment and community: Communes and utopias in sociological perspective*. Cambridge: Harvard Univ. Press, 1972.

Kantrowitz, N. *Pre-Civil War political realignment*. Unpublished Ph.D. dissertation, University of Chicago, 1965.

Key. V. O., Jr. A theory of critical elections. *Journal of Politics*, 1955, **17**, 3–18.

Key, V. O. Jr., & Munger, F. Social determinism and electoral choice:

The case of Indiana. In E. Burdick & A. J. Brodbeck (Eds.), *American voting behavior*. Glencoe, Ill.: Free Press, 1959.

Kleppner, P. Lincoln and the immigrant vote: A case of religious polarization. *Mid-America*, 1966, **48**, 176–95.

Kleppner, P. *The cross of culture: A social analysis of Midwestern politics 1850–1900*. New York: Free Press, 1970.

Kleppner, P. Beyond the "new political history": A review essay. *Historical Methods Newsletter*, 1972, **6**, 17–26.

Knox, R. *Enthusiasm: A chapter in the history of religion with special reference to the XVII and XVIII centuries*. Oxford: Clarendon Press, 1950.

Kousser, J. M. The new political history: A methodological critique. *Reviews in American History*, 1976, **4**, 1–14.

Kraditor, A. S. *Means and ends in American abolitionism: Garrison and his critics on strategy and tactics 1834–1850*. New York: Vintage, 1970.

Krout, J. A. *The origins of prohibition*. New York: Russell & Russell, 1967.

Lane, R. E. *Political ideology: Why the common man believes what he does*. New York: Free Press, 1962.

Lenski, G. *The religious factor: A sociologist's inquiry*. Garden City, N.Y.: Doubleday Anchor, 1963.

Lipset, S. M. Religion and politics in the American past and present. In R. Lee & M. E. Marty (Eds.), *Religion and social conflict*. New York: Oxford Univ. Press, 1964.

Lipset, S. M., & Rokkan, S. Cleavage structures, party systems, and voter alignments: An introduction. In S. M. Lipset & S. Rokkan (Eds.), *Party systems and voter alignments: Cross-national perspectives*. New York: Free Press, 1967.

Litwack, L. F. *North of slavery: The Negro in the free states 1790–1860*. Chicago: Univ. of Chicago Press, 1961.

Loveland, A. C. Evangelicalism and "immediate emancipation" in American antislavery thought. *Journal of Southern History*, 1966, **32**, 172–88.

Macrae, D., Jr. Occupations and the congressional vote, 1940–1950. *American Sociological Review*, 1955, **20**, 332–40.

MacRae, D., Jr. *Issues and parties in legislative voting*. New York: Harper & Row, 1970.

MacRae, D., Jr. & Meldrum, J. A. Critical elections in Illinois: 1888–1958. *American Political Science Review*, 1960, **54**, 669–83.

MacRae, D., Jr., & Meldrum, J. A. Factor analysis of aggregate voting statistics. In M. Dogan & S. Rokkan (Eds.), *Quantitative ecological analysis in the social science*. Cambridge, Mass.: MIT Press, 1969.

Mannheim, K. The sociological problem of generations. In B. McLaughlin (Ed.), *Studies in social movements: A social psychological perspective*. New York: Free Press, 1969.

Mathews, D. G. *Slavery and Methodism: A chapter in American morality 1780–1845*. Princeton, N.J.: Princeton Univ. Press, 1965.

Mathews, D. G. The Methodist schism of 1844 and the popularization of antislavery sentiment. *Mid-America*, 1968, **41**, 3–23.

Mathews, D. G. The second great awakening as an organizing process, 1780–1830: An hypothesis. *American Quarterly*, 1969, **21**, 23–43.

Mathews, L. K. *The expansion of New England: The spread of New England settlement and institutions to the Mississippi River 1620–1865*. Boston and New York: Houghton Mifflin, 1909.

Mazmanian, D. A. *Third parties in presidential elections*. Washington: Brookings Institution, 1974.

McCormick, R. L. Ethno-cultural interpretations of nineteenth-century American voting behavior. *Political Science Quarterly*, 1974, **89**, 351–78.

McCormick, R. P. Political development and the second party system. In W. N. Chambers & W. D. Burnham (Eds.), *The American party systems: Stages of political development*. New York: Oxford Univ. Press, 1967.

McLoughlin, W. G., Jr. *Modern revivalism: Charles Grandison Finney to Billy Graham*. New York: Ronald Press, 1959.

McLoughlin, W. G. Introduction to Finney, C. G., *Lectures on revivals of religion*. Cambridge, Mass.: Belknap, 1960.

McLoughlin, W. G. Pietism and the American character. *American Quarterly*, 1965, **17**, 163–186.

McPherson, J. M. *The struggle for equality: Abolitionists and the Negro in the Civil War and Reconstruction*. Princeton, N.J.: Princeton Univ. Press, 1964.

McSeveney, S. T. *The politics of depression: Political behavior in the northeast, 1893–1896*. New York: Oxford Univ. Press, 1972.

Mead, S. E. *The lively experiment: The shaping of Christianity in America*. New York: Harper & Row, 1963.

Merton, R. K. *Social theory and social structure*. New York: Free Press, 1957.

Miller, P. From the covenant to the revival. In J. W. Smith & A. L. Jamison (Eds.), *The shaping of American religion*. Princeton, N.J.: Princeton Univ. Press, 1961.

Miller, P. *The life of the mind in America: From the revolution to the Civil War*. New York: Harcourt Brace & World, 1965.

Murray, A. E. *Presbyterians and the Negro—A history*. Philadelphia: Presbyterian Historical Society, 1966.

Myers, J. L. The agency system of the antislavery movement, 1832–1837, and its antecedents in other benevolent and reform societies.

Unpublished Ph.D. dissertation, University of Michigan, 1960.

Myers, J. L. The beginning of anti-slavery agencies in New York state, 1833–1836. *New York History*, 1962, **43**, 149–81.

Myers, J. L. The major efforts of national anti-slavery agents in New York State, 1837–1838. *New York History*, 1965, **46,** 162–86.

Myers, J. L. Organization of "the seventy": To arouse the north against slavery. *Mid-America*, 1966, **48**, 29–46.

New York, Secretary of State. *Manual for the use of the legislature of the state of New York*. Albany: Lyon, 1916.

Nichols, R. H. *Presbyterianism in New York state: A History of the synod and its predecessors* (J. H. Nichols, Ed.). Philadelphia: Westminster, 1963.

Niebuhr, H. R. *The kingdom of God in America*. New York: Harper & Row, 1937.

Odegard, P. H. *Pressure politics: The story of the Anti-Saloon League*. New York: Octagon, 1966.

Opie, J. Jr. Conversion and revivalism: An internal history from Jonathan Edwards through Charles Grandison Finney. Unpublished Ph.D. dissertation, University of Chicago Divinity School, 1963.

Parsons, S. B. *The Populist context: Rural versus urban power on a Great Plains frontier*. Westport, Conn.: Greenwood, 1973.

Parsons, T. *Structure and process in modern society*. New York: Free Press, 1960.

Parsons, T. Durkheim and religion revisited: Another look at *The elementary forms of the religious life*. In C. Y. Glock & P. E. Hammond (Eds.), *Beyond the classics: Essays in the scientific study of religion*. New York: Harper & Row, 1973.

Pessen, E. *Jacksonian America; Society, personality, and politics*. Homewood, Ill.: Dorsey, 1960.

Pomper, G. Classification of presidential elections. In J. M. Clubb & H. W. Allen (Eds.), *Electoral change and stability in American political history*. New York: Free Press, 1971.

Pomper, G. M. *Elections in America: Control and influence in democratic politics*. New York: Dodd, Mead, 1970.

Porter, G. H. *Ohio politics during the Civil War period*. New York: n.p., 1906.

Pratt, J. W. Governor Seward and the New York City school controversy, 1840–1842. *New York History*, 1961, **42,** 351–64.

Presbyterian Church in the United States of America, General Assembly. *Minutes*. Philadelphia: Stated Clerk of the Assembly, 1822–1835.

Presbyterian Church in the United States of America [New School],

General Assembly. *Minutes*. New York: Daniel Fanshaw, 1841–1843.

Presbyterian Church in the United States of America, Presbytery of Ohio. One hundred fifty years of Presbyterianism in the Ohio Valley 1790–1940. Cincinnati: 1941.

Pye, L. W. *Politics, personality, and nation building*. New Haven: Yale Univ. Press, 1962.

Quarles, B. *Black abolitionists*. New York: Oxford Univ. Press, 1969.

Radcliffe-Brown, A. R. *Structure and function in primitive society*. New York: Free Press, 1965.

Rayback, J. G. The Liberty party leaders of Ohio: Exponents of anti-slavery coalition. *Ohio Archaeological and Historical Quarterly*. 1948, **42**, 165–79.

Rayback, R. J. *Millard Fillmore: Biography of a president*. Buffalo, N.Y.: Buffalo Historical Society, 1959.

Richards, L. L. *Gentlemen of property and standing: Anti-abolition mobs in Jacksonian America*. New York: Oxford Univ. Press, 1970.

Roach, G. W. The presidential campaign of 1844 in New York State. *New York History*, 1938, **19**, 153–72.

Robinson, W. S. Ecological correlations and the behavior of individuals. *American Sociological Review*, 1950, **40**, 351–57.

Rogin, M. P. *The intellectuals and McCarthy: The radical specter*. Cambridge, Mass.: MIT Press, 1967.

Rokkan, S. Geography, religion and social class: Cross-cutting cleavages in Norwegian politics. In S. M. Lipset & S. Rokkan (Eds.), *Party systems and voter alignments: Cross-national perspective*. New York: Free Press, 1967.

Roseboom, E. H., & Weisenburger, F. P. *A history of Ohio*. New York: Prentice-Hall, 1934.

Roseboom, E. H. *The Civil War era: 1850–1873*. Vol. 4 of the History of the State of Ohio (C. Wittke, Ed.). Columbus, Ohio: Ohio State Archaeological and Historical Society, 1944.

Schattschneider, E. E. *The semi-sovereign people: A realist's view of democracy in America*. New York: Holt, Rinehart & Winston, 1960.

Scisco, L. D. *Political nativism in New York State*. Studies in History, Economics and Public Law, Columbia University, Vol. 13, No. 2, 1901.

Sellers, C. *James K. Polk, Continentalist 1843–1846*. Princeton, N.J.: Princeton Univ. Press, 1966.

Sellers, C. The equilibrium cycle in two-party politics. In J. M. Clubb & H. W. Allen (Eds.), *Electoral change and stability in American political history*. New York: Free Press, 1971.

Silbey, J. H. The Civil War synthesis in American history. *Civil War*

History, 1964, **10**, 120–40.

Silbey, J. H. *The shrine of party: Congressional voting behavior 1841–1852*. Pittsburgh, Pa.: Univ. of Pittsburgh Press, 1967. (a)

Silbey, J. H. *The transformation of American politics 1840–1860*. Englewood Cliffs, N.J.: Prentice-Hall, 1967. (b)

Simmel, G. *Conflict and the web of group affiliations* (K. H. Wolff & R. Bendix, trans.). Glencoe, Ill.: Free Press, 1955.

Skotheim, R. A. The 'status revolution' thesis criticized. In R. O. Curry (Ed.), *The abolitionists: Reformers or fanatics?* New York: Harper & Row, 1965.

Smith, T. C. *The Liberty and Free Soil parties in the northwest*. Harvard Historical Studies, Vol. VI. New York: Longmans, Green, 1897.

Smith, T. C. *Parties and slavery 1850–1859*. Vol. 18 of *The American nation: A history* (A. B. Hart, Ed.). New York: Harper, 1906.

Smith, T. L. *Revivalism and social reform: American protestantism on the eve of the Civil War*. New York: Harper & Row, 1957.

Sorauf, F. J. Political parties and political analysis. In W. N. Chambers & W. D. Burnham (Eds.), *The American party systems: Stages of political development*. New York: Oxford Univ. Press, 1967.

Sorin, G. *The New York abolitionists: A case study of political radicalism*. Westport, Conn.: Greenwood, 1971.

Sorin, G. *Abolitionism: A new perspective*. New York: Praeger, 1972.

Staiger, C. B. Abolitionism and the Presbyterian schism of 1837–1838. *Mississippi Valley Historical Review*, 1949, **36**, 391–414.

Stanley, J. L. Majority tyranny in Tocqueville's America: The failure of Negro suffrage in 1846. *Political Science Quarterly*, 1969, **84**, 412–35.

Stewart, J. B. *Joshua R. Giddings and the tactics of radical politics*. Cleveland, Ohio: The Press of Case Western Reserve Univ., 1970.

Stokes, D. E. Parties and the nationalization of electoral forces. In W. N. Chambers & W. D. Burnham (Eds.), *The American party systems: Stages of political development*. New York: Oxford Univ. Press, 1967.

Sundquist, J. L. *Dynamics of the party system: Alignment and realignment of politics parties in the United States*. Washington: The Brookings Institution, 1973.

Sweet, W. W. The churches as moral courts of the frontier. *Church History*, 1933, **2**, 3–21.

Sweet, W. W. *Revivalism in America: Its origin, growth and decline*. New York: Scribner, 1944.

Tocqueville, A. de. *Democracy in America* (P. Bradley, Ed.). New York: Knopf, 1945.

Tyler, A. F. *Freedom's ferment: Phases of American social history from the colonial period to the outbreak of the Civil War*. New York: Harper & Row, 1944.

U.S. Department of Commerce. Bureau of the Census. *State censuses: An annotated bibliography* . . . . Prepared by Henry J. Dubester. Washington: Government Printing Office, 1948.

Van Deusen, G. G. *The Jacksonian era*. New York: Harper Torchbooks, 1959.

Walker, J. L. Protest and negotiation: A case study of Negro leadership in Atlanta, Georgia. *Midwest Journal of Political Science*, 1963, **7**, 99–124.

Walzer, M. *The revolution of the saints: A study in the origins of radical politics*. New York: Atheneum, 1969.

Weber, M. *From Max Weber: Essays in sociology* (H. H. Gerth & C. W. Mills, Eds.). New York: Oxford Univ. Press, 1958.   (a)

Weber, M. *The Protestant ethic and the spirit of capitalism*. New York: Scribner, 1958.   (b)

Weber, M. *Economy and society: An outline of interpretive sociology*. (G. Roth & C. Wittich, Eds.), 3 vols. New York: Bedminster, 1968.

Weld, T. W. *The Bible against slavery: or, an inquiry into the genius of the Mosaic system, and the teachings of the Old Testament on the subject of human rights*. Pittsburgh, Pa.: United Presbyterian Board of Publications, 1864 (first published 1837).

Wesley, C. H. The Negroes of New York in the emancipation movement. *Journal of Negro History*, 1939, **24**, 65–103.

Whitlock, B. *Forty years of it*. New York: Appleton, 1914.

Wiles, P. A syndrome, not a doctrine: Some elementary theses on populism. In G. Ionescu & E. Gellner (Eds.), *Populism: Its meaning and national characteristics*. London: Weidenfeld & Nicolson, 1969.

Wilson, B. R. *Religion in secular society: A sociological comment*. Baltimore, Md.: Pelican, 1969.

Woodward, C. V. The Populist heritage and the intellectual. *The American Scholar*, 1959–60, **59**, 55–72.

Wolfinger, R. E., & Field, J. O. Political ethos and the structure of city government. *American Political Science Review*, 1966, **60**, 306–26.

Worsley, P. The concept of populism. In G. Ionescu & E. Gellner (Eds.), *Populism: Its meaning and national characteristics*. London: Weidenfeld & Nicolson, 1969.

Wright, J. E. The ethnocultural model of voting: A behavioral and historical critique. *American Behavioral Scientist*, 1973, **16**, 653–74.

Wyatt-Brown, B. *Lewis Tappan and the evangelical crusade against slavery*. Cleveland, Ohio: The Press of Case Western Reserve Univ., 1969.

Wyatt-Brown, B. Prelude to abolitionism: Sabbatarian politics and the rise of the second party system. *Journal of American History*, 1971, **58**, 316–41.

Yinger, J. M. *The scientific study of religion*. New York: MacMillan, 1970.

Zeitlin, M. Political generations in the Cuban working class. *American Journal of Sociology*, 1966, **71**, 493–508.

Author Index

Subject Index